IMAGES
of America

AROUND LA PORTE

Ann Uloth Malone and Dan Becker

ARCADIA
PUBLISHING

ISBN 978-0-7385-8490-4

Published by Arcadia Publishing
Charleston, South Carolina

Printed in the United States of America

Library of Congress Control Number: 2011922713

For all general information, please contact Arcadia Publishing:
Telephone 843-853-2070
Fax 843-853-0044
E-mail sales@arcadiapublishing.com
For customer service and orders:
Toll-Free 1-888-313-2665

Visit us on the Internet at www.arcadiapublishing.com

To the memory of my husband, Norman Malone,
who always knew I could

And to my beautiful children and grandchildren—always try

—Ann Malone

To Mom and Dad—this is for you, thank you

To Ann—I love you, thank you

To Charlie and Mary—for remembering our past, thank you

—Dan Becker

Contents

ACKNOWLEDGMENTS

Our sincere gratitude goes to all the people who worked so diligently to organize the La Porte Bay Area Heritage Society over 30 years ago. The organization has gathered and shared the vital and interesting history of the La Porte Bay Area. Special thanks must go to Gordon Black, his mother, Arbela Ralston, and especially his grandmother, Gertrude Ackerly, who began collecting history and stories while the city was still young, and the earliest settlers were still here. We also thank the many people who happily shared their stories and photographs with us.

Thanks to those who graciously allowed the use of their photographs and stories for our book: The La Porte Bay Area Heritage Society Archives, Joel Draut and the Houston Metropolitan Research Center, Harris County Public Library Archives, Margaret Anderson, Karen Rigby, Lola and Marvin Phillips, Rose Hall, the City of La Porte, Stacey Osbourne, Mary Gay, J.J. and Patsy Meza, Charlotte Boudreaux, Dennis Dunham, Sam (Dora) Akkerman, Julia Green Dautriel, Georgia Malone, Diana Sutherland, Randy Pace, Sarah Duncan, Ellen Stuart, Louis F. Rothermel II, and Buck Bonner. Unless otherwise noted, images are courtesy of the La Porte Bay Area Heritage Society.

INTRODUCTION

The city of La Porte is situated in what is known as the Johnson Hunter Survey. Hunter acquired the property under an original land grant from Stephen F. Austin. Johnson Hunter was a doctor who moved to the area in 1822 with his wife and five children. They landed near what is now Morgan's Point. Years later as an old man, Hunter's oldest son relates the first few days in Texas. From their point of arrival, they could see across the bay to Little Cedar Bayou where Indians were waylaying another group of settlers. A rescue party was gathered, and they sailed to Little Cedar Bayou (on the edge of what is now Sylvan Beach) where they found the Indian attackers eating the settlers. Original tribes in the area included the Attacapa and the Karankawa Indians. The Karankawas are generally acknowledged as being cannibals, but there is some dispute regarding the Attacapa.

Through a series of transactions, most of the land covered under the Johnson Survey eventually passed into the hands of two men well known in Texas history, Gen. Sidney Sherman, hero of the Battle of San Jacinto, and Col. James Morgan. Most of the land covered by the survey was thus once under the ownership of two of the greatest and most colorful men in the pantheon of Texas history.

Shortly after his heroics at the Battle of San Jacinto, General Sherman asked his friend Daniel Burnet, the future president of the Republic of Texas and a neighbor of Colonel Morgan, to secure a property on San Jacinto Bay. Sherman resided with nine family members in a log cabin (he called it Mount Vernon in jest) overlooking the bay for a year during the construction of his home, Crescent Place. Sherman resided on the bay for several years until his great hope of establishing a railroad from Harrisburg to the Brazos River led him to resettle in Harrisburg. No photograph exists of the one-room log cabin. Among the family sometimes residing at Crescent Place was his young brother-in-law Cornelius Cox, who recorded his experiences in the community:

> It may be proper now, to say something of the personnel of the people who preceded us to this part of Texas and who now constituted the citizenship of the Bay Country, for it must be remembered that Texas was very new. . . . The families settled along the Bay shore, on either side were mainly from the different southern states, and came in with Austin's Colony. . . . . We had one near neighbor within a half mile, this was Enoch Brunson [Brinson], two miles further down we came to Morgan's Point or New Washington . . . the most beautiful site on the bay, being at the junction of the San Jacinto and Galveston Bays. . . . I have met at the home President Burnet, General Houston, Sidney Johnson, Barnard E. Bee, Dr. Ashbel Smith, Mosely Baker, Mr. Anderson, the naturalist, the son and daughter of J.N. Moffit-Com Moore and hundreds of other prominent citizens.

One of the earliest inhabitants of the area was Nicholas Rightor, a surveyor whose vessel wrecked on Galveston Bay and washed him ashore on what would become Morgan's Point. It is unknown precisely how long Rightor resided in the area before leaving. Of anecdotal interest is that several years later when Rightor married, Jefferson Davis served as best man at his wedding.

Another somewhat notorious resident of the Bay Area is the pirate Jean Lafitte. It is known that Lafitte worked out of a Galveston base of operations for three years. Some local legends assert that Lafitte occasionally set up operations on the bay shore, and one local legend says he built a one-room safe house for temporary quarters and the division of his piratical spoils. One of the earliest residents of the La Porte area was Abner Beazley, who built a home near Sylvan Beach where several generations of Beazley's grew up. Legend has it that the Beazley home was built onto Lafitte's one-room safe house and that the structures stood intact until the Beazley home burned in 1928. Granddaughter Julia Beazley wrote a story entitled "The Uneasy Ghost of Lafitte." J. Frank Dobie includes a version of the legend in one of his *Legends of Texas* compilations.

Many other colorful and famous individuals—men like Lorenzo de Zavala, women such as Emma Seelye, and others—resided in the La Porte area before the city's founding. Indeed, it is claimed that Sam Houston, a frequent guest at James Morgan's home and on his boats, resided for a time just across the bay from Morgan at the head of Cedar Bayou and on the line between what is now Chambers and Harris Counties.

La Porte was incorporated on August 10, 1892, the result of a vigorous marketing campaign by a group of businessmen known as the Nebraska Syndicate. Precarious financing and national economic scares seemed to rank slightly ahead of fire as the most chronic and severe disaster to hammer Bay Area communities early in their histories. Most recently, Hurricane Ike reminded all La Portians of the continuing threat natural disasters, particularly those heading in from the Gulf, present to our communities. But Ike also reminded us all of the strength and boldness, the poise and kindness, the courage, and the selflessness that have defined the growth and daily life of La Porte and its neighbors for over 100 years. The pictures in this collection help to illustrate these qualities better than words can hope to.

Morgan's Point has a long, distinguished, and complicated history. It is located east of La Porte on Galveston Bay, and the area has been known as Hunter's Point, Rightor's Point, and Clopper's Point (all names coming from men who had owned or settled on the land before James Morgan). The area was previously home to the town of New Washington, which some allege existed in a prior incarnation near Lynchburg. Santa Anna set fire to and destroyed New Washington. Much of what currently stands in Morgan's Point was once part of the Bayridge community. The Point was incorporated in 1949 with a population of roughly 350. The city is now the hub for the Barbour's Cut container terminal, one of the largest and finest such facilities in the world.

Shoreacres is a small town south of La Porte on Galveston Bay with a population varying from about 1,000 to 2,000 residents. It initially functioned as a corporation jointly owned by the homeowners (The Shoreacres Development Co.), and shortly after World War II, it was incorporated (in 1949). Professional golfer J. Val Dealy carried the laboring oar in civic affairs during the city's corporate years. The city had its own golf course, which Dealy kept open until the mid-1930s. The Houston Yacht Club, which began operating under that name in 1927, calls Shoreacres home. It had previously been known as the Houston Yacht & Power Boat Club (1897) and the Houston Launch Club (from 1906 to 1926). "Just take the Harrisburg Trolley to the end of the line," read an advertisement for the Houston Launch Club. For a period, the yacht club had its own airport, the Houston Yacht Club Airport. It is one of the finest such clubs in the South, and its members have a long and proud history.

Lomax is on the prairie west of La Porte. It is separated from La Porte by the Strang railroad yard. It has historically been a farming and ranching community and it retains that agrarian and Western culture to this day. Ike Shireman was one of the first residents, but it is named for the first man to purchase land in the area, which is today primarily residential homesteads with large country-like lots. Lomax was annexed by La Porte in 1940 and de-annexed in 1952; it then incorporated in 1953 and was re-annexed by La Porte in 1980. Many descendants of the early farmers who settled the area still remain or maintain ties to the community.

La Porte and its neighbors constitute separate cities with their own histories and traditions. But they are also a part of the larger community containing Houston, and Galveston and the plethora of Bay Area communities that surround them. A.O. Blackwell, general counsel to La

Porte's founding Nebraska Syndicate and one of the finest and most civic-minded men the city can boast, tells of how the initial gatherings of the Nebraska Syndicate were feted with banquets sponsored by Spencer Hutchins at the Cotton Exchange building in Houston (which still stands). When construction of the La Porte, Houston & Northern Railroad stalled, Blackwell notes how Houston luminaries like T.W. House, J.H. Tennant, and M.T. Jones contributed to moving the line along to reach Sylvan Grove. Thus began the special excursion train rides to Sylvan Beach that would become such a huge part of life for generations of Houstonians and La Portians alike. Today, the entrance to the Port of Houston starts in La Porte and Morgan's Point, and the spread of mass transit and rapid transit seems to reduce the distance between La Porte and its larger neighbors and remind Houstonians of the Little Jewel by the Bay.

Finally, an acknowledgments page does not seem sufficient to state the huge debt of gratitude the authors feel towards those who have preserved our history as well as those who have given so freely of their time and collections to help in the making of this book. Our sincere gratitude to Gertrude Ackerley, Gordon Black, Arbela Ralston, and all of La Porte's local historians. We wish to especially thank the members of the Houston Yacht Club and Sam Ackerman for sharing their photographic collections and personal recollections with us, and finally, our deepest gratitude goes to all the members, past and present, of the La Porte Bay Area Heritage Society.

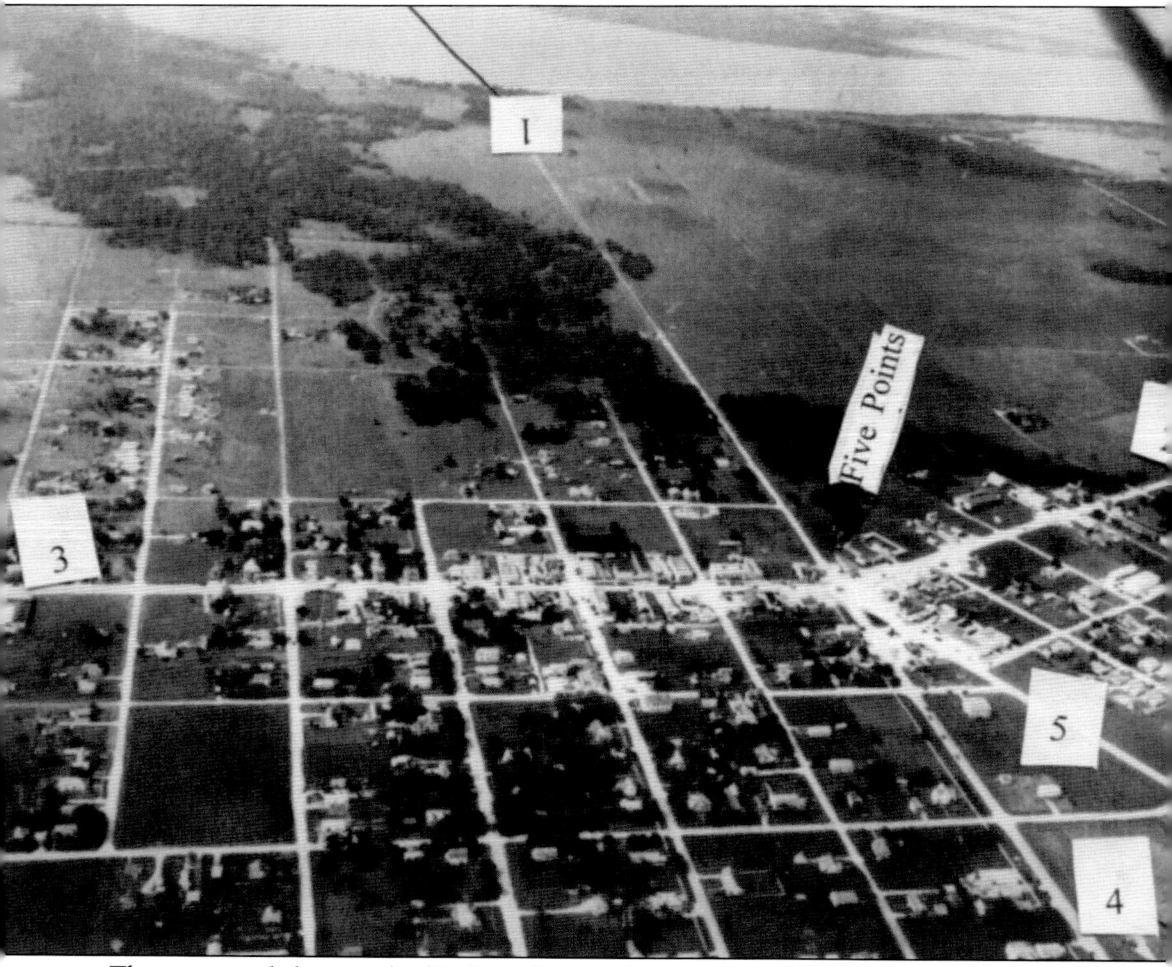

This is an aerial photograph of La Porte showing the centrality of the Five Points. The name came from the meeting of the five roads shown. Number 1 is North Broadway to the shipping wharf on San Jacinto Bay. Number 2 is East Main to Morgan's Point. Number 3 is Main or West Main to Houston and places west. Number 4 is South Broadway to Seabrook or old Highway 146, and Number 5 is San Jacinto Street, which goes directly to Sylvan Beach Park and Galveston Bay. This meeting of these roads at Five Points is the heart of old La Porte.

One

Beginnings and Town Builders

The San Jacinto Battleground, the place where Texas gained its independence, is five miles from downtown La Porte and lies within the cities' extra territorial jurisdiction and the La Porte School District. Many of the giants of early Texas (including Lorenzo de Zavala, David Burnet, James Morgan, Sidney Sherman, and Andrew Jackson Houston to name a few) fell in love with the areas that would become La Porte and Morgan's Point and settled nearby.

Upon James Morgan's death, Capt. Frederick Leon Allien purchased his plantation. In 1887, Allien took passengers from Houston, a group of corporate officers with the Interior Land and Immigrant Co. On his vessel were Ira Holmes (president of the company), brothers A.M. and J.H. York, John Thayer (former governor of Nebraska), and Tom Lee. The company is also known as the Nebraska Syndicate. A.C. Blackwell had been added as general counsel. The Syndicate bought 600 acres from John Beazley.

The year 1892 saw the incorporation of La Porte, the designation of La Porte's first mayor (J.H. York), and the establishment of Sylvan Beach (simply called the Grove at first). Also in 1892, the Ballentine Hotel, the Palace Livery, and the Artesian Hotel were constructed, and the first city lots were sold to Emil P. Sereau. The new city's first child (Daisy La Porte Ballentine) was born in 1892, the first Sunday school was held at the Tabernacle Union Church on July 17, 1892, and the La Porte, Houston & Northern Railroad was chartered that year.

An early pamphlet published as a sales advertisement for La Porte stated the four objectives of the towns' founders: (1) the establishment of a great commercial center and leading harbor on the coast of Texas, (2) the establishment of a natural summer and winter resort area, (3) the building of a manufacturing center for the Southwest, and (4) the establishment of an educational center second to none in the Southwest. The city was blessed with energetic and visionary men at the beginning and has been blessed with bright, dedicated, hardworking men and women who have carried the torch ever since.

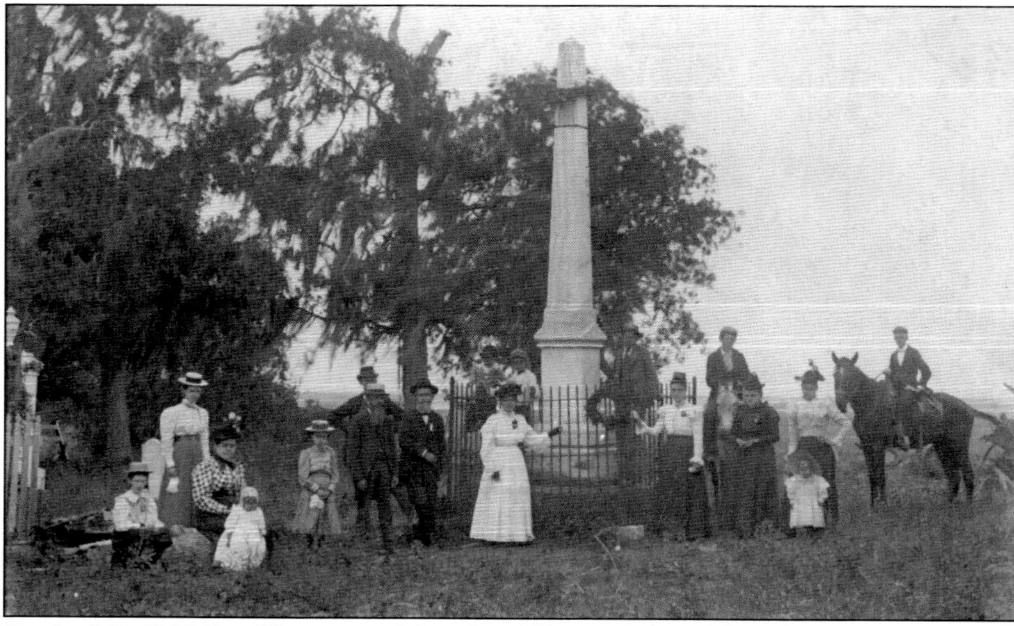

On April 21, 1836, Sam Houston, with less than 800 men, defeated the 1,500-man army of Santa Ana and won independence for Texas. Days before, Santa Anna had burned New Washington at Morgan's Point, where legend says he met Emily West Morgan, musically known as "The Yellow Rose of Texas." Here, family members gather at the Brigham Memorial Shaft, which marks the resting place of the nine Texans who lost their lives in the battle at San Jacinto.

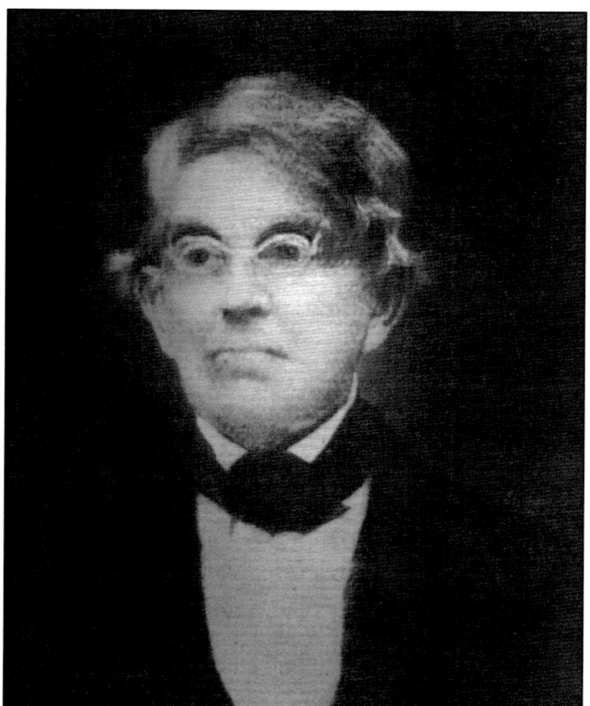

Morgan's Point was originally acquired from Mexico by Johnson Hunter with help from Stephen F. Austin. Nicholas Clopper purchased the land from Hunter and later sold it to George Patrick. James Morgan purchased the land from Patrick and established the town of New Washington, which Santa Anna burned days before the Battle of San Jacinto.

The city of La Porte is said to be the brainchild of Capt. Frederick Leon Allien. He and his wife became enamored with Morgan's Point and in 1885 bought James Morgan's Orange Grove home site near New Washington. Captain Allien had dreams of building a town and port there. He and his wife built a large home and began inviting groups of people to visit.

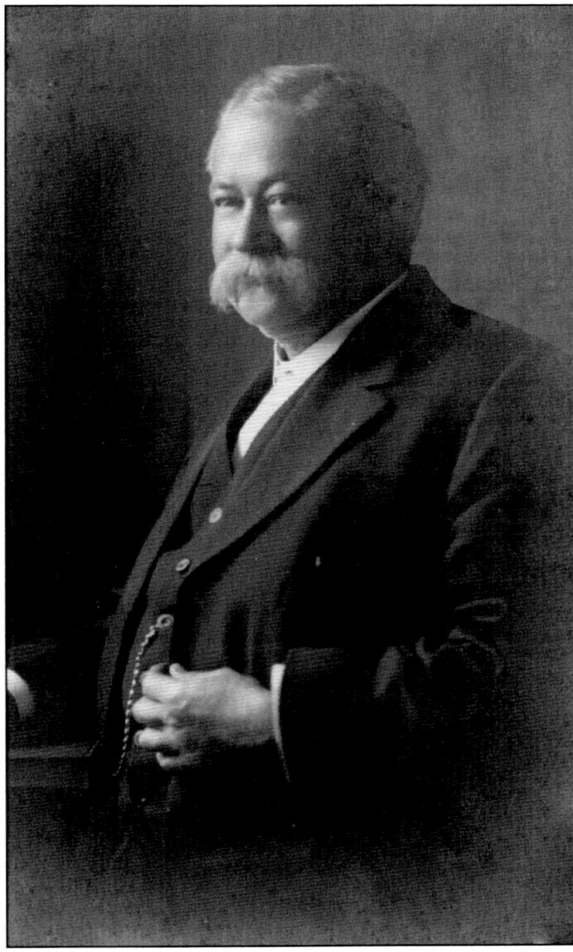

Here is the photograph of Captain Allien's boat, the *Eugene*, which is named for his wife. The passengers are disembarking at his home in Morgan's Point for a day of picnicking and fun on the beautiful bay, which was how Allien met the promoters instrumental in building La Porte.

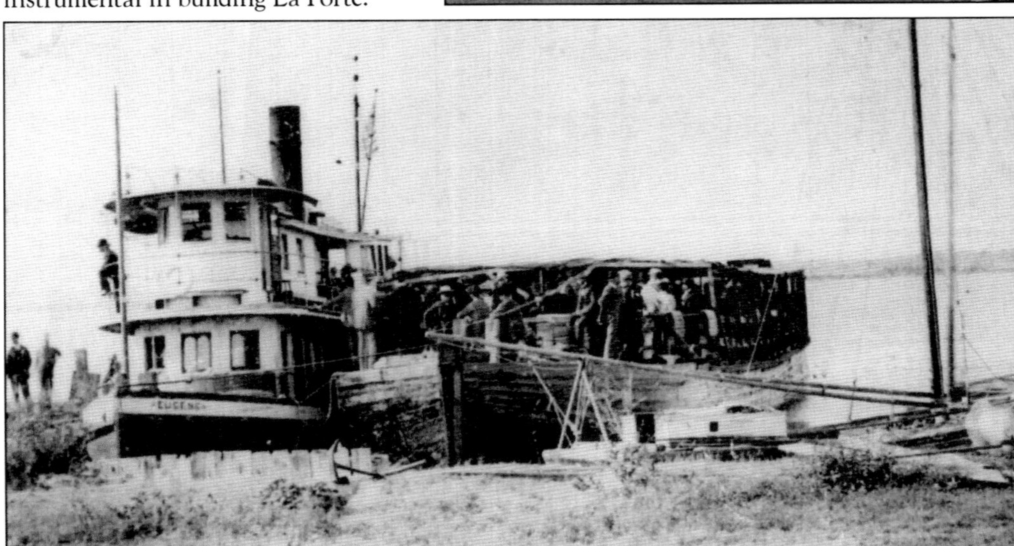

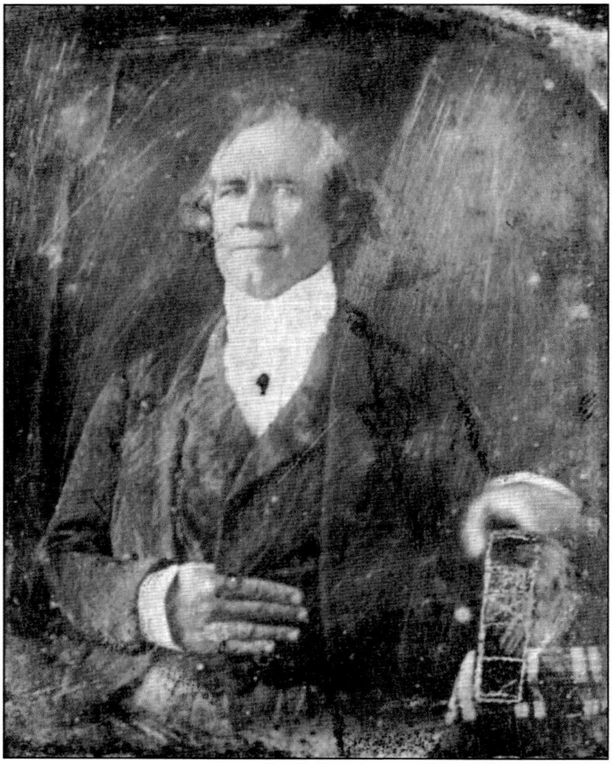

This is a scarce photograph of Sam Houston as a younger man. On the back of the photograph is written, "4-2-36 Please return to Colonel A.J. Houston, La Porte, Texas." When Houston was a young man, La Porte did not yet exist, but Houston is well known to have frequented the area and was fond of accompanying James Morgan on regattas down through Buffalo Bayou and San Jacinto Bay to what is now Morgan's Point, where he was many times a guest. (Courtesy of Randy Pace.)

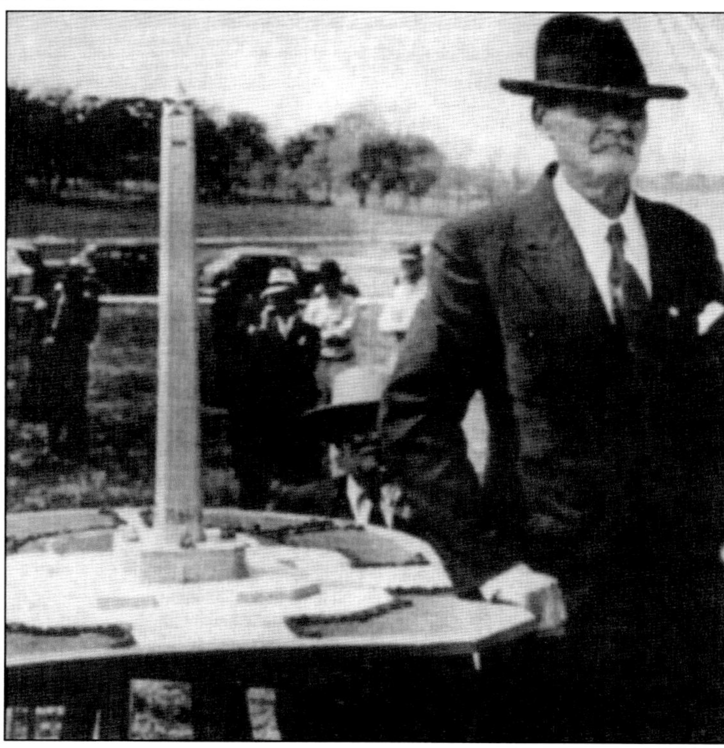

Andrew Jackson Houston stands proudly beside the replica of the San Jacinto monument in La Porte, which commemorates the battle where his father won independence for the state. Houston was living in La Porte at the time of the photograph. He retired from St. Mary's Seminary where he taught military science for years. In 1941, Gov. W. Lee O'Daniel appointed Houston to fulfill a recently vacated senate seat; he died shortly thereafter.

The Allien home was not just the first post office; it was also the unofficial entertainment center. Mrs. Allien is shown tending her plants.

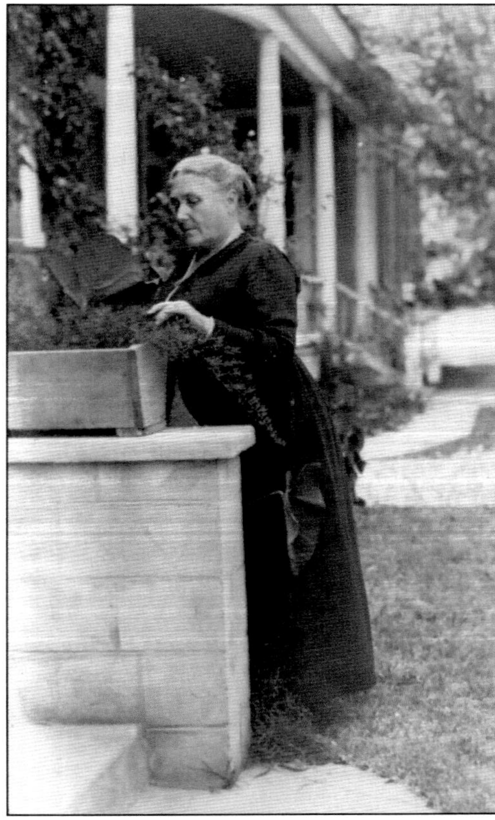

In 1892, Emil P. Sereau bought lots from the steps of the Harris County Courthouse in Houston. He built his general store at the corner of Main and Third Streets to be ready for the expected land buyers and settlers. He and his family lived above the store, as was the custom in those days. The store pictured burned in one of La Porte's three great fires, but Sereau rebuilt.

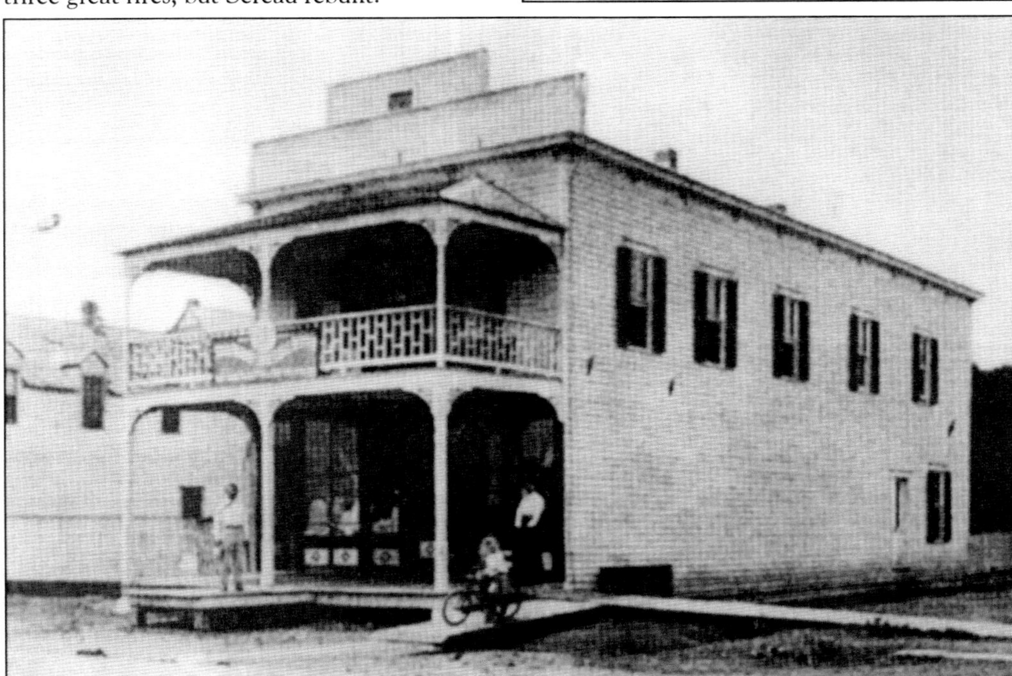

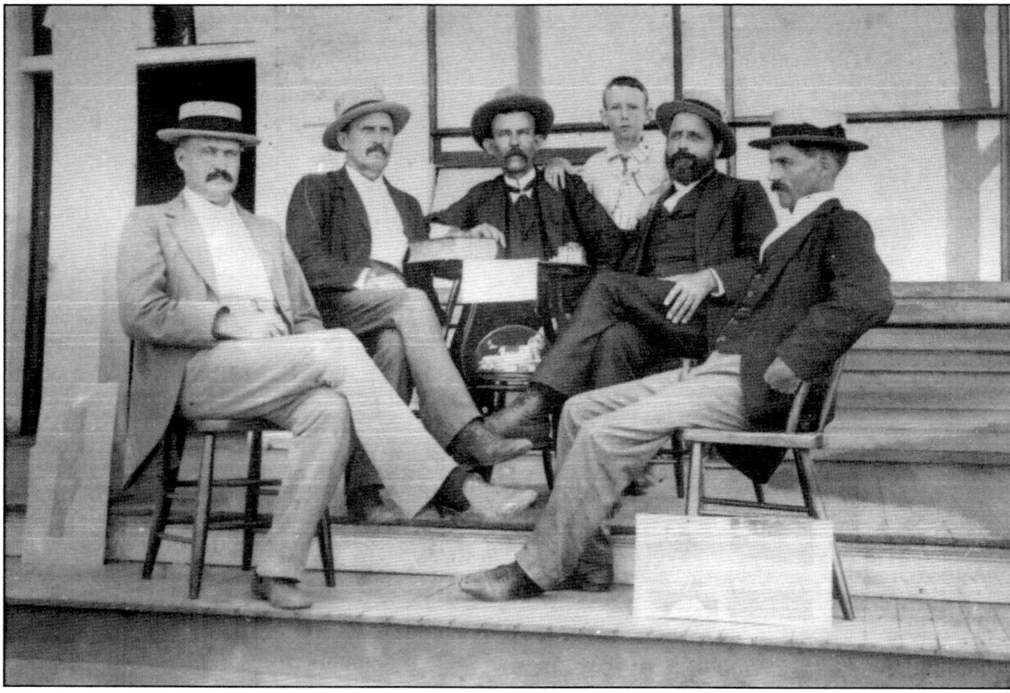

At the Printers Association gathering at his home, Allien met I.R. Homes, a land developer, and his partners, the Nebraska Syndicate. Allien's dream of building a port and a city was discussed, and the Syndicate agreed with his idea. In this group photograph are, from left to right, J.H. York, Ed York, John Caplan with son I.R. Holmes, and attorney A.O. Blackwell.

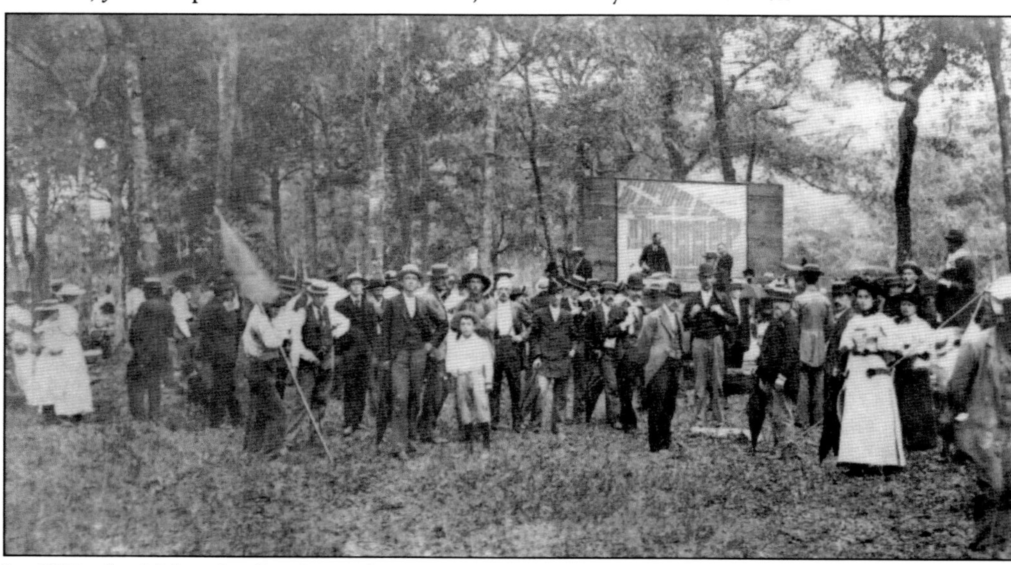

In 1891, the Nebraska Syndicate began an extensive promotional campaign for La Porte that spanned the country. They later held auctions in La Porte, as shown in the photograph. On New Year's Day 1892, lots were sold from the County Courthouse steps in Houston for $25 apiece to people all over the country, and excursion trains were being planned to bring property owners and land speculators to La Porte.

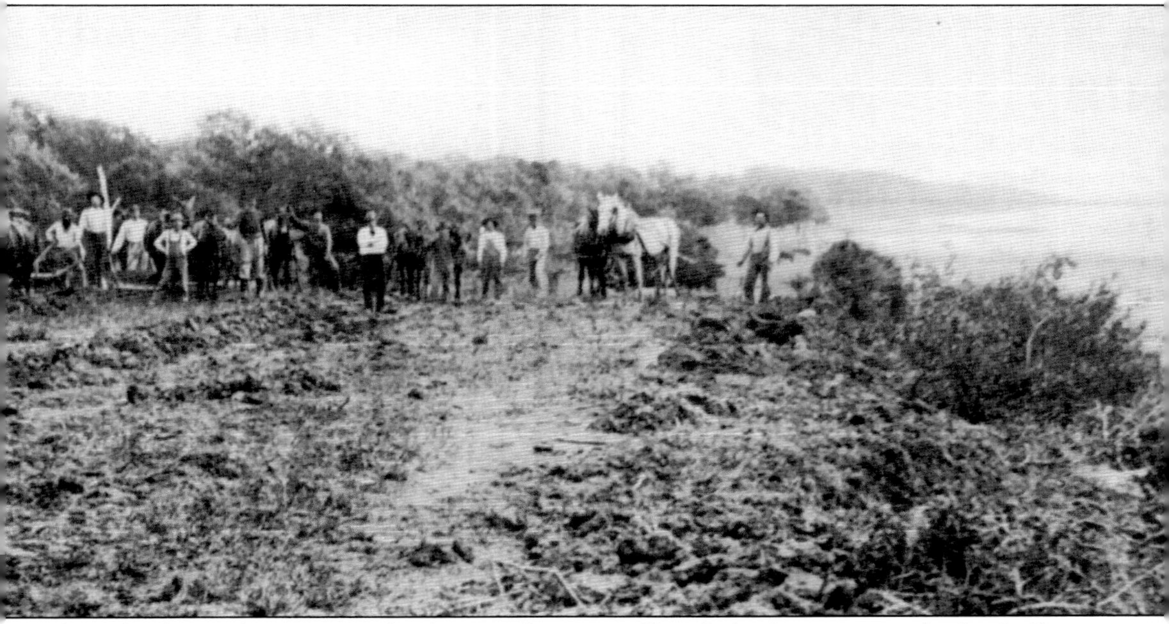

The Nebraska Syndicate operated under several names and bought land as a group and individually. The group acquired 800 acres from Captain Allien and another 600 acres from John Beazley, an early settler. The group discovered that James Morgan had a family cemetery at Morgan's Point, and because nothing could be built there, the Syndicate decided to leave the Point area and moved the town site inland a few miles. The Syndicate also had set aside 22 acres for a park site. This was how the location of La Porte was chosen. Surveyors began to layout the town and started grading the streets as shown in the photograph. The town name that was agreed on was La Porte, which means "the door" in French—and now the door was open to all new settlers. La Porte incorporated in 1892, and I.R. Holmes of the Nebraska Syndicate was appointed town manager. Thus La Porte was born.

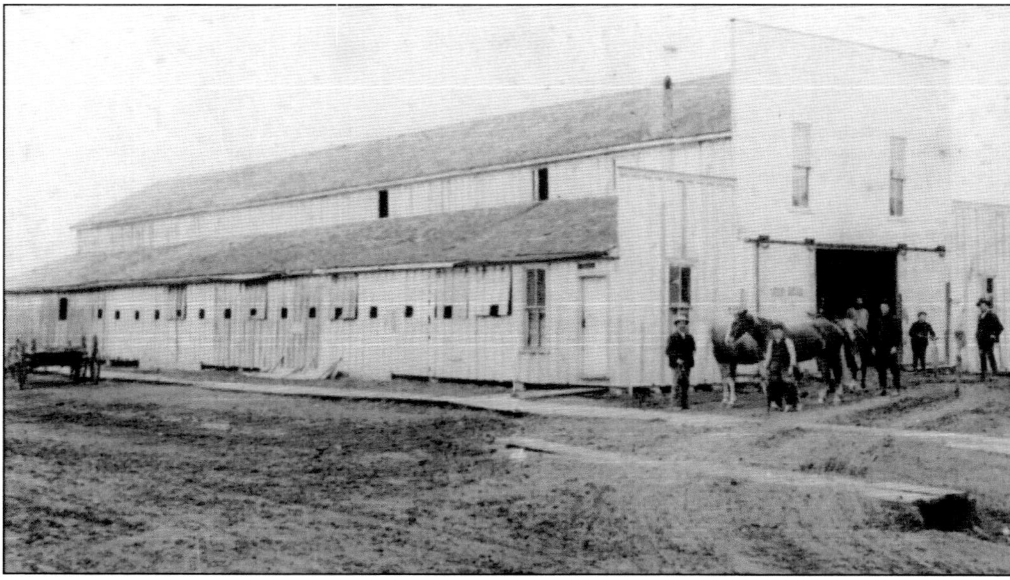

On New Year's Day 1892, the Nebraska Syndicate began building accommodations for the expected hoards of people coming from all over the country. A stable to house horses, wagons, hacks, and equipment was the first building constructed. Many workers decided to live in the stable instead of camping in tents or commuting and said it was like living in a palace; thus the name Palace Livery Stable.

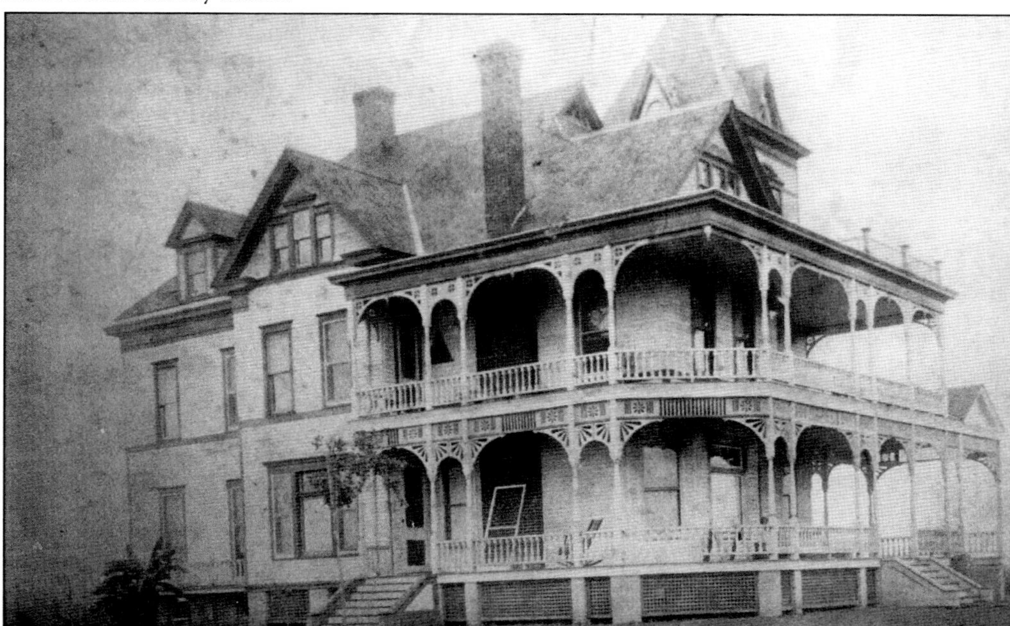

J.H. York was La Porte's first mayor. He built his mansion, which was designed by architect Frank Kirkland, near present-day Broadway Street and Fairmont Parkway. York named the 15-room mansion Grasmere. Construction cost was quoted at $10,000–$27,000. After York left, the mansion passed through several hands, mostly wealthy Houstonians looking for summer homes. On May 14, 1946, it was struck by lightning and burned.

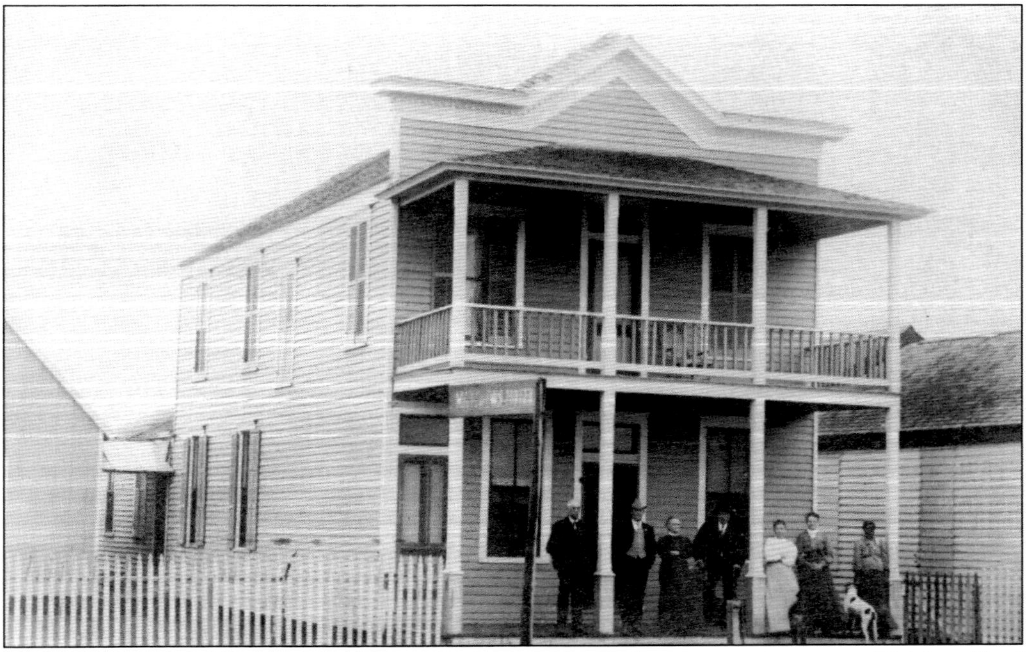

Also, in 1892, a small hotel was built near the Artesian for workers coming into town. This hotel had several monikers during its existence, including the Ballentine, named after the gentleman who built it, and the Matthews Hotel after it was sold. The hotel was moved four times, finally coming to rest across the street from where it originated. It was renamed once again—the Heartbreak Hotel.

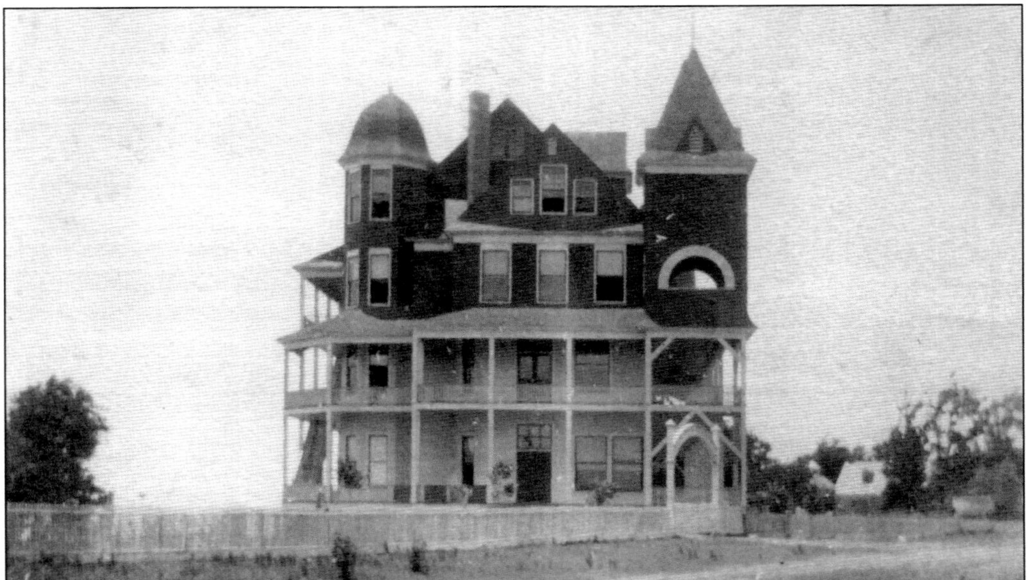

The original members of the Nebraska Syndicate began the Sylvan Hotel in 1893 with financing from Adoue & Lobit of Galveston. A series of natural and financial calamities ruined the Syndicate and financiers took over both the hotel and Sylvan Beach Park. A *Galveston Daily News* article in 1895 touts the coming dance pavilion, gardens, promenade, and the 1,200-foot pier.

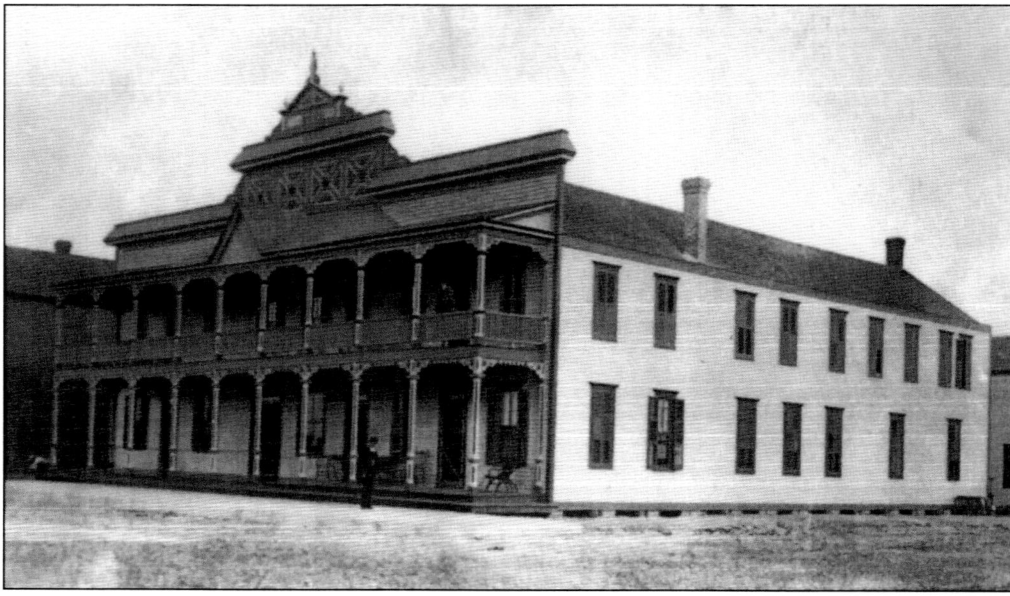

In 1892, with the big promotions over, the Artesian Hotel was constructed across the street simultaneously with the Sereau building. The hotel began with 40 rooms and later added an annex of 30 more rooms. Behind the structure was a laundry building and servants' quarters. The hotel got its name from the artesian well that was discovered while drilling for water.

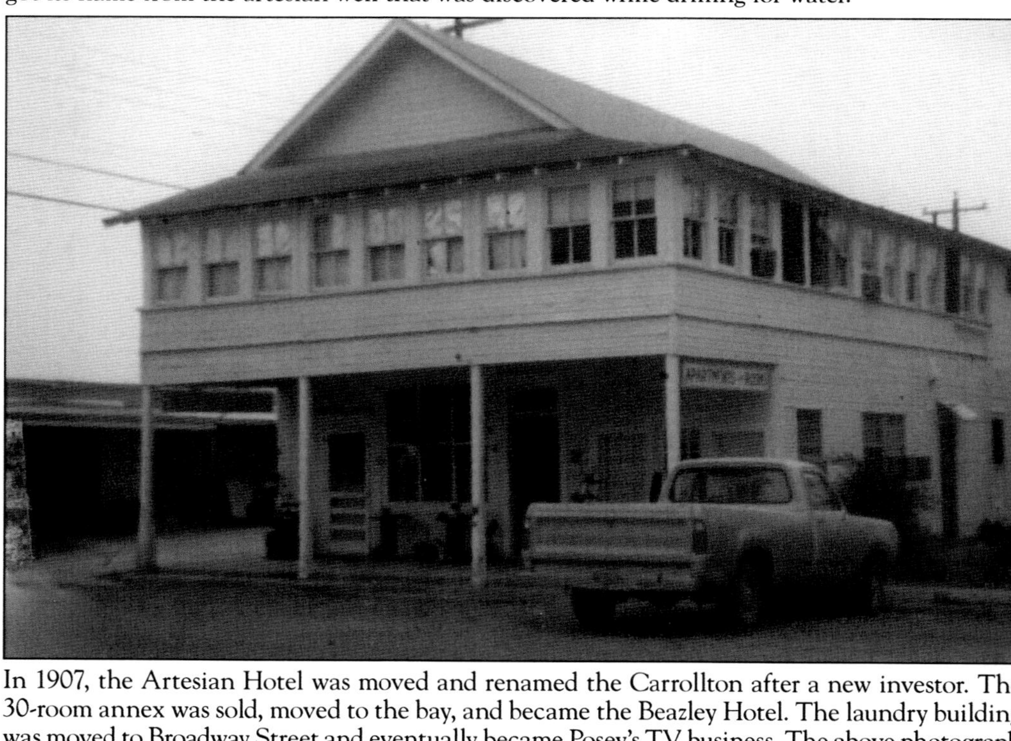

In 1907, the Artesian Hotel was moved and renamed the Carrollton after a new investor. The 30-room annex was sold, moved to the bay, and became the Beazley Hotel. The laundry building was moved to Broadway Street and eventually became Posey's TV business. The above photograph is believed to be the servant quarters. This and a few photographs are all that remain of the Artesian Hotel.

Gen. Sidney Sherman was a hero of San Jacinto and a pioneer of the fledgling Texas railroad industry. A county and a town in Texas are named after him, and a monument was erected in his honor in Galveston. He first settled on San Jacinto Bay in a log cabin he named Mount Vernon. In 1839, Sherman built a new, grander home—Crescent Place—on San Jacinto Bay about two miles above Morgan's Point.

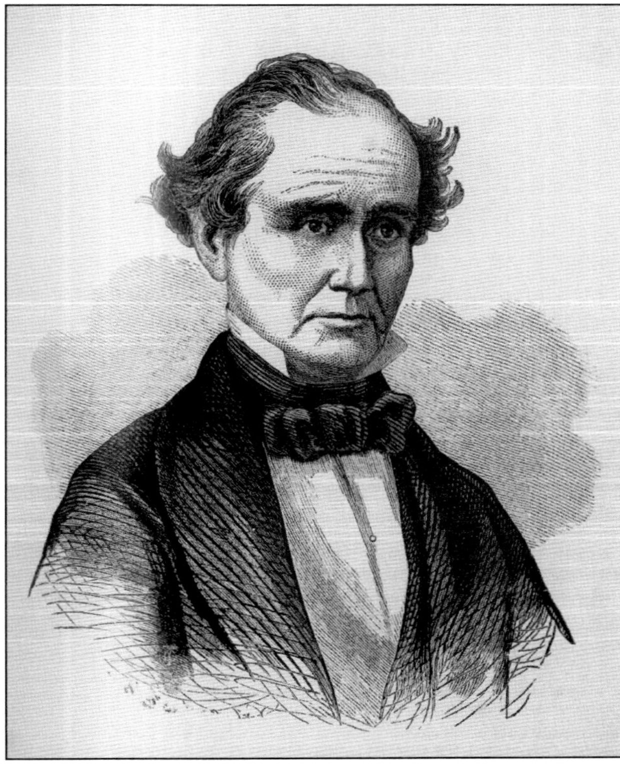

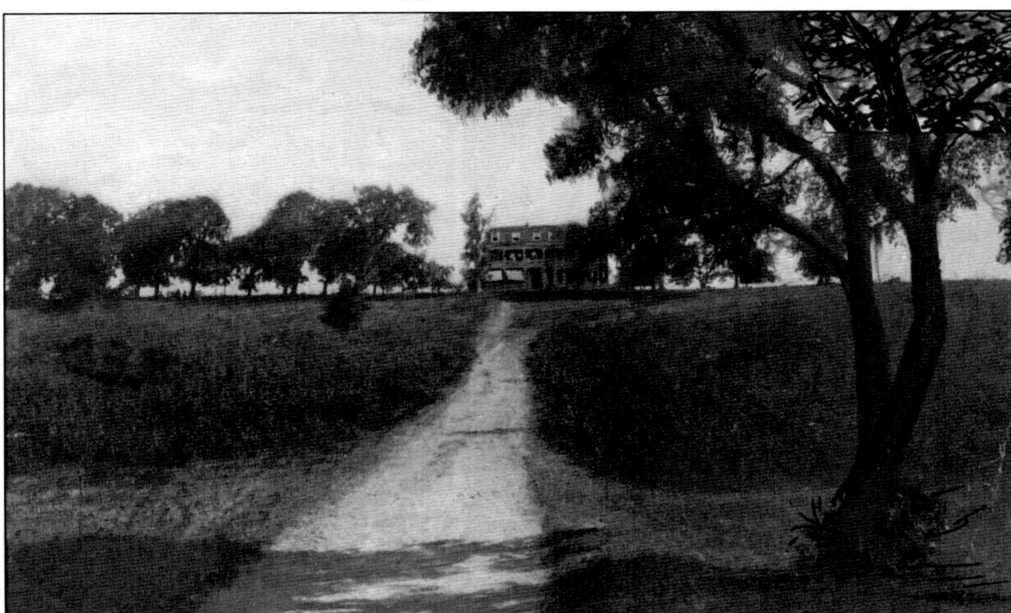

Ed York purchased the old home of Gen. Sydney Sherman, a hero of the Battle of San Jacinto, turning the home into the Crescent Hotel. Visitors could come down Buffalo Bayou by boat, land at the hotel's doorstep, and take a short walk to the center of town. Later, the hotel became the Texas Military Institute and was eventually destroyed by fire.

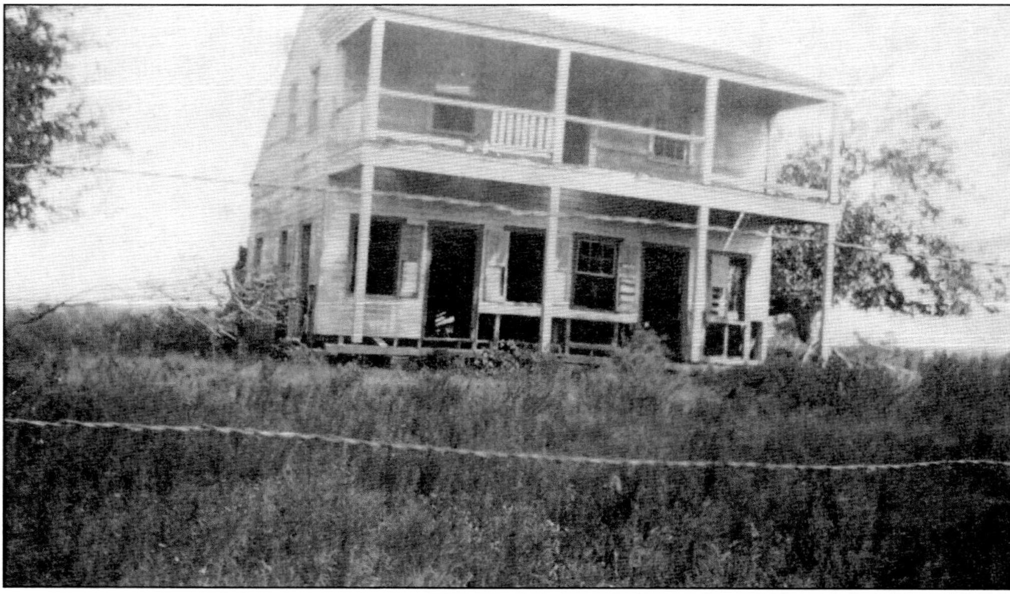

Pictured is the pioneer home of the first vice president of the Republic of Texas, Lorenzo De Zavala. He was also a hero of the Battle of San Jacinto. Many wounded soldiers were nursed back to life and health by the capable nursing of de Zavala's wife and other neighbors. Although his home was not in La Porte proper, he was a part of the early community that predated the cities in the area.

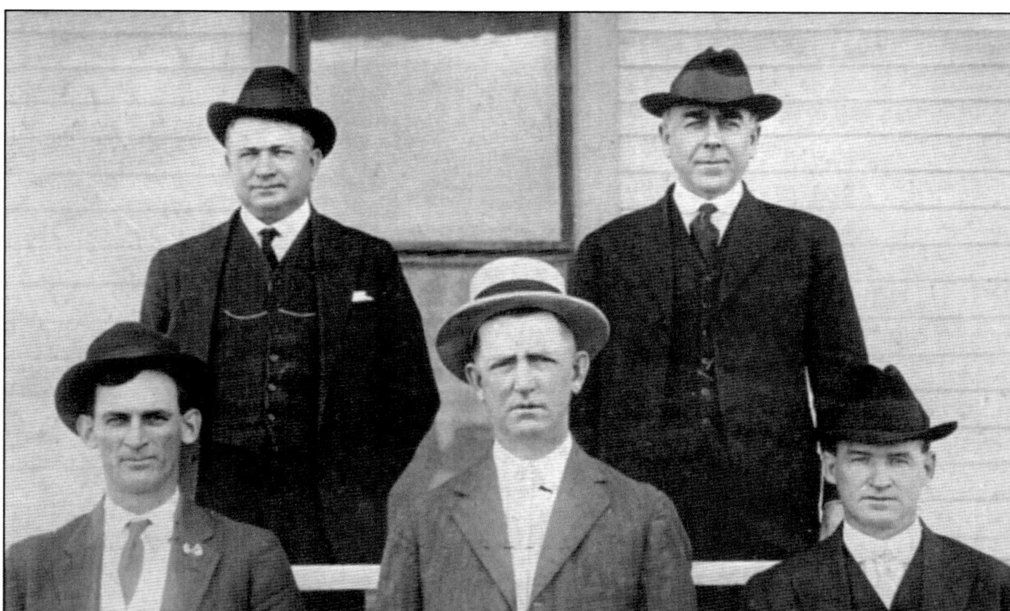

These five gentlemen are some of La Porte's earliest settlers and great supporters of the city. Anything written about the history of La Porte includes their names. This photograph is from the 1900s and includes, from left to right, (first row) fire chief Chris Isensee, Herb Neal, and F.W. Reynolds, who had been a city councilman; (second row) councilman F.C. Dorgan and mayor A.N. McKay.

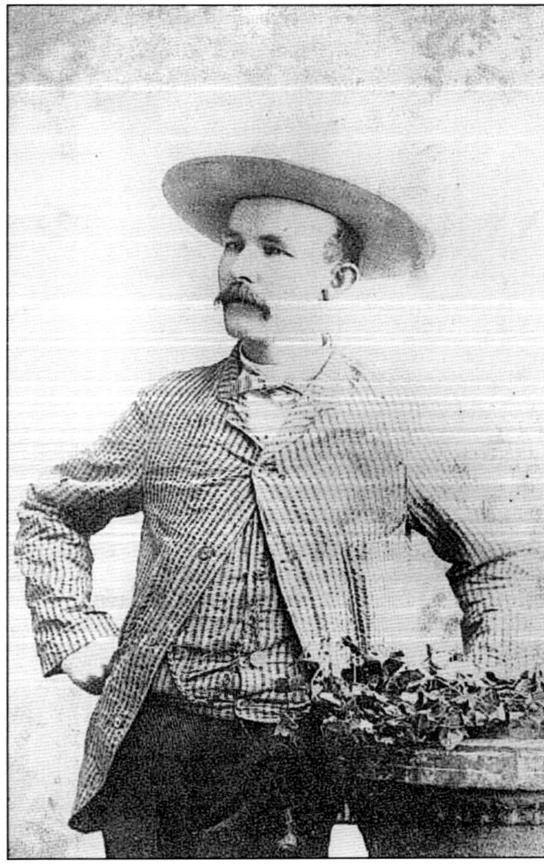

John Caplan was one of La Porte's original developers and promoters. According to Daisy La Porte Ballentine, the first baby born in La Porte after incorporation in 1892, Caplan and J.H. York, another developer, built the hotel where she was born and sold it to her father. It was across Third Street from the first hotel built in La Porte. Daisy's mother recalled seeing the artesian well come in that became the namesake of the Artesian Hotel. Caplan also gave property to the town on which La Porte's first permanent school was built.

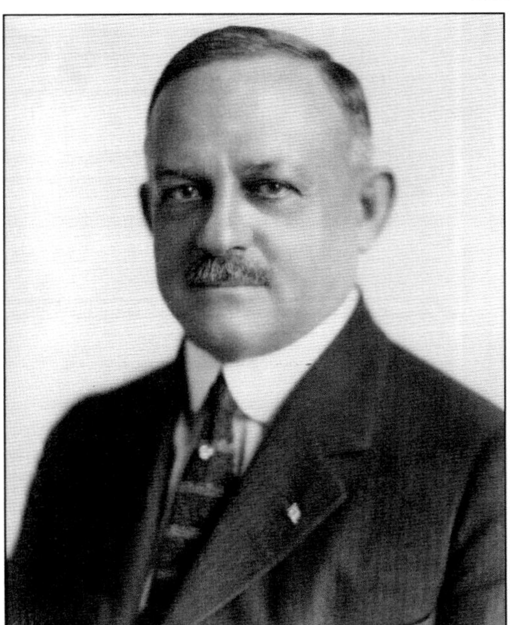

In 1928, Capt. Clyde Barbour acquired 1,435 acres at Morgan's Point with the goal of creating a maritime terminal to rival the Port of Houston. He succeeded in dredging a canal off the main ship channel called Barbour's Cut, but the Great Depression ended his dream. In 1952, the Port Authority purchased land on Barbour's Cut property as the nucleus for the terminal. (Courtesy of Julie Potter Treece.)

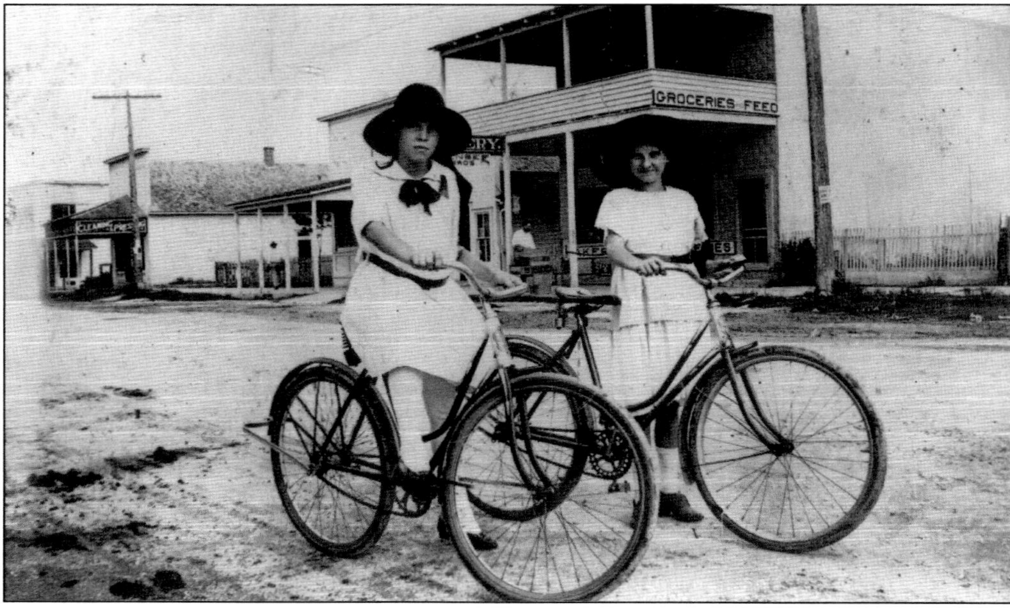

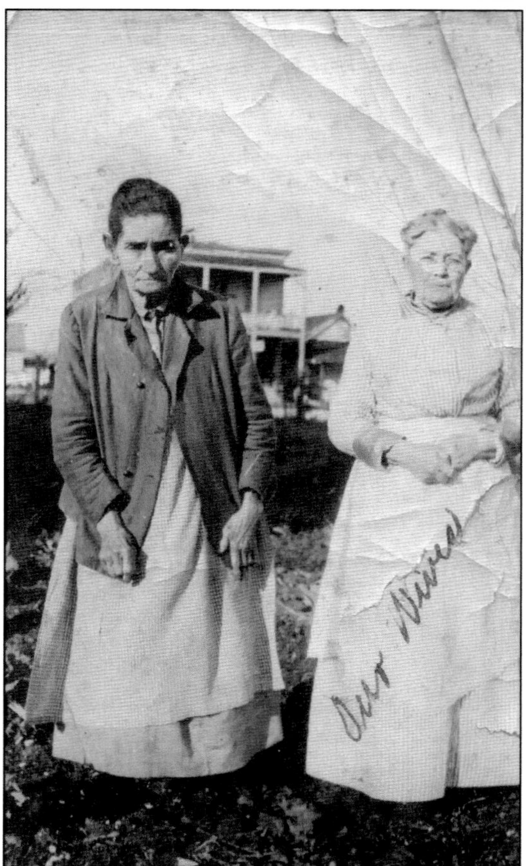

Gertrude Ackerly and her friend cycle down Main Street during the 1920s. Cycling was a popular pastime. Ackerly is responsible for the preservation of many of the photos in this collection and the recording of much of La Porte's early history. She was nearing completion of her history of La Porte when her untimely death stopped her.

Alas, we were unable to turn up a companion photograph labeled "Our Husbands," leaving readers to their imagination, if they wish, to picture the spouses of these two early La Portians. What this photograph says about the lifestyle in La Porte back then probably depends on whether you are a man or a woman.

A.N. McKay was a longtime supporter of La Porte and eventually became mayor of the city. His interests were varied and included banking and other endeavors. People like McKay were vital to the success of La Porte.

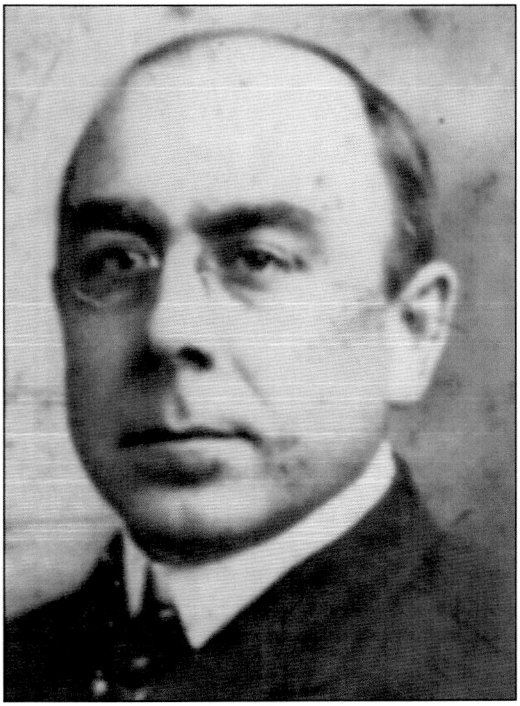

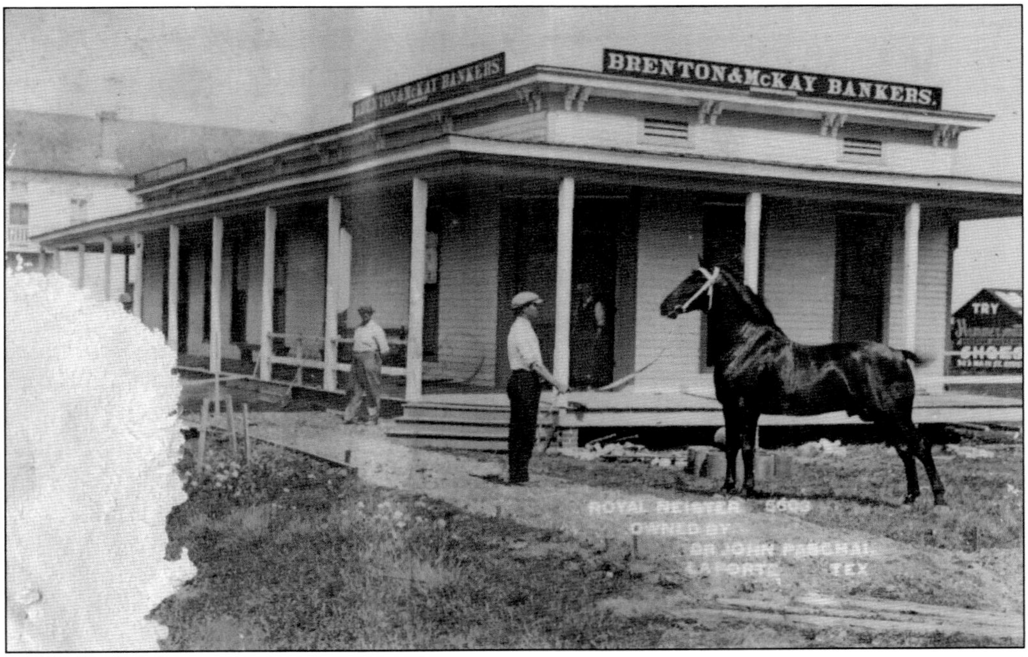

The Brenton & Mckay Bank was established in La Porte in 1901 at its location at Main and Broadway Streets in the Five Points area. The Brentons were not local, but A.N. Mckay was, making him responsible for running the bank. Early La Porte settlers and families describe Mckay as an enthusiastic promoter for the city and a good friend. Across the street from the bank stood the cafe and movie house operated by Maybell Howell.

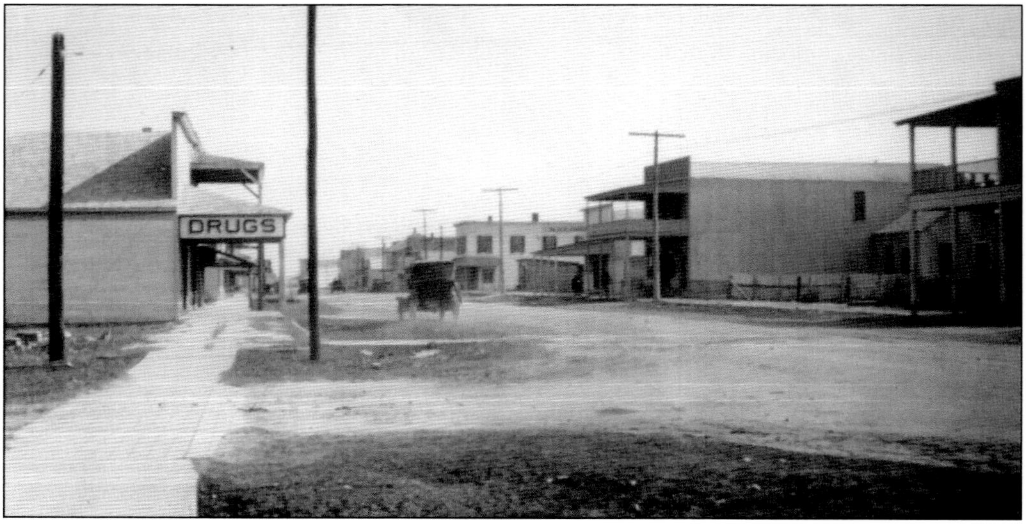

This photograph shows Main Street in La Porte shortly after the turn of the century—just after cars had arrived on the scene, but before Main Street was paved. For a couple decades, cars shared the road with hackneys and lone horsemen. Oyster shell was the most widely used base coating for roads prior to paving. The oyster industry in the Bay Area was and still is a huge employer.

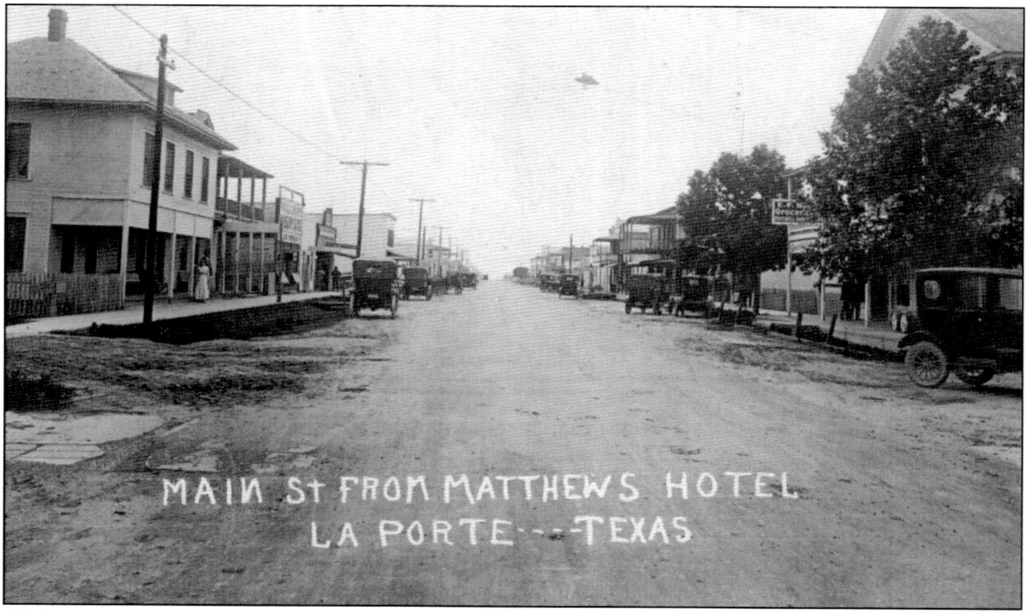

Although the streets were not yet paved, and automobiles had to traverse uneven streets, La Porte was home to a large number of new car owners. This view of Main Street shows a bustling town with many early-model cars and a sign advertising the Maxwell House Coffee available from the grocer.

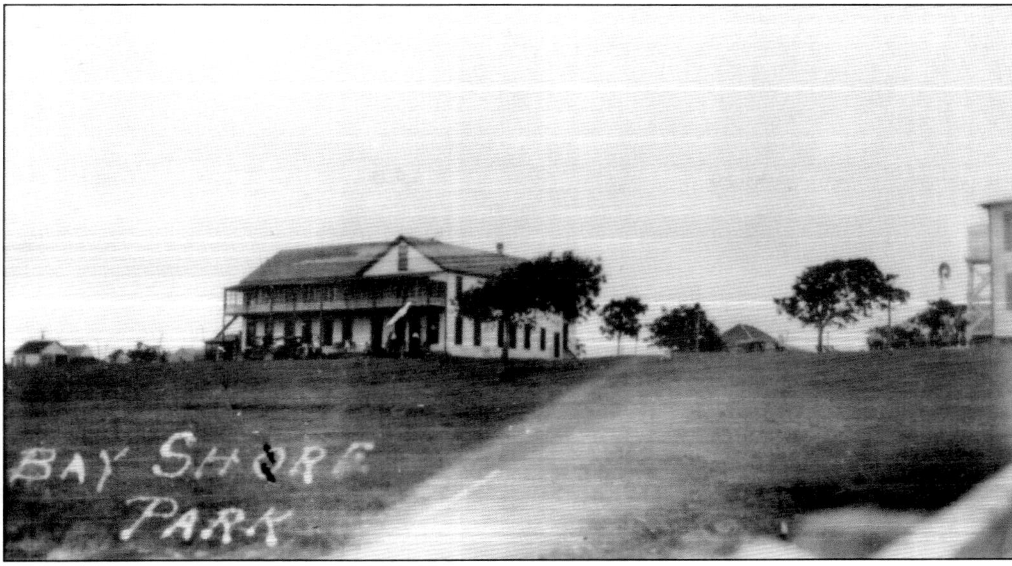

The Bay Shore Park Hotel was built near the site of the John Beazley home. His was one of the two original families residing in what became La Porte. Beazley built the Bay Shore Park Hotel to compete with the Sylvan Beach Hotel. After varying degrees of success, Beazley's hotel later became the Happy Harbor Retirement Home.

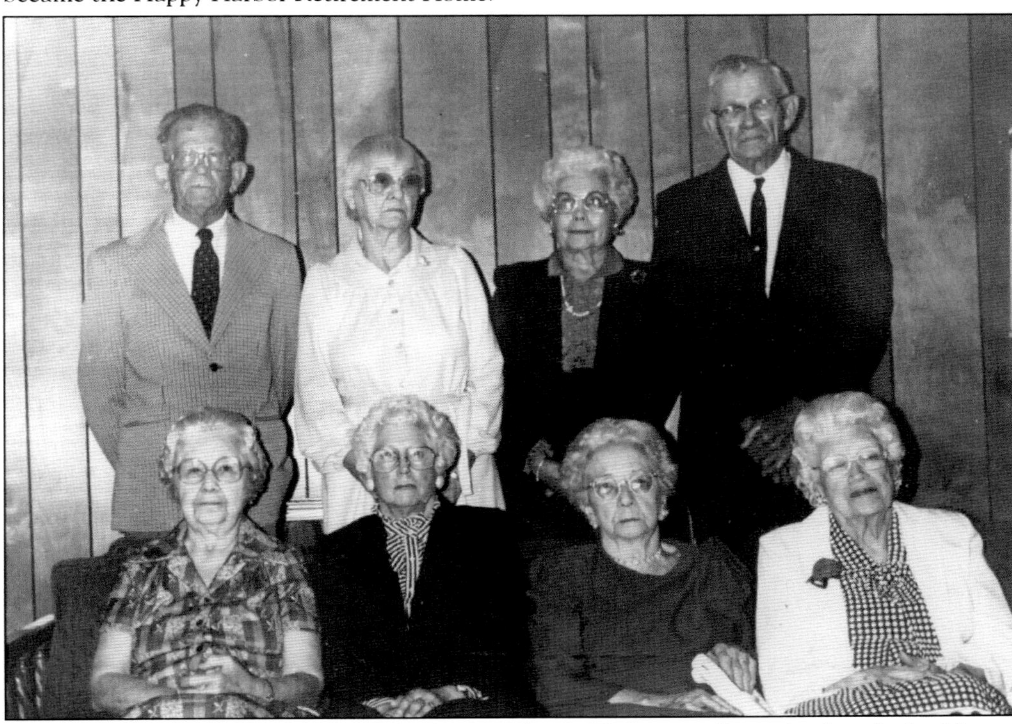

This is a group of some of La Porte's leading residents. They were all involved in the building of the city in some way. The following appear, from left to right: (first row) Florence Counts, Rena Vickers, unidentified, and Gladys Harrison; (second row) unidentified, Arbela Ralston, and Mr. and Mrs. Roper.

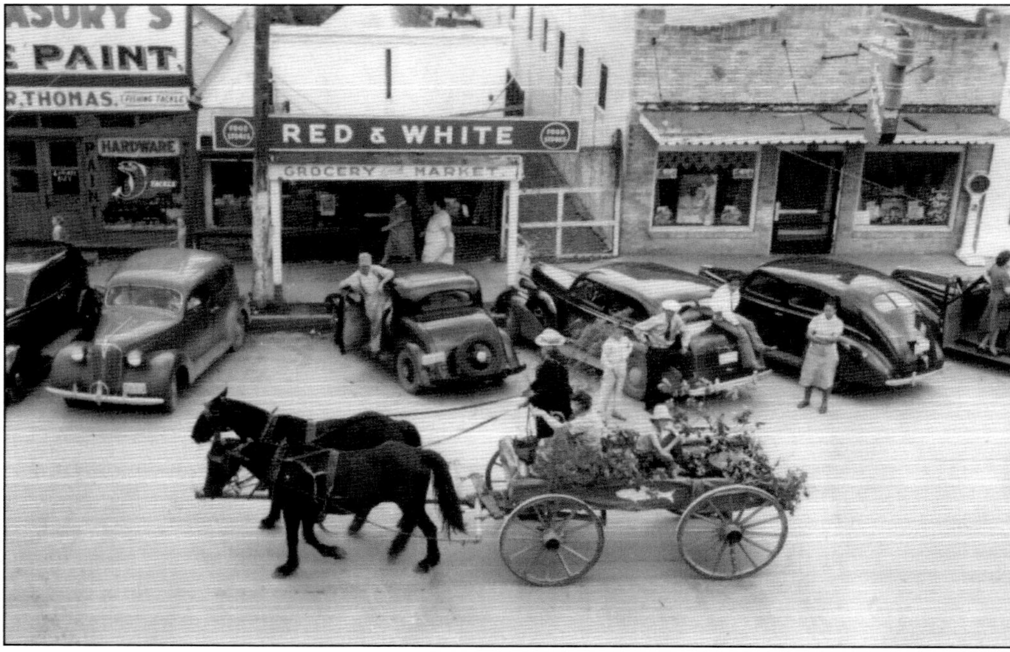

La Porte is a big parade town. The city holds parades every year for the Fourth of July, Sylvan Beach Day, Juneteenth, and for any other opportunities that come up. The residents in this photograph from the late 1930s seem to be celebrating the beginnings of La Porte. Local businesses have always supported the parades.

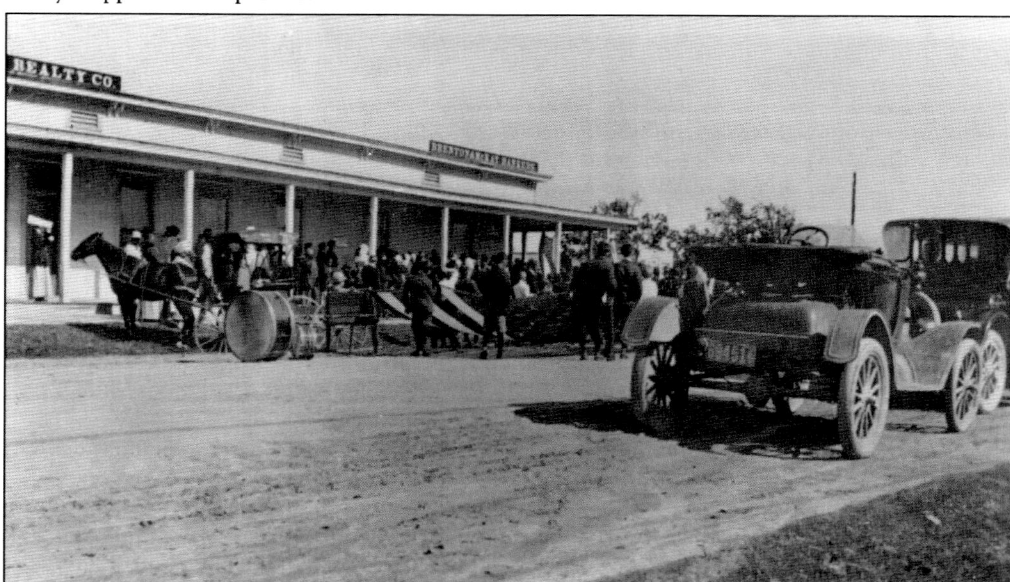

A crowd congregates in preparation for another parade in front of the Brenton & Mckay Bank at Five Points. Before the parade could begin, pretty girls would sit in the jump seat of the roadster shown, and some poor soul would have to carry the massive drum sitting on the ground in the left of the photograph, which was taken in 1934. At this time, the *Baytown Daily Sun* had just opened an office in La Porte and Erna Beth (Foxworth) Seamman had been hired as their local rep.

Nebraska Syndicate promoters appointed the first mayor of La Porte. As the city evolved during the late 1890s and early 1900s, the need for better facilities became apparent. On July 31, 1907, the city council voted to build La Porte's first city hall and jail, which would replace the old freight car used as a makeshift holding cell for criminals and miscreants. George Van Pelt was contracted to construct the new facility at a cost of $660.85. It was erected on Second Street and remained there until 1932 when it was moved across the street (where it still stands).

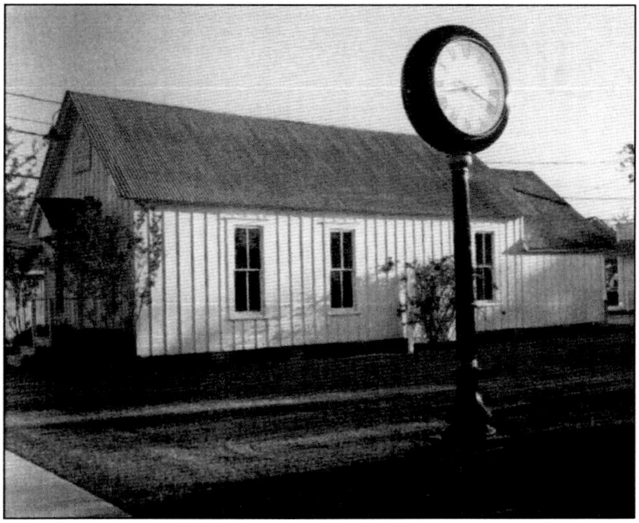

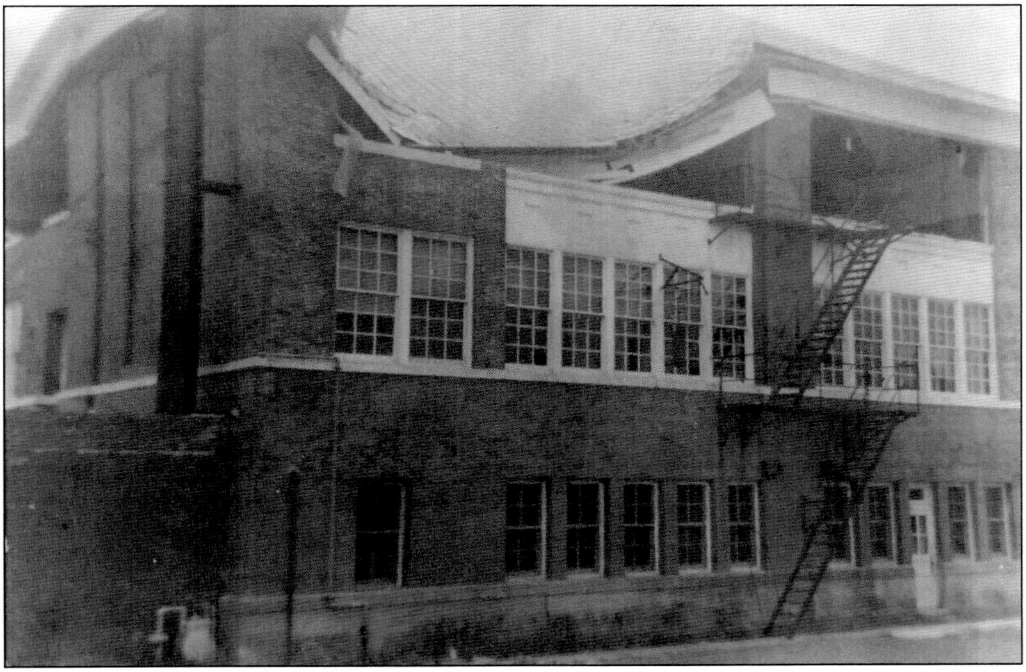

This photograph shows some of the devastation following the "Surprise Hurricane" that hit La Porte on July 27, 1943. The *Galveston Daily News* reported that more than 6,000 homes were damaged in Goose Creek, and La Porte and listed the death toll at 20. La Porte High School was damaged in the hurricane, and students had to meet in ad hoc arrangements until repairs were completed.

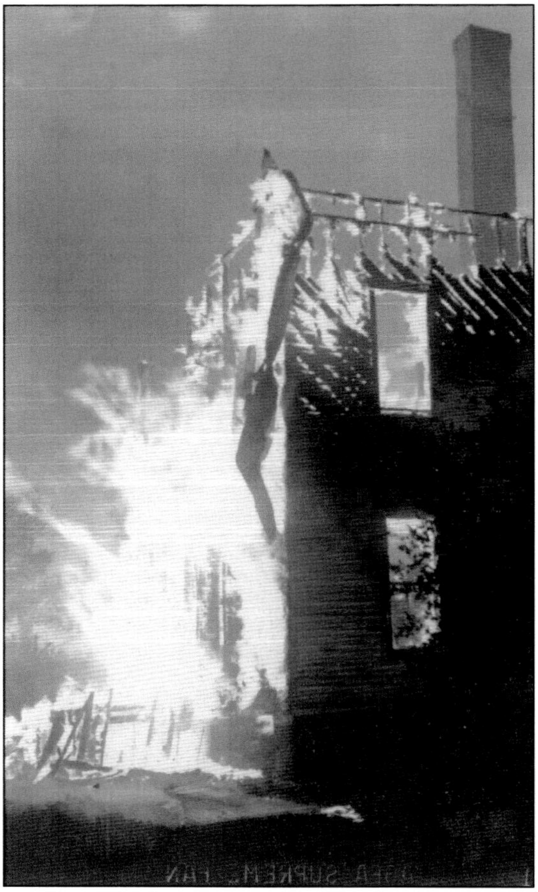

La Porte has had three disastrous fires. The first occurred in 1893 in the 300 block of Main Street; the second in 1898 around the time of Halloween, and the third fire was in 1915. The photograph at left shows a raging fire, and below is the aftermath of that fire, which ultimately burned much of the town. It started in the Besson building where automobile services were performed. A spark from fixing a tire ignited the gasoline barrel nearby. The Besson building was a three-story brick structure and the pride of La Porte. The city was rebuilding from the fire when the Great Storm of 1915, which wreaked havoc on the entire Bay Area, occurred. The fires and hurricanes over the years have dealt La Porte many devastating blows, but the city has always recovered quickly.

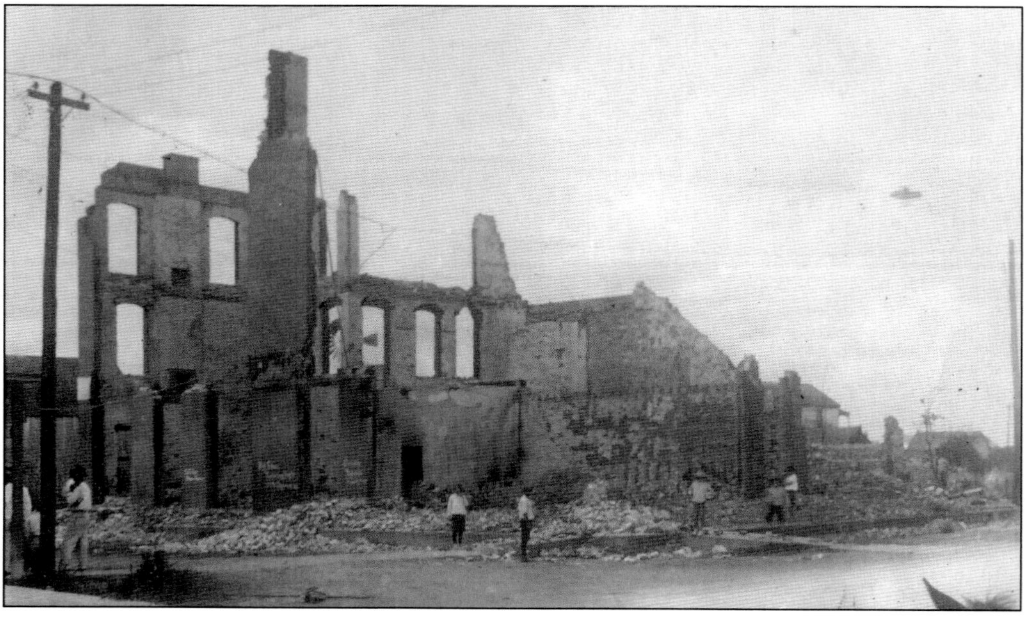

Two

THE BUSINESS COMMUNITY

Despite the ravages of fires and storms over the centuries, the La Porte business community has continued to thrive. Some of the first buildings erected were the hotels. The Ballentine of La Porte Hotel, erected by early pioneer McElroy Ballentine, was built facing east on the 100 block of Third Street. In 1896, Ballentine sold the property to Tom Matthews, at which time it became the Matthews Hotel; Matthews moved the structure to the 200 block of Second Street. Moving buildings like this was quite commonplace in early La Porte. The Artesian Hotel, with its more than 60 rooms, was built in 1893. Col. A.M. York built the Sylvan Hotel near the present location of St. Mary's Catholic Church.

Guy Hopkins ran the Palace Livery Stable on Second Street, and he advertised, "60 horses were available for lease or sale." The *La Porte Chronicle* began publication almost contemporaneously with the incorporation of the town in 1892, and in 1899, Joe Williams began publishing the *La Porte Herald*. Sharp's Ice Cream was a favorite of the Sylvan Beach crowd. Operated by Mrs. Sharp, the ice cream shop offered fresh dairy products from husband John's dairy.

M. Figley was a leading local photographer, and his son ran an apothecary. A.O. Blackwell was an attorney, John Baker had lumberyards, and M.K. Morris started the La Porte Lumber Company in 1894. Important family names in the community included Kirkland, McKay, Isensee, Agees, Parker, Johnson, and many others. The Shannon, Hovey, and Slusher families ran hardware stores, and the Bush and Baker families had a popular meat market. Ed Pfeiffer supplied both La Porte and Sylvan Beach with electricity, A.H. Willetts sourced bricks for construction, and Frank W. Kirkland and F.L. Putnam advertised their services as architects. A restaurant owned by the Simpson family catered to the likes of famous entertainer Rudy Vallée.

One of the stated goals of the founders of La Porte was "the establishment of a great commercial center and leading harbor on the coast of Texas." This goal was achieved, but the La Porte community also managed to strike a balance among quality of life, integrity in business, responsible civic-minded growth, and aesthetics—a balance that was not always easy for growing cities to achieve at this time.

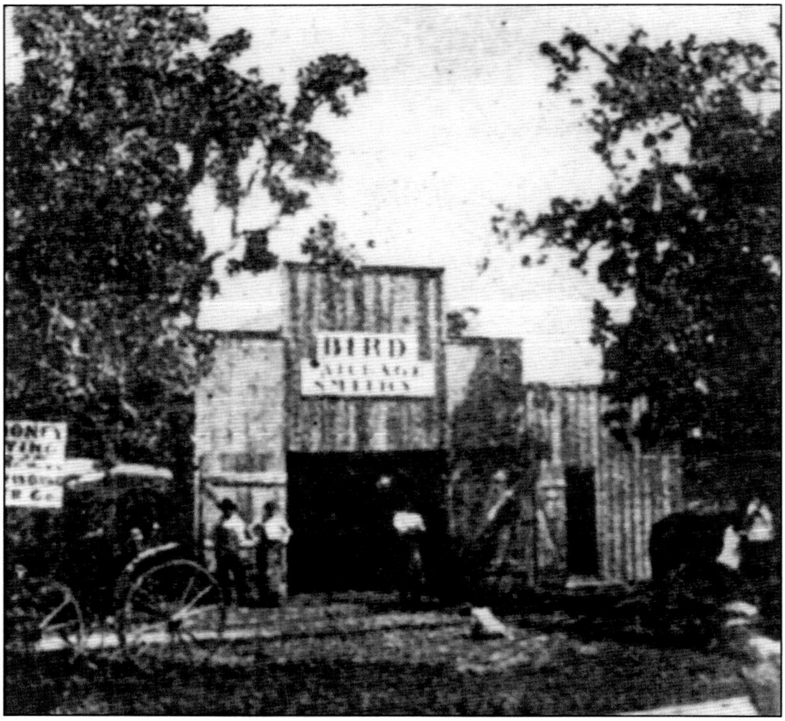

Bird Sharp bought this business in 1906 from Tommy Sullivan. It was a popular location to get horses shod and buggies and wagons repaired. Six years later, Bird left this business to develop and market an invention that replaced the singletree, a device that helped distribute the strain on the horses shoulders when they are pulling large loads. He obtained a patent, and this invention was sold on the open market.

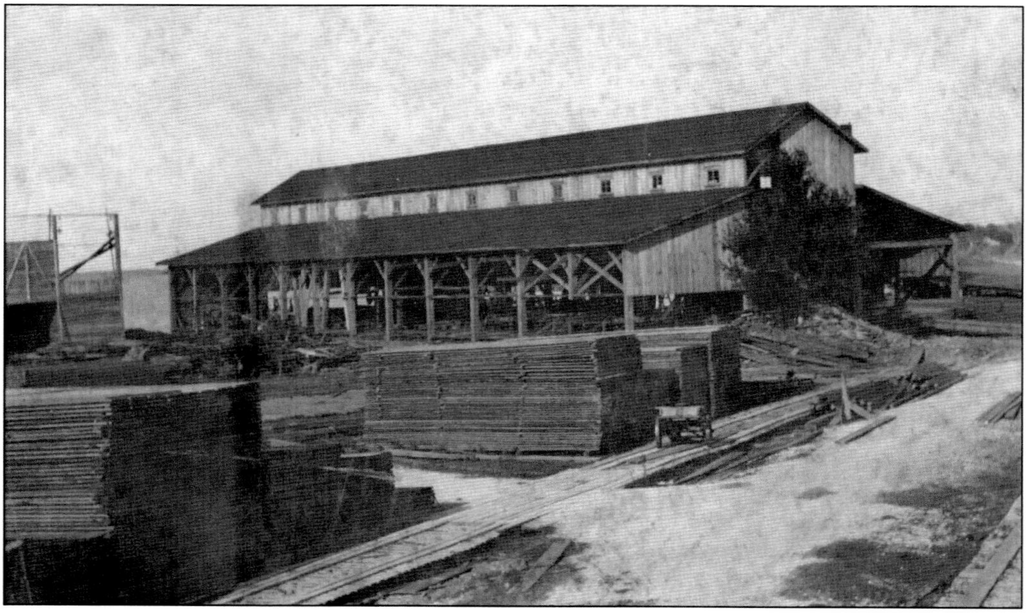

The edition of the *Galveston Daily News* from June 6, 1903, states, "La Porte Saw and Planing mill is located on the banks of San Jacinto Bay. It has a capacity of 50,000 feet daily and seems to be doing a prosperous business." The La Porte Saw and Planing Mill burned on January 28, 1906. At the time, it was the largest employer in La Porte. The mill was never rebuilt.

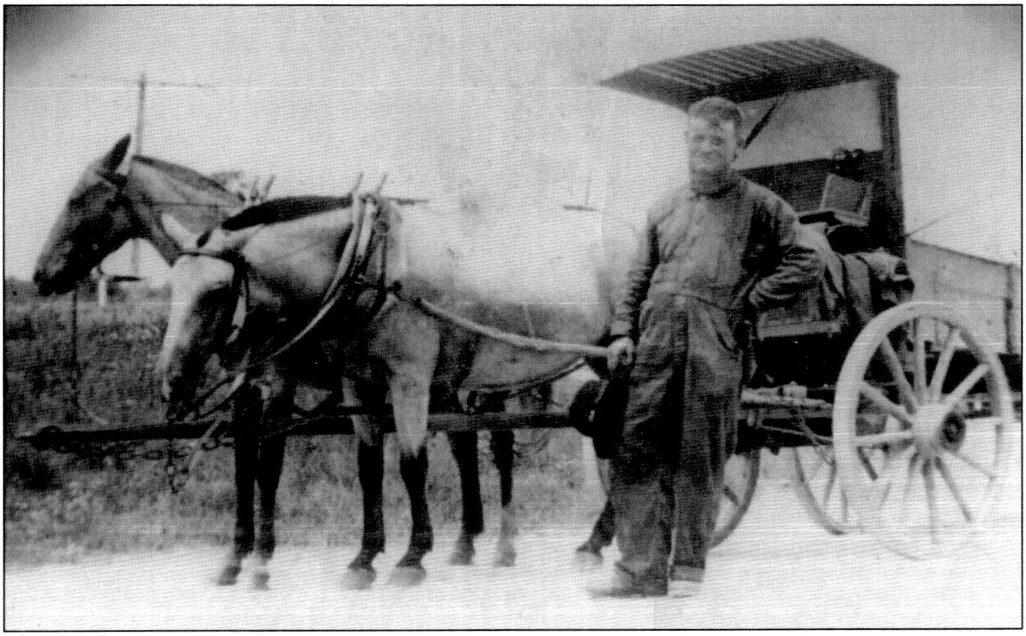

Hayes Hamilton, one of the earlier settlers of La Porte, became an iceman. He traveled to Houston every two weeks to get ice. The photograph shows Hamilton standing by his ice wagon, which was the first one in town.

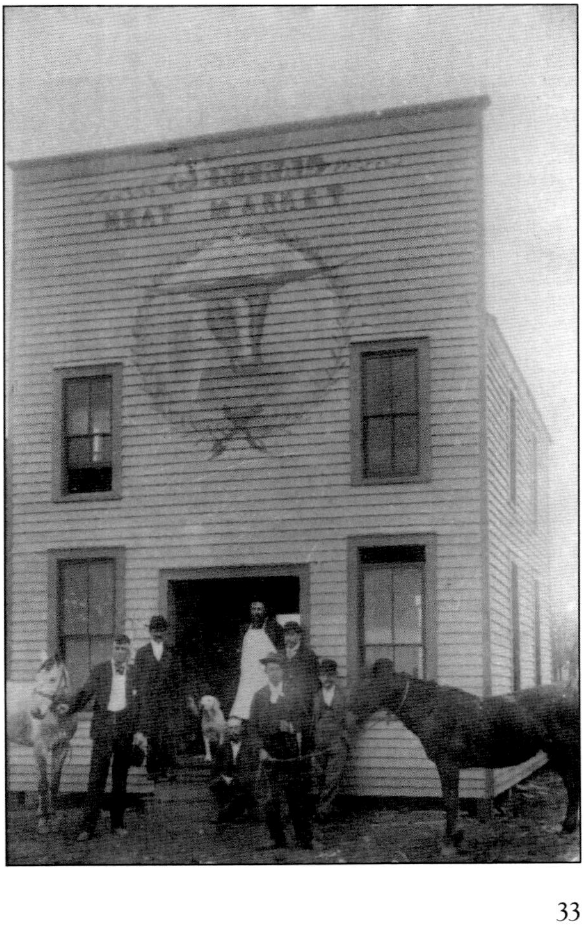

In 1895, Richard Baker came to La Porte from Baytown. He and wife May Busch operated several establishments, including the Panama Grocery. La Porte had several groceries and meat markets at various times during the days before supermarket chains began dominating the grocery business.

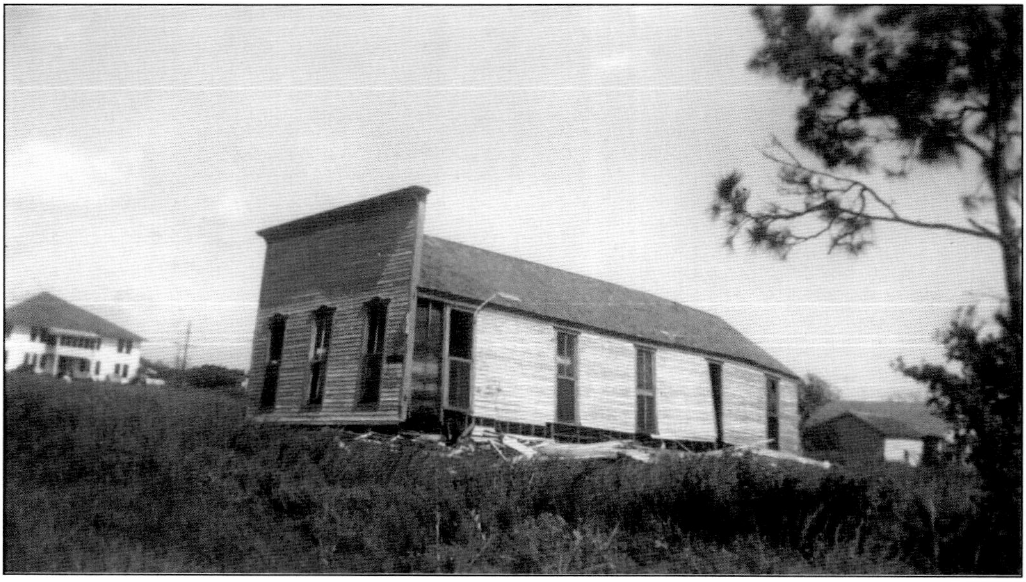

The B.F. Howald building was once a two-story structure and was, in fact, described as the largest mercantile building in New Town. Like many of La Porte's early buildings, it was moved. In 1915, it was located at Five Points, and after the great fire, it temporarily served as the post office and a movie house. Unlike most buildings around it, the Howald building sustained only minor damage in the hurricane of 1915.

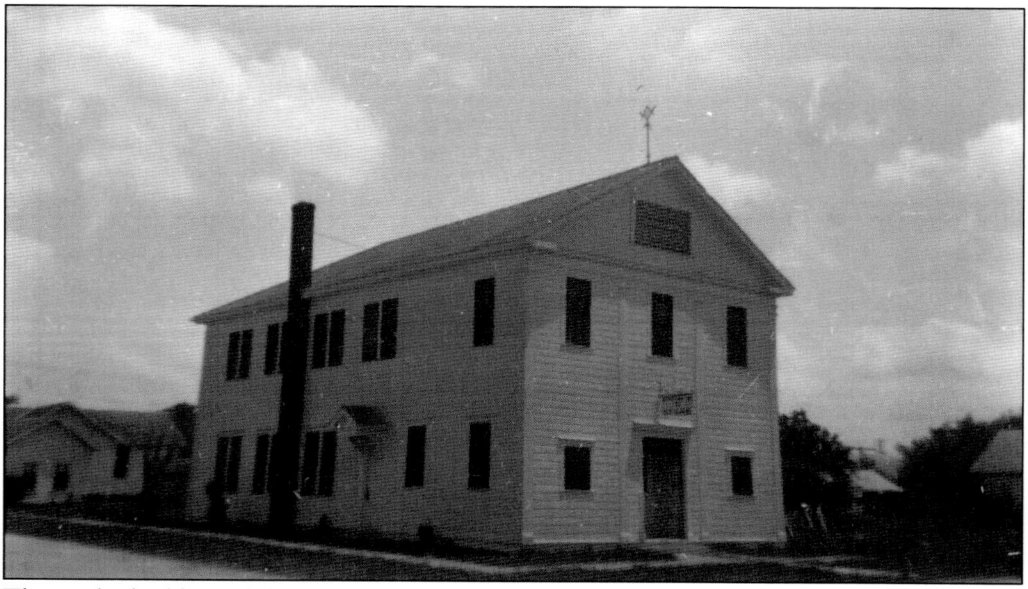

This is the building of the Fraternal Order of Freemasons AF & AM Lodge 857 in La Porte. The Masons organized in La Porte on January 16, 1902. Many of La Porte's leading residents and several of its mayors over the years have been members of this lodge.

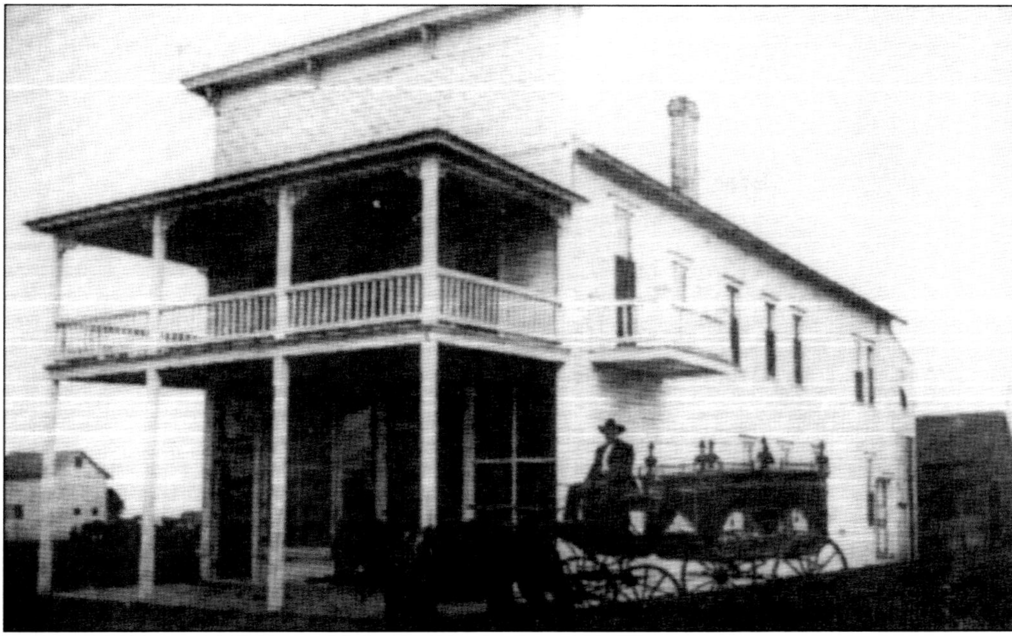

This is the Johnson building on Main Street in La Porte around 1900. The Johnsons moved to La Porte from Illinois via Pearland in 1896. They owned a funeral parlor located in the Johnson building, which was sometimes referred to as the Johnson Hotel. The Johnsons are said to have come to Texas in a covered wagon.

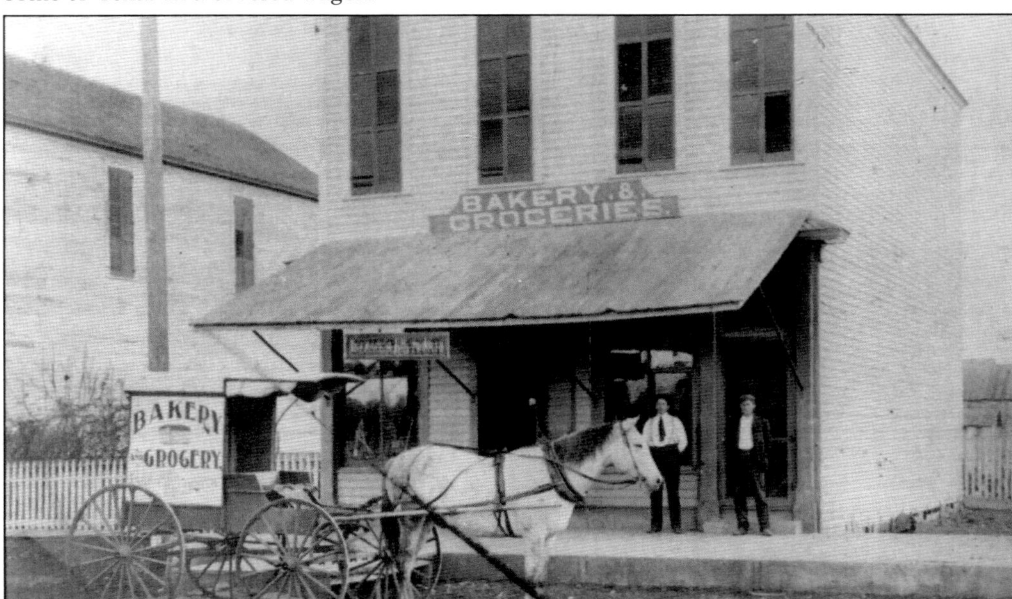

This is the Isensee Grocery, sometimes called the IGA grocery. Judge Stovall described it as a place where housewives could go to "gossip and grab groceries." The Isensees were longtime La Portians and, at one time, they owned the property upon which the Artesian Hotel was first located. They operated various businesses in La Porte, including a grocery and a saloon, and John Isensee played in La Porte's first band.

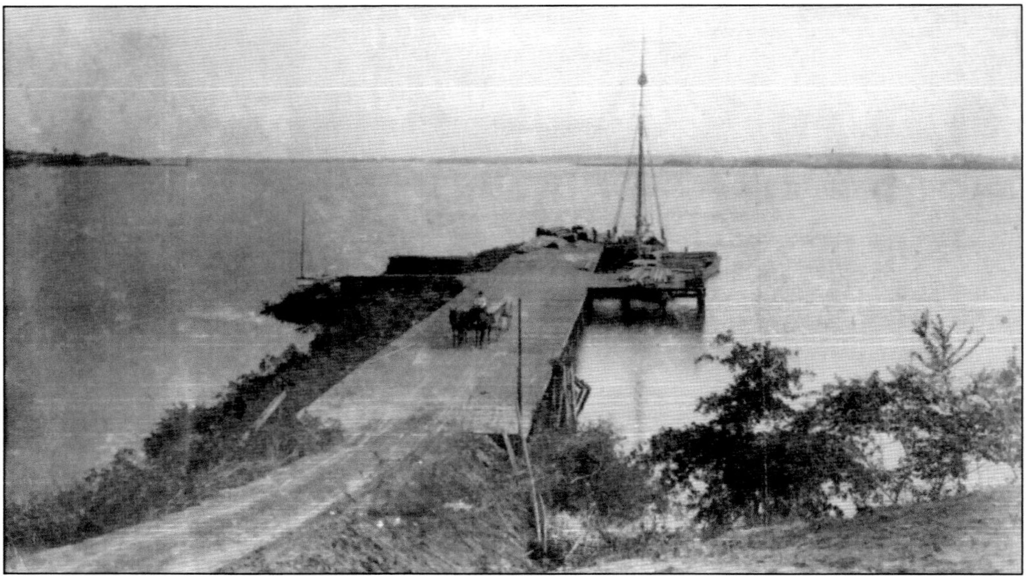

This is the Broadway Wharf at the foot of Broadway Street, near where the Barbour's Cut Container Terminal now stands. This photograph shows the wharf on San Jacinto Bay in 1892. It was used to transship and offload lumber and materials from Houston, Harrisburg, and Cedar Bayou. Soon thereafter, a sawmill opened nearby on the San Jacinto Bay.

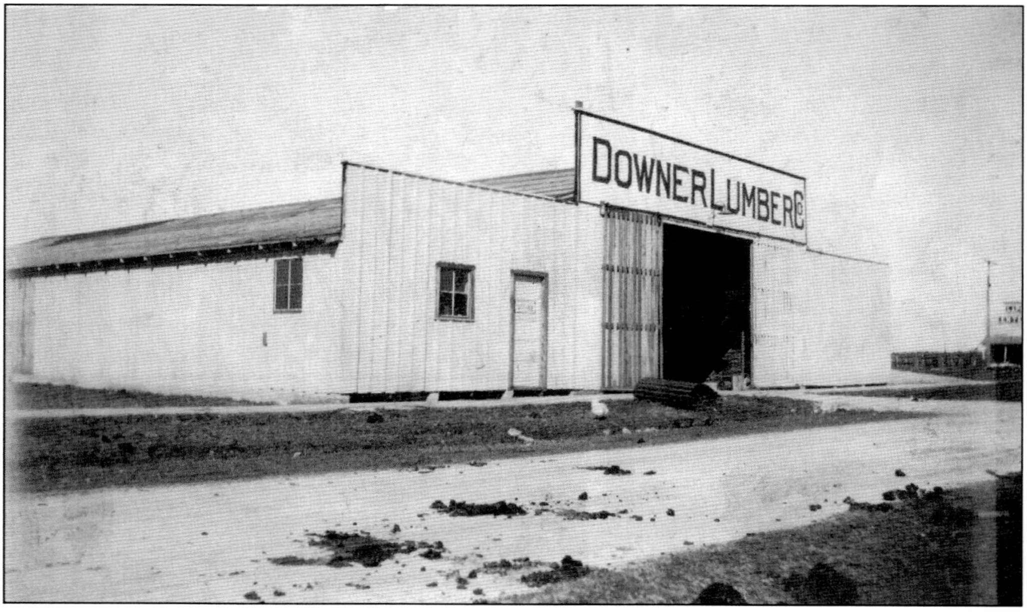

This photograph, taken in 1916, shows the Downer Lumber Company. Mrs. Downer also rented out a house across the road from the Ferris wheel and merry-go-round at Sylvan Beach around 1923. The *Galveston Daily News* contains the announcement that E.C. Downer had completed his new building on Second Street in 1921.

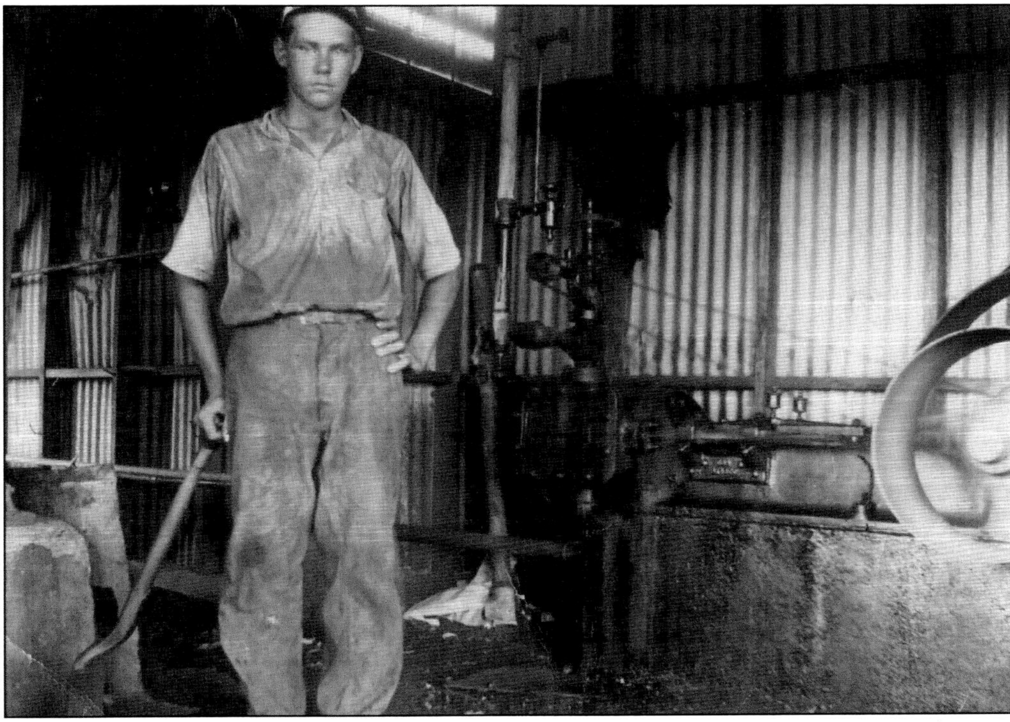

Farmers attempted to cultivate various agricultural products, including oranges, pecans, and cotton, until they determined that fig trees flourished the best in La Porte's climate. Close inspection shows the streets and glades in La Porte still teeming with fig trees. The factory in the photograph above was probably the one started by Henry Benjamin "Happy" Harrison, a professional baseball player whose career was ended by an injury sustained while barnstorming at Sylvan Beach. He stayed on to found a fig farm and cannery and later served as mayor. The bottom photograph displays the exterior of Harrison's factory, which was located near Lomax.

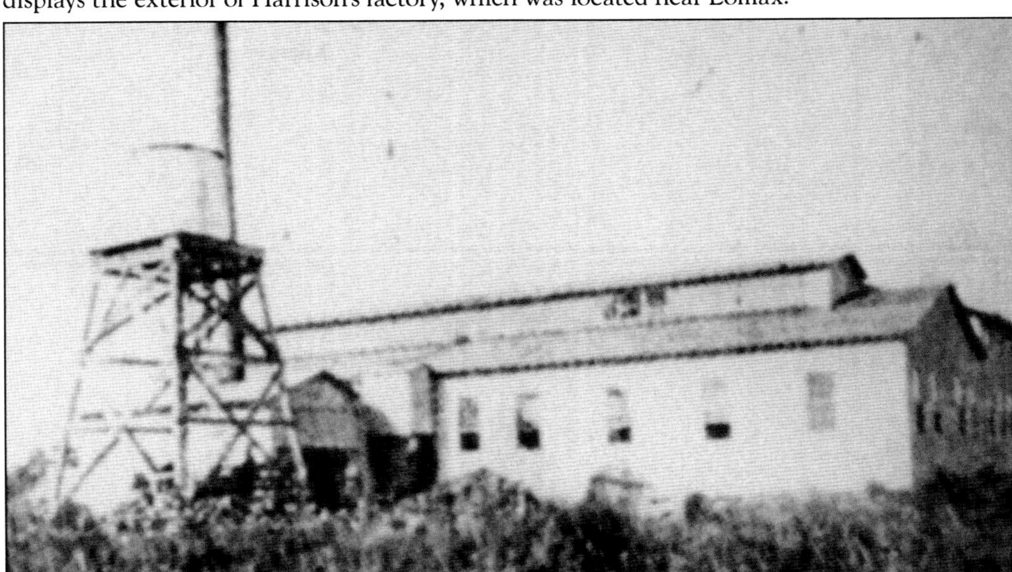

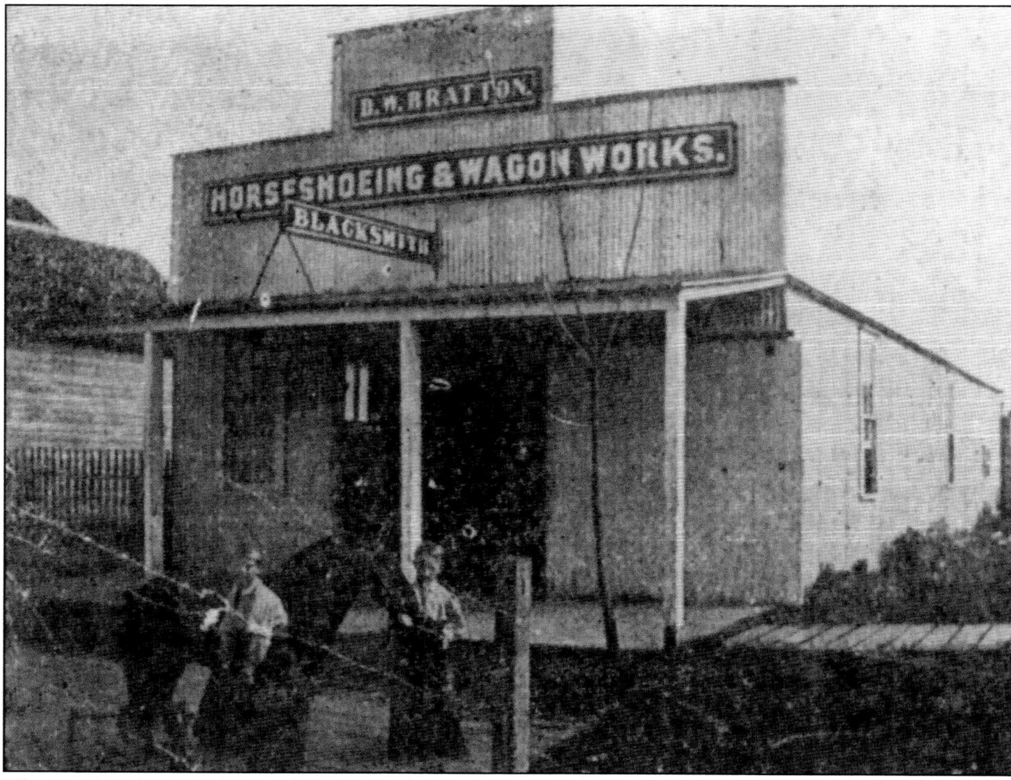

This is the Bratton Horseshoeing and Wagon Works circa 1895. Blacksmithing in La Porte in 1895 was very hot work. David William Bratton was the only blacksmith in town at that time. The Brattons had five surviving children, and many of their descendants (including the Rosses and the Riemens) still live in La Porte.

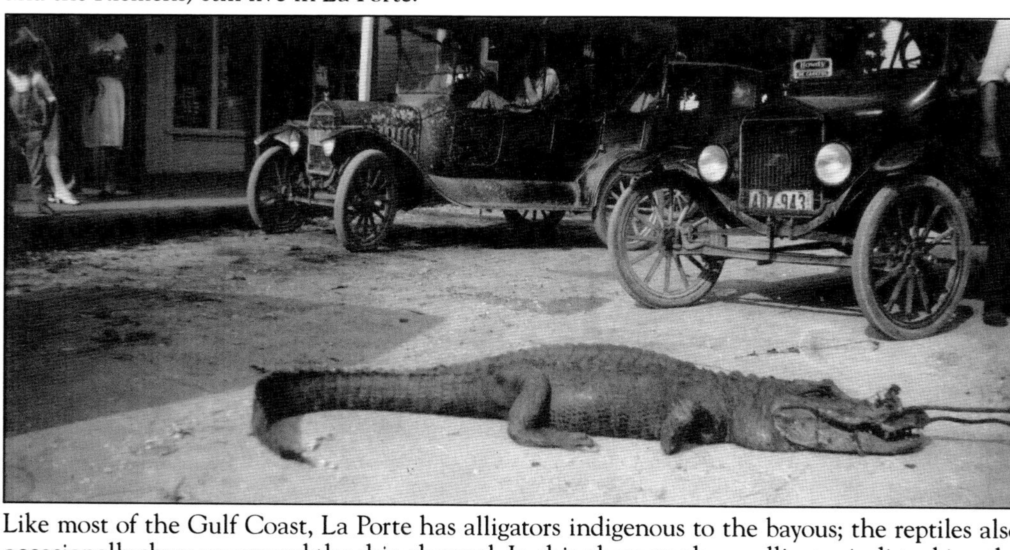

Like most of the Gulf Coast, La Porte has alligators indigenous to the bayous; the reptiles also occasionally show up around the ship channel. In this photograph, an alligator is disturbing the normal course of business on La Porte's Main Street around 1910 and has had his jaws trussed preliminary to removal.

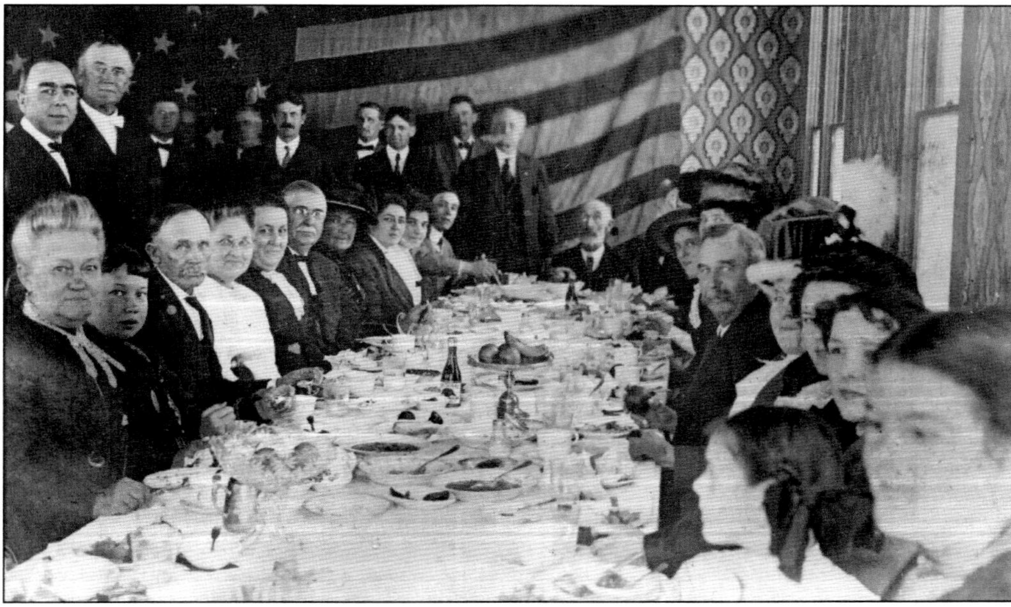

The banquet in this picture is being held on the top floor of the three-story Besson building. The members pictured here represent three generations of the Chamber of Commerce, and by the time of this photograph, they had survived a severe financial panic that gripped Harris County the year before. The Besson building was lost in a devastating fire in 1915.

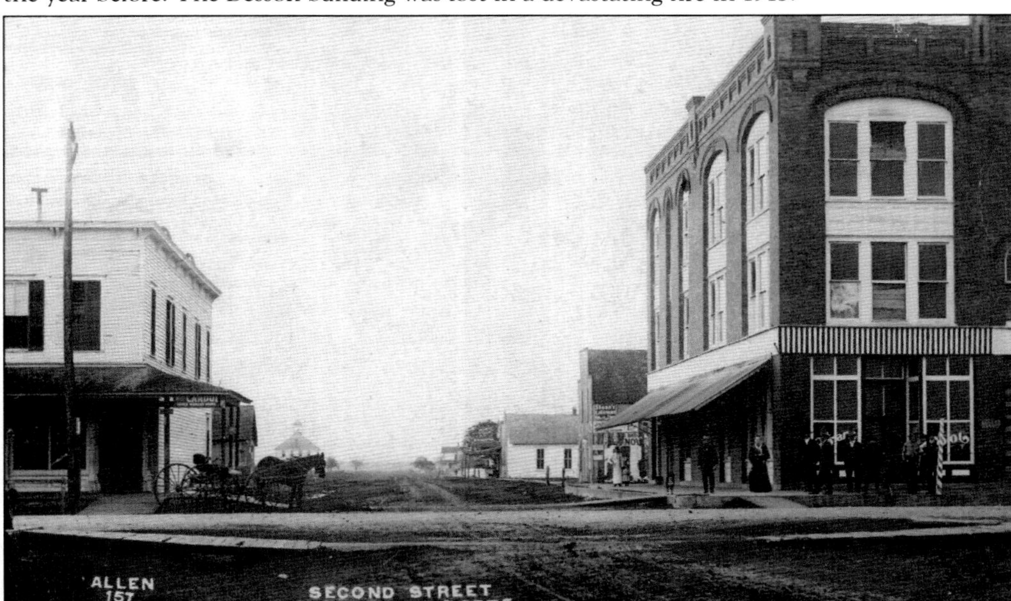

Madame Besson came from London to the 1893 World's Fair in Chicago and saw promotions for La Porte. She came down to visit and was so impressed she purchased several properties and commissioned the Besson building at Second and Main Streets. The first floor contained a facility for fueling cars from gasoline stored in barrels inside the building. This is where the fire that destroyed La Porte in 1915 started. The first permanent schoolhouse can be seen in the background.

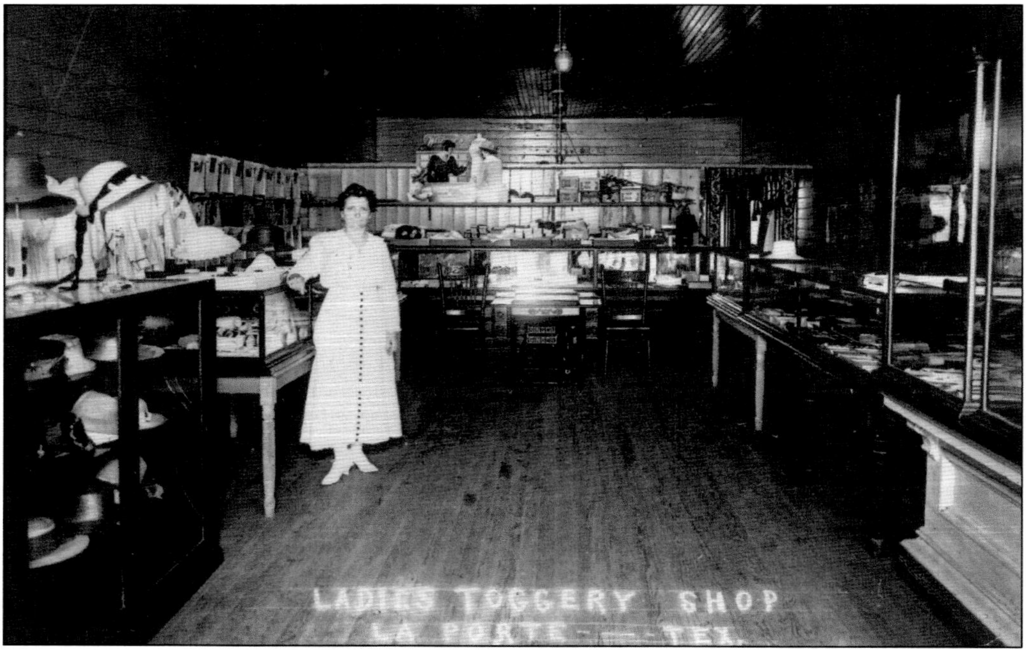

Gertrude Ackerly is pictured in her ladies shop on Main Street. She not only was a businesswoman but also took an interest in local history and the early residents of La Porte. Without her diligence at collecting that information, writing this history would have been difficult. She passed this interest along to daughter Arbela Ralston and grandson Gordon Black who graciously shared it for the writing of this book.

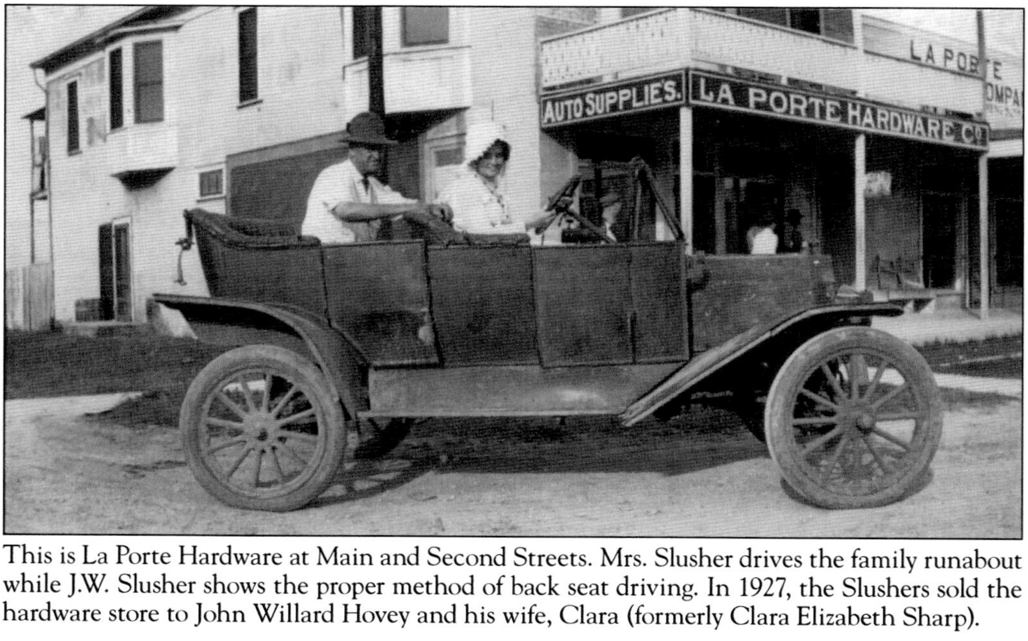

This is La Porte Hardware at Main and Second Streets. Mrs. Slusher drives the family runabout while J.W. Slusher shows the proper method of back seat driving. In 1927, the Slushers sold the hardware store to John Willard Hovey and his wife, Clara (formerly Clara Elizabeth Sharp).

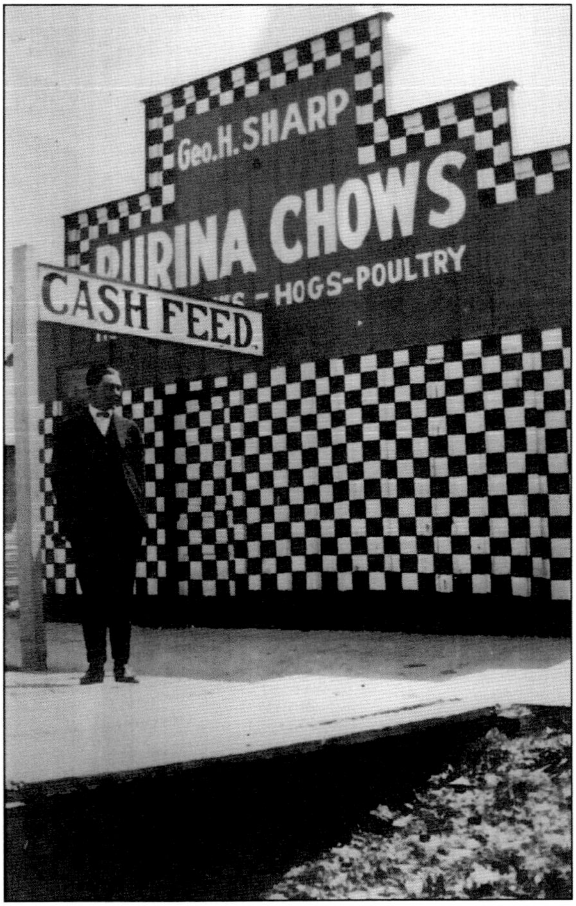

The Sharp family was one of the first families to settle in La Porte. They have contributed in a great way to the growth of the city. John Z. Sharp was a dairyman, among other things. He and his wife, Sarah (Johnson), raised a family in La Porte. Together, they opened Sharp's Confectionery on the corner of Main and Second Streets. It became popular with local residents and tourists. These photographs show George Sharp, John's son, in front of the business, which he and his wife, Irene (Kropet), ran for 58 years. George opened Sharp's Grain and Feed at the age of 18. Sharp descendants still live in the area.

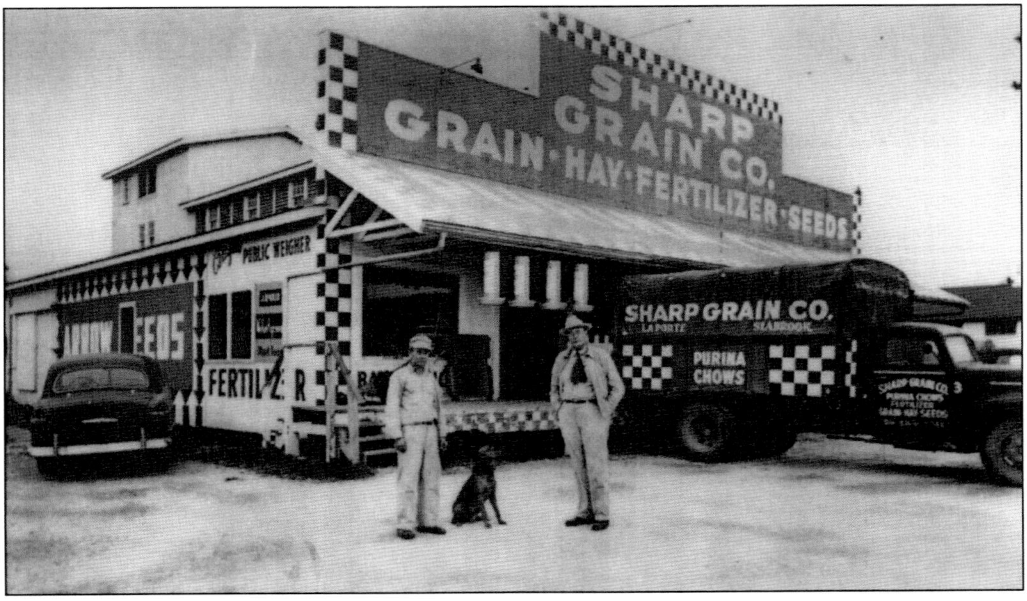

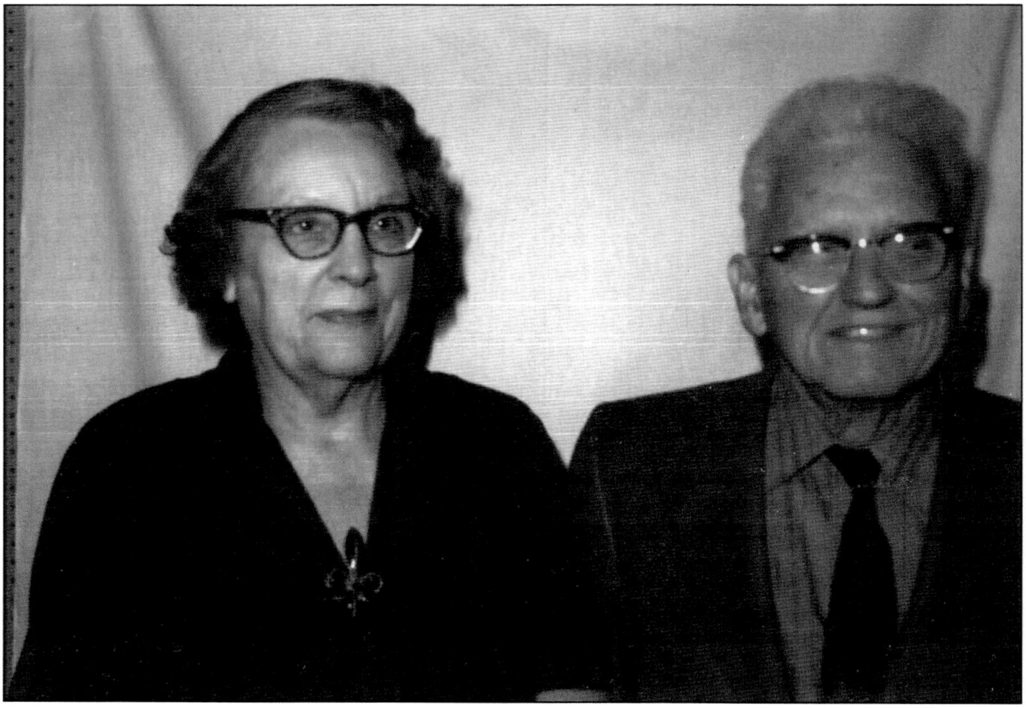

John Willard Hovey and his wife bought the hardware store from the Slushers. His parents, Leroy Gould Hovey and wife Mary, moved to La Porte in 1895 from Lincoln, Nebraska and were in business in La Porte for a long time. Hoveys still reside in the area.

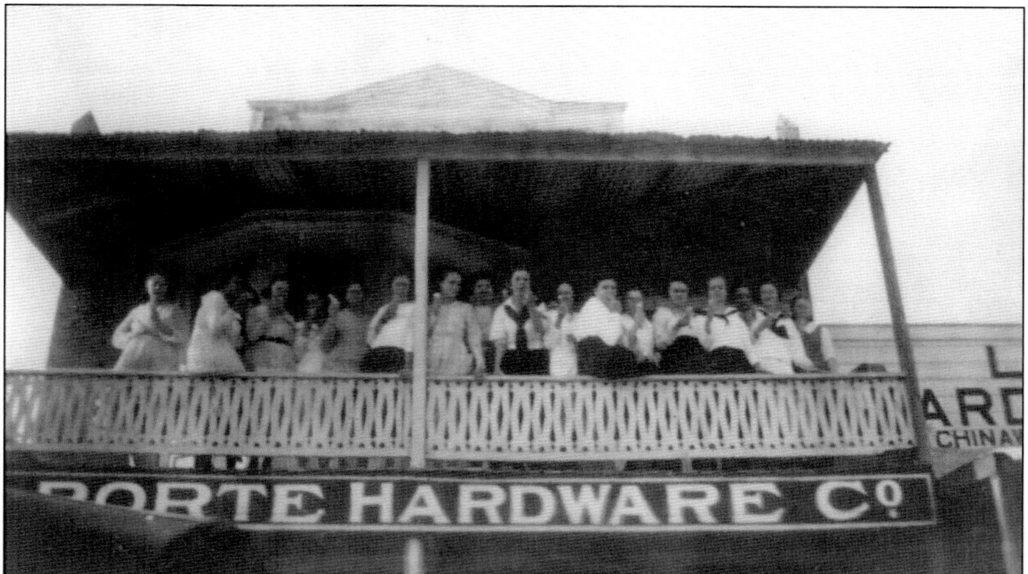

The Slusher family owned a hardware store and sold to the Hoveys in 1927. The Hoveys were original members of the La Porte Community Church when it was chartered in 1925. The Shannons also owned a hardware store in La Porte. This photograph shows the stores upstairs packed with people, probably enjoying one of La Porte's many parades.

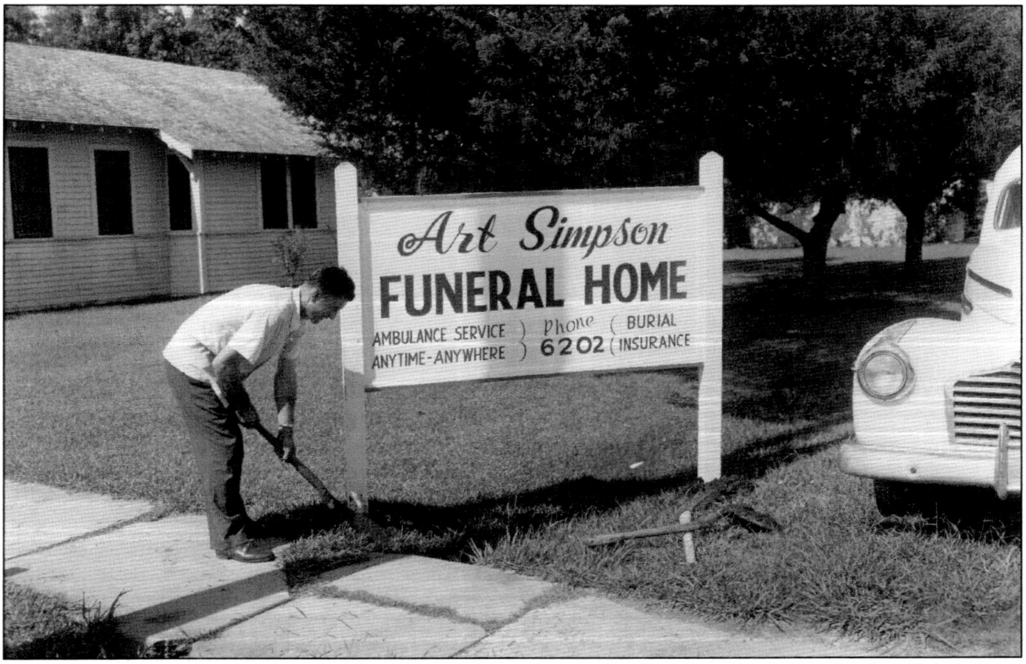

The Art Simpson Funeral Home began operations in 1949, and it was rebuilt at Third and A Streets in 1954 and it remains at that location today. Members of the Simpson family still reside in the area. It is now the Paul U. Lee Funeral Home and is still caring for the needs of the La Porte community.

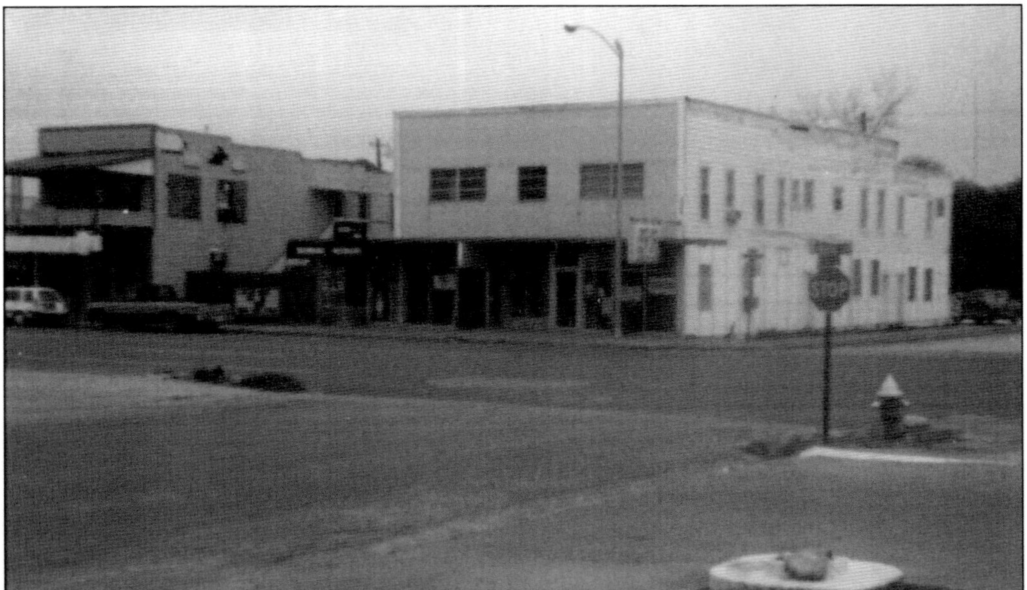

The Sayres building was at the corner of Main and First Streets. In 1929, it briefly served as the first home of the *La Porte News Tribune*, run initially by C.M. Bond, who brought La Porte's first typesetting machine to town for the purpose of this paper. The previously shell-covered Main Street was paved with concrete for the first time in 1928.

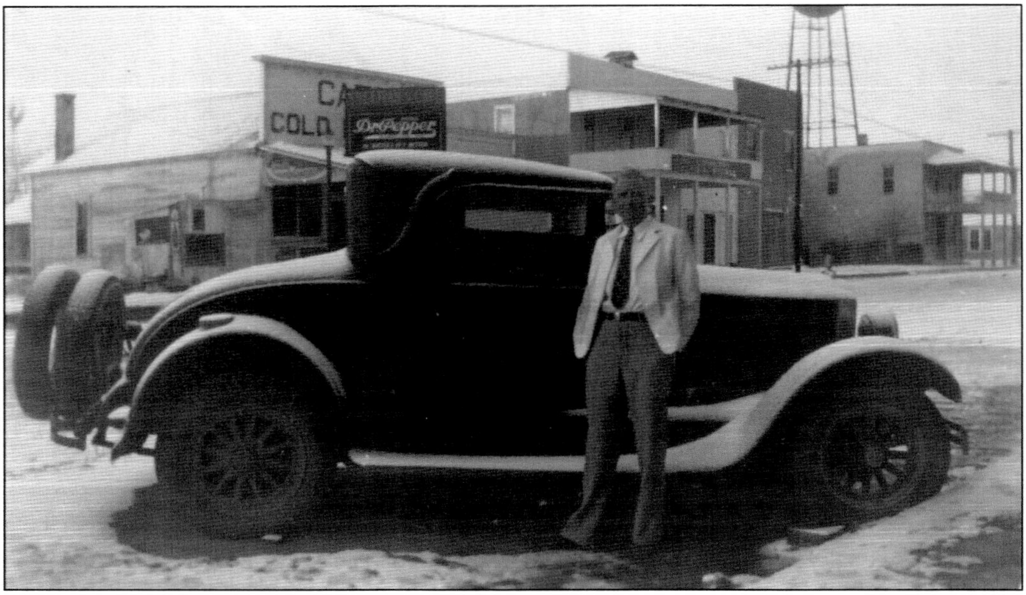

Jim Simpson stands beside his 1929 automobile on Main Street in La Porte. His pharmacy was located on Main Street between Second and Third Streets. Main Street had only recently been paved when this photograph was taken.

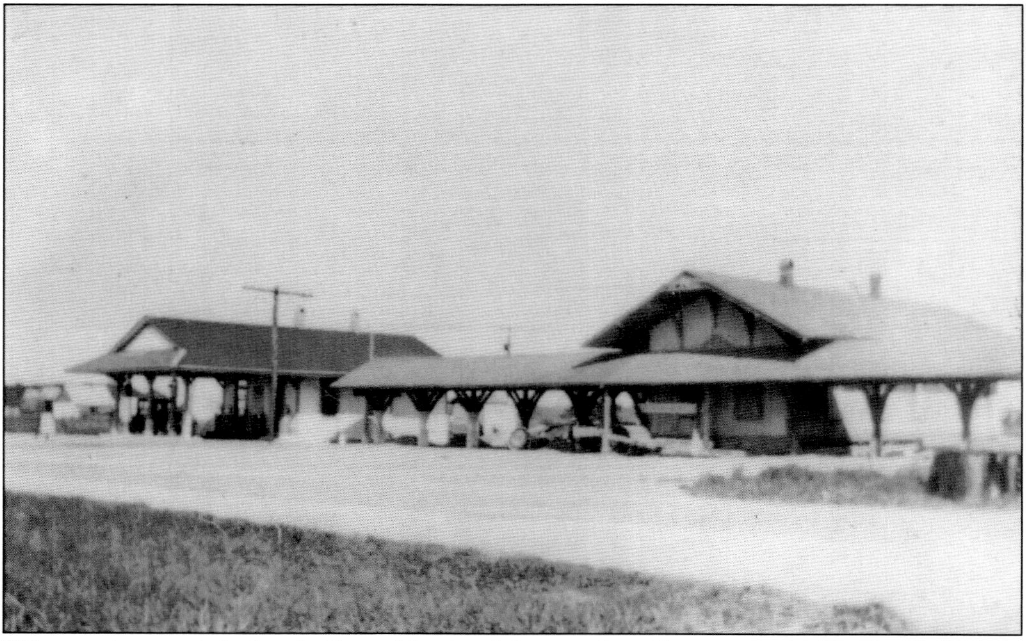

When train travel declined, Capt. Charles Ashton, a local businessman, bought the Sylvan Beach and Morgan's Point Depots. He moved them to Main Street near Five Points and had them remodeled into a service station and store. The businesses eventually closed and sat dormant until the Sylvan Depot was moved back to Sylvan Beach Park and renovated for use as a museum by the La Porte Bay Area Heritage Society.

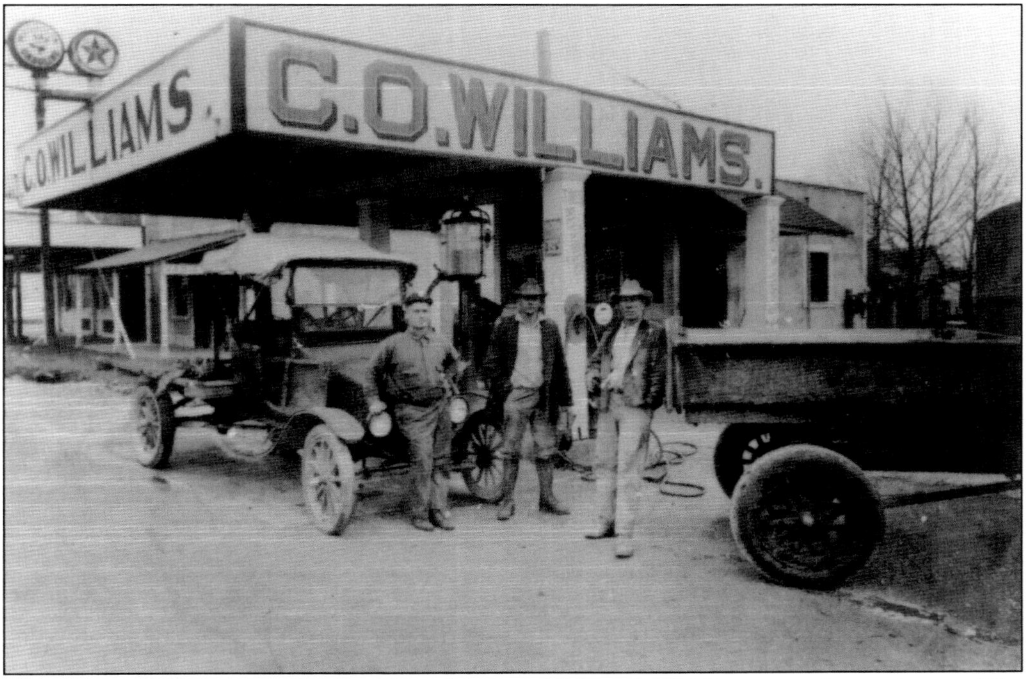

Charles O. Williams married Josephine Mary Andel in 1923. They were descendants of Ike Shireman and America Jane Paige. This photograph shows the C.O. Williams filling station. His first filling station was a small, wooden building at 409 West Main Street. It was later rebuilt into the building pictured.

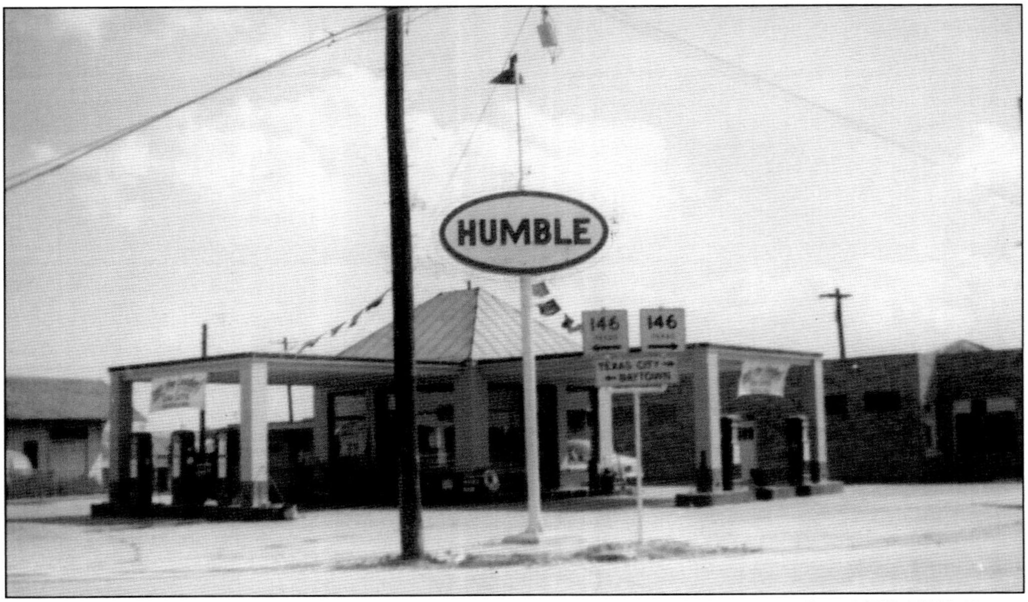

This is the Humble filling station, built in 1933 at Five Points, as it appeared in 1953. F.W. Carey is the owner of this station. Jimmy Crate ran the business before Carey. Another owner was Mr. Deloach. An advertisement for the station states, "We pick up and deliver your car." Times have certainly changed over the years.

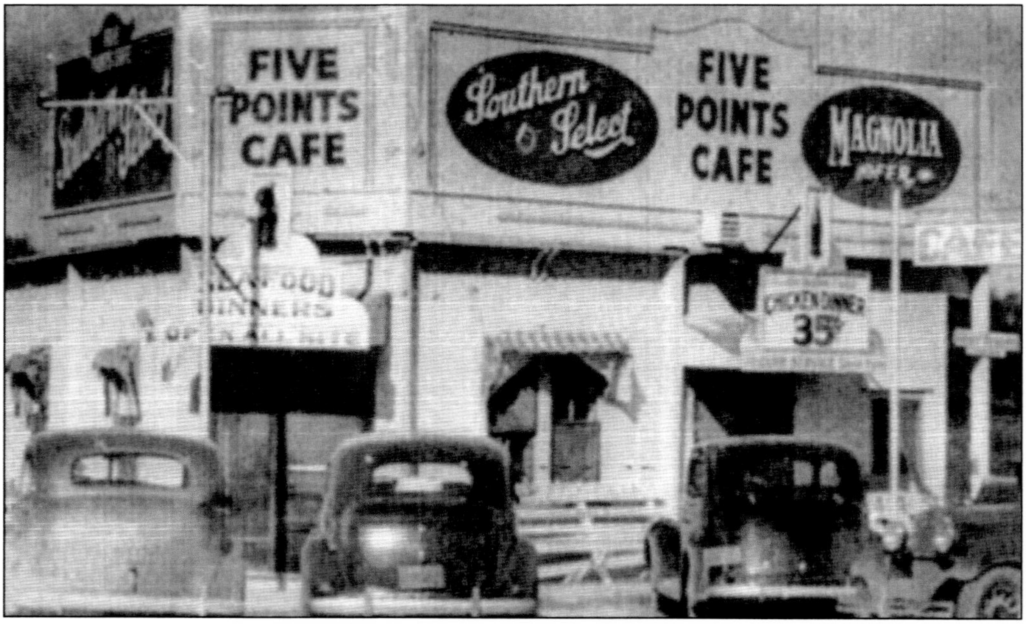

The above photograph shows the Five Points Cafe. In the 1920s and 1930s, as automobiles became the primary means of travel, 10,000–20,000 people would come to Sylvan Beach on the weekend; they would come down Main Street to Five Points and from there, down San Jacinto through the gates of the park. Business at the cafe boomed. Five points is the historical heart of La Porte and was recently beautifully landscaped and embellished by the city. In 1937, contracts were awarded for two traffic lights in La Porte; one was at Five Points, and the other, shown below, was at Main and Second Streets.

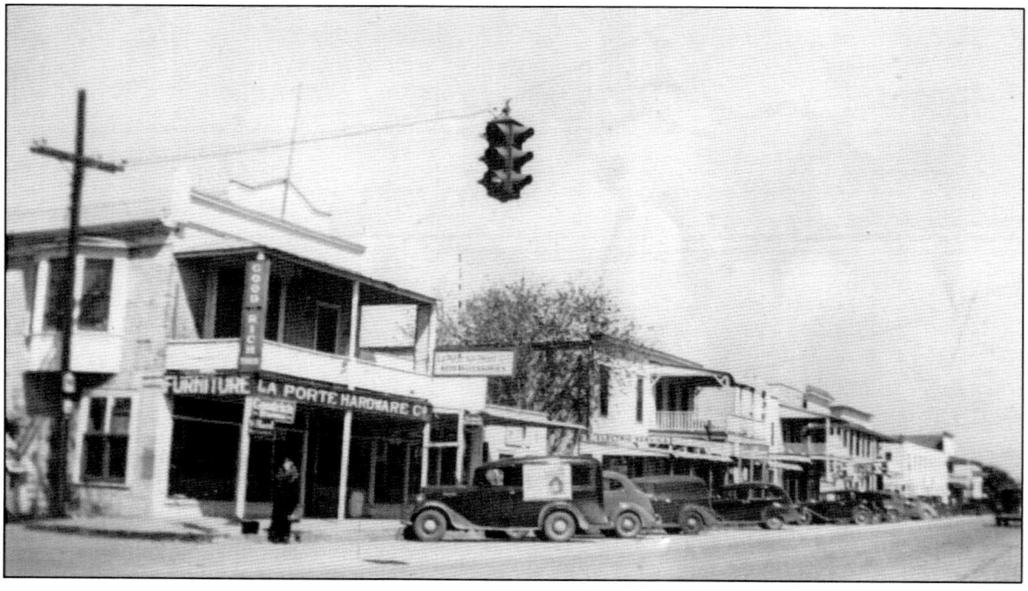

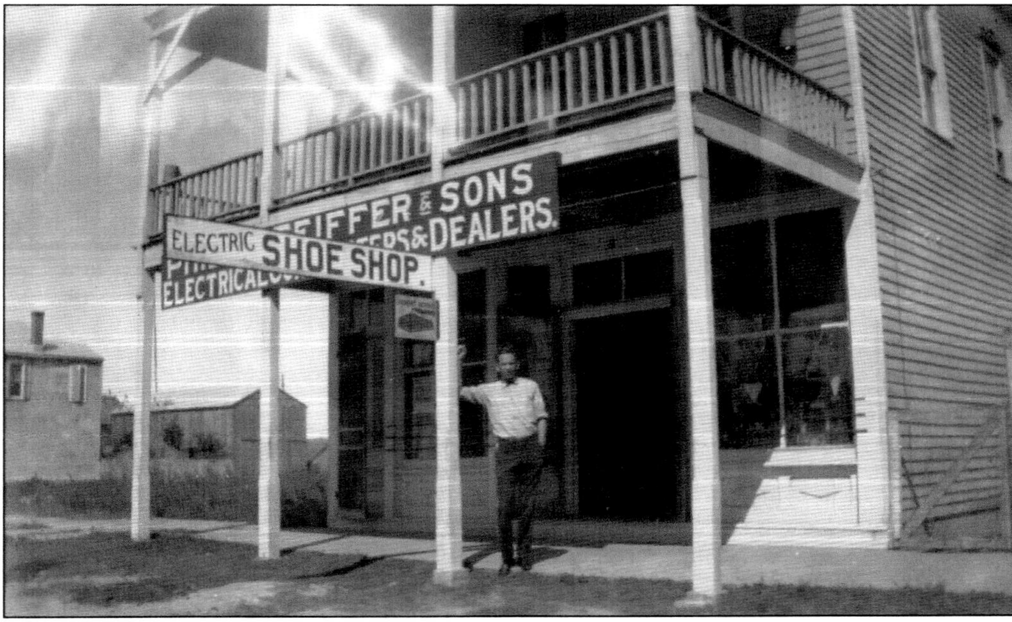

Pfeiffer Electric Company and Counts Shoe Repair shared this building around 1922. Phillip Pfeiffer moved to La Porte in 1913 and started his electric company. He built La Porte's first so-called light plant. His grandson, Harold, was mayor from 1958 to 1970, and their descendants still live in the area. George Counts owned the shoe shop and later served as a judge. His family members are still active in La Porte.

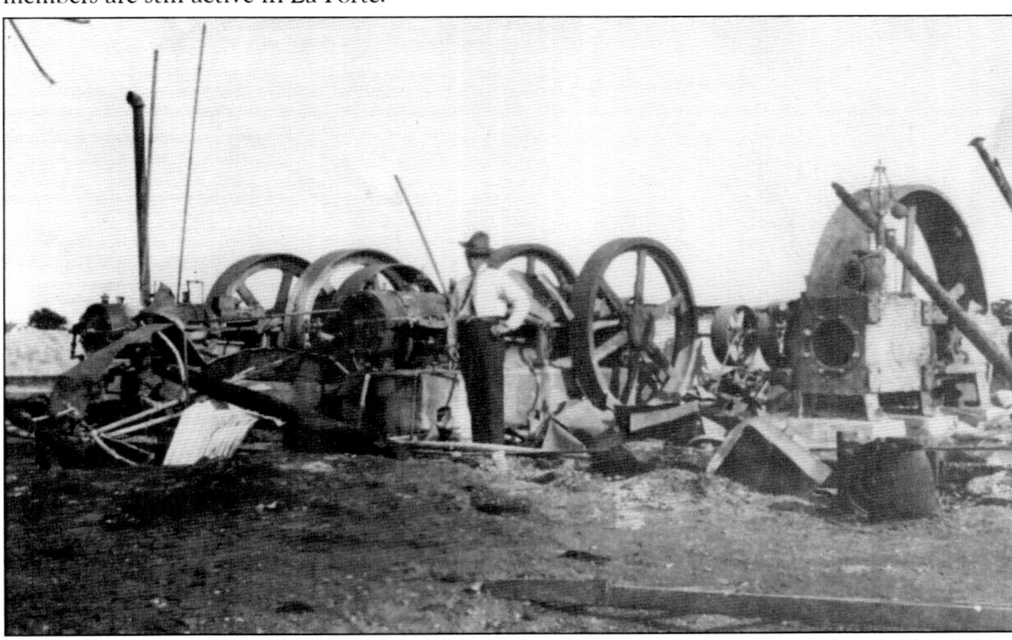

This photograph shows the destruction of the light plant after the devastating fire on September 30, 1921. Undaunted, Pfeiffer rebuilt the plant. An article in the *Galveston Daily News* announced that the plant destroyed by the fire was built under a license that had only just been granted in March of 1921.

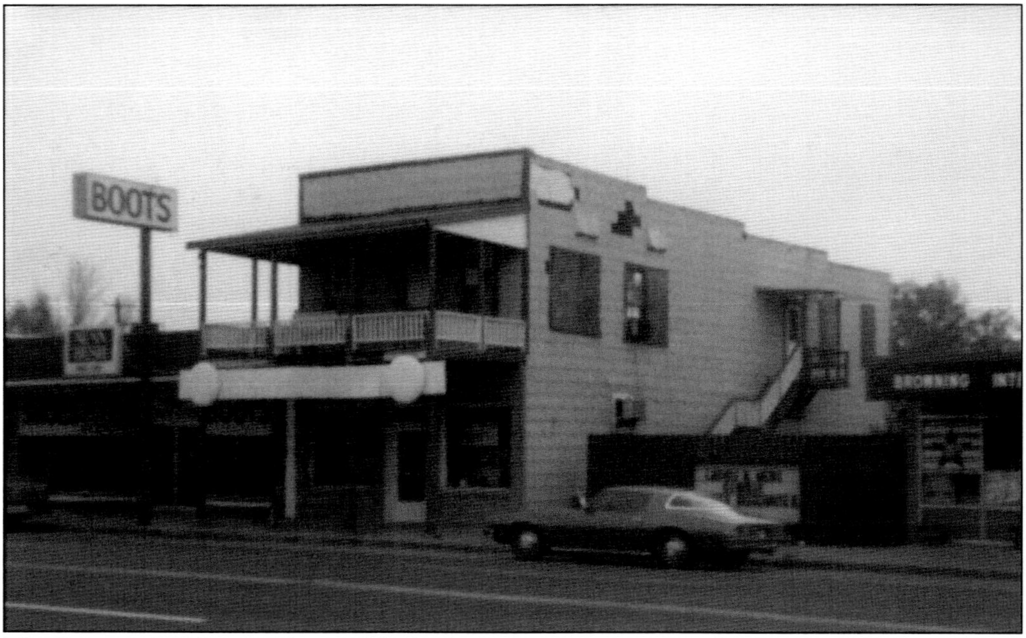

The Simpson building on the 200 block of Main Street was originally built in the 1920s to house the Simpson Cafe. Over the years, it housed a number of other restaurants, including one run by longtime La Porte restaurant owners L.B. and Opal Parker. Then the Lynnwood Shoe Store, which had been next door, moved into the Simpson building, where it operated for many years, albeit under several different names.

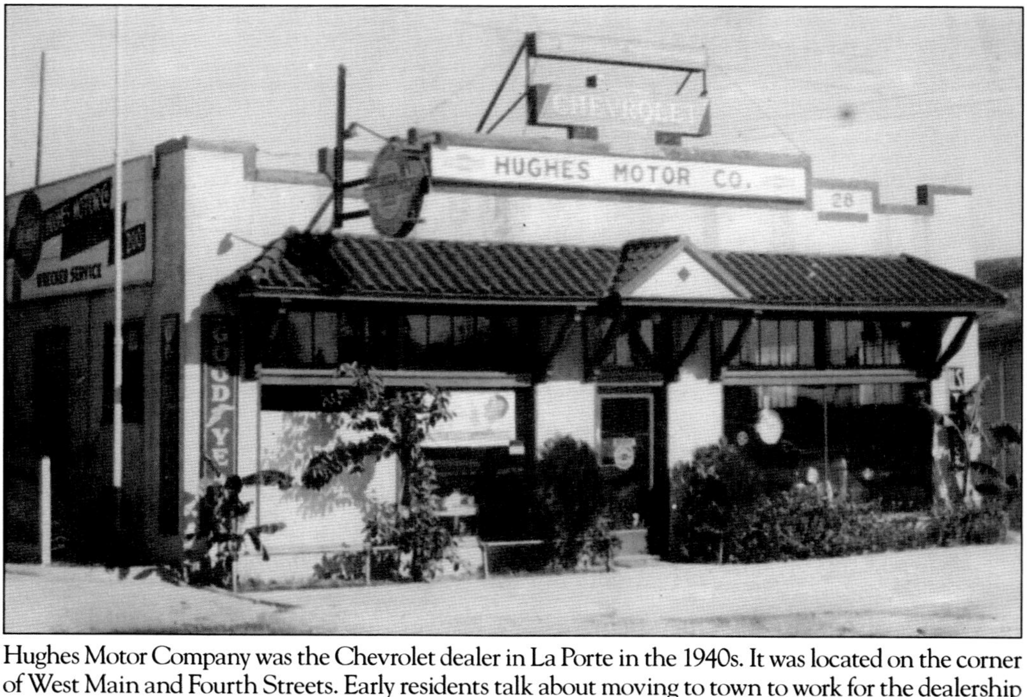

Hughes Motor Company was the Chevrolet dealer in La Porte in the 1940s. It was located on the corner of West Main and Fourth Streets. Early residents talk about moving to town to work for the dealership for the then lucrative sum of $15 per week. Hughes Motor later became Macmillan Chevrolet.

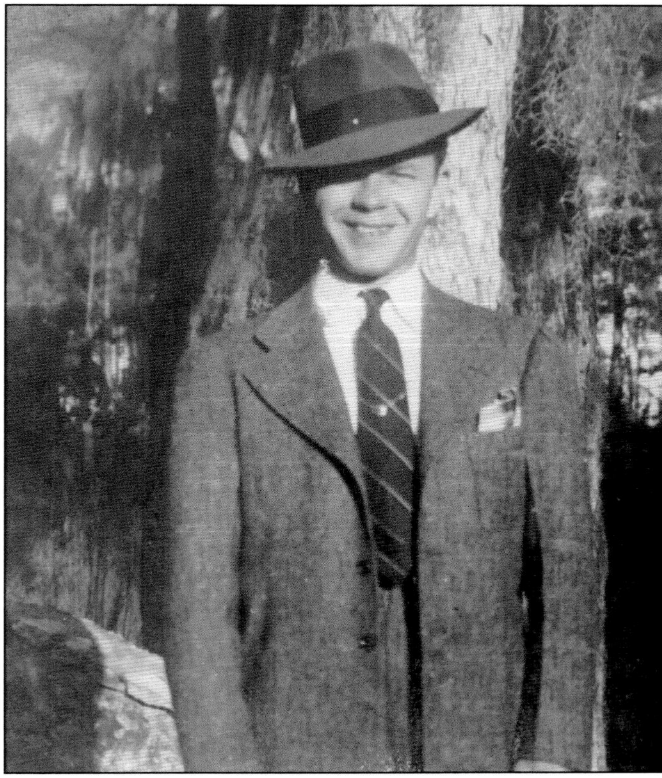

In 1939, Lynnwood Anderson came to the La Porte area and bought three and a half acres in Shoreacres. His first business venture was a Texaco station at Five Points, where Main Street, San Jacinto Street, and Broadway Street met. Since then, he has had several other business ventures, among them the Shoe Stop. He and his wife raised a family of seven children. Some are still in the La Porte area. (Courtesy of Margaret Anderson.)

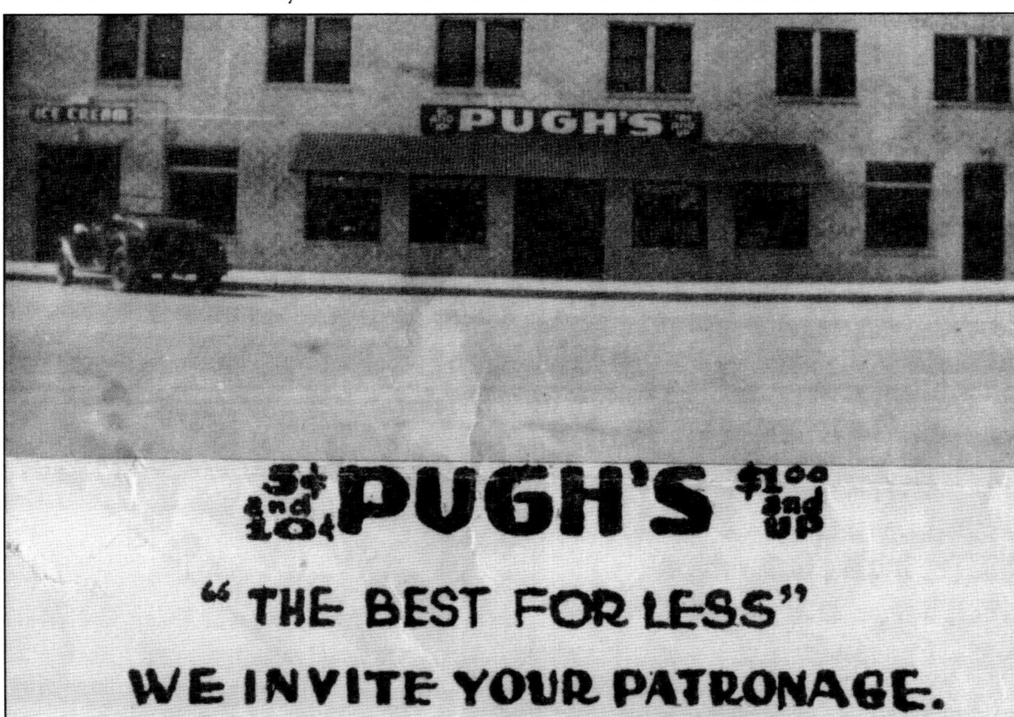

Pugh's was always a favorite during the 1940s and 1950s. They always seemed to have what was needed at any time. They opened early to accommodate parents of children who remembered that they needed something for school while on the way.

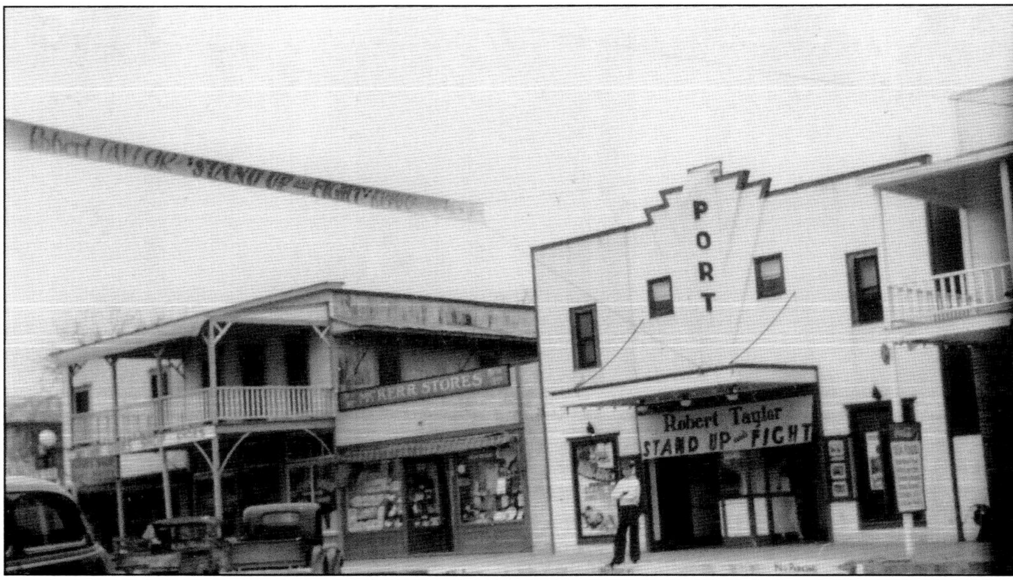

La Porte has always been fortunate to have a theater. The top photograph shows the original Port Theater on Main Street before the new Port was built. Other theaters serving La Porte were the Mac La Theater and the Picture Show at Five Points. The Picture Show was La Porte's first permanent theater. The Mac La Theater opened on the southeast corner of First and Main Streets. Below, is the new Port Theater, opened in 1948 with much fanfare and said to be Harris County's finest. A ribbon cutting and music by La Porte's high school band were the events of the day. Louis "Doodle" Rigby was the Port's manager for many years. Everyone who went to the movies remembers him. Other than being the manager of the theater, Rigby had a great interest in all civic affairs. (Courtesy of Karen Rigby.)

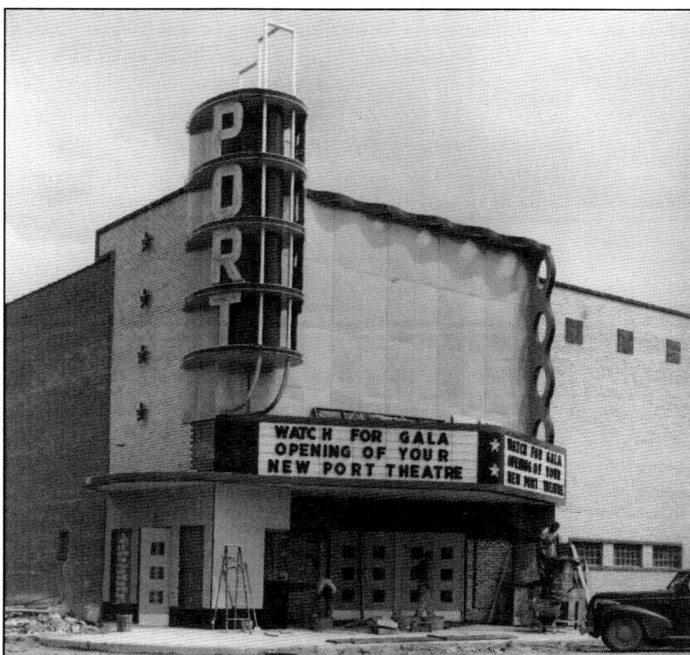

Three

History of Education

One of the goals of the promoters of La Porte was to establish an education center that was "second to none." With that in mind, these town builders set aside a plot of land between La Porte and Shoreacres for a college and prepared for an influx of new children. Sadly, the college did not immediately come to fruition, but a place was found for the younger students. La Porte was incorporated in 1892; when a building owned by A.B. Prince was completed in 1893, he offered it for educational use, and school began in earnest. The Prince building remained La Porte's only school for the next four years.

A permanent school was built on land donated by another promoter, John Caplan, and the growing student body finally had a place of its own. That building served La Porte well until 1916 when a beautiful three-story brick structure became the pride of La Porte and was one of the outstanding school buildings in Harris County. It was partially destroyed by hurricane in 1943 but was rebuilt as a single-story building and continued as La Porte's only school until more room was needed.

Several schools have been built for the student body over the years, but that single-story building still stands in La Porte and serves as a reminder of the city's educational past. It is now La Porte Intermediate. Although the first attempt at bringing a college to La Porte failed, the Catholic Diocese purchased the Sylvan Hotel in early 1902 after a storm damaged it in 1900. The hotel became the dormitory for the soon-to-be St. Mary's Seminary. The seminary was a four-year college for young men and seminarians and an elementary school for young boys. St. Mary's remained in La Porte until 1954 when it moved to Houston. Today, the same interest in education is as prevalent as it has always been. Morgan's Point, Lomax, and Shoreacres are in the La Porte's school district. La Porte is always ready to give students the finest education possible.

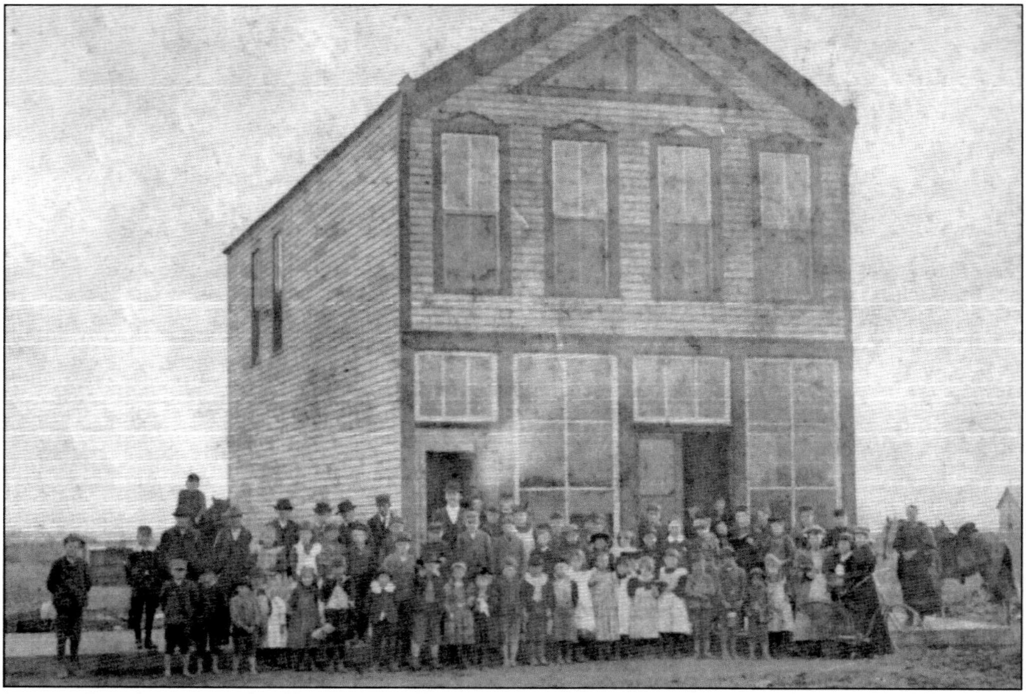

Pictured is the Prince building, located on the corner of Main and Fourth Streets. Opened in 1893, it housed the first school in La Porte, which was for younger children. The popular mode of travel, as shown, was by horseback or walking. Below is the new school.

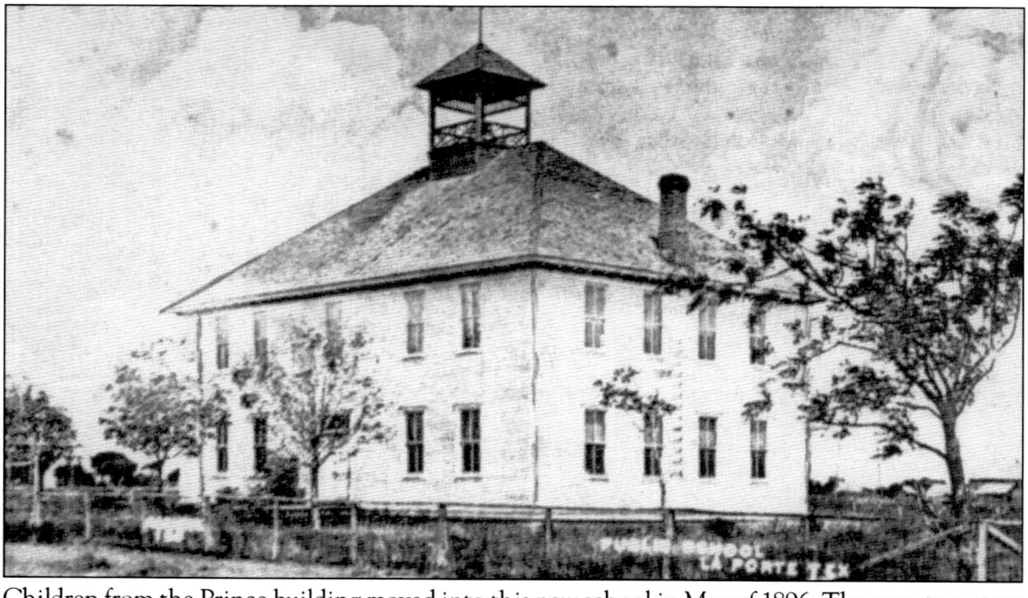

Children from the Prince building moved into this new school in May of 1896. The new, two-story La Porte school was located on Second and C Streets and had three teachers who led students from primer through high school. The school had four rooms with a large hallway down the middle. It served the community until 1916. Later, Mr. Nickle bought the building and remodeled it into a duplex.

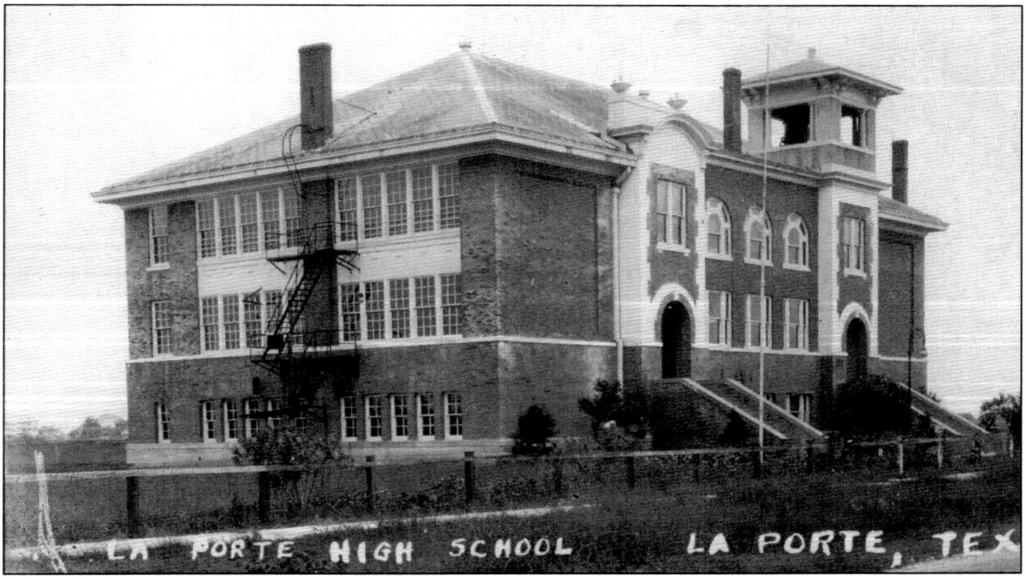

La Porte's new high school, a three-story brick structure, was completed in 1916. Located on Broadway Street, the school was the pride of La Porte. Its 500-seat auditorium, which was on the third floor, was filled to capacity when it was dedicated. Many businesses closed to allow employees to attend the ceremony. This building was used until 1943 when a hurricane destroyed the upper floors.

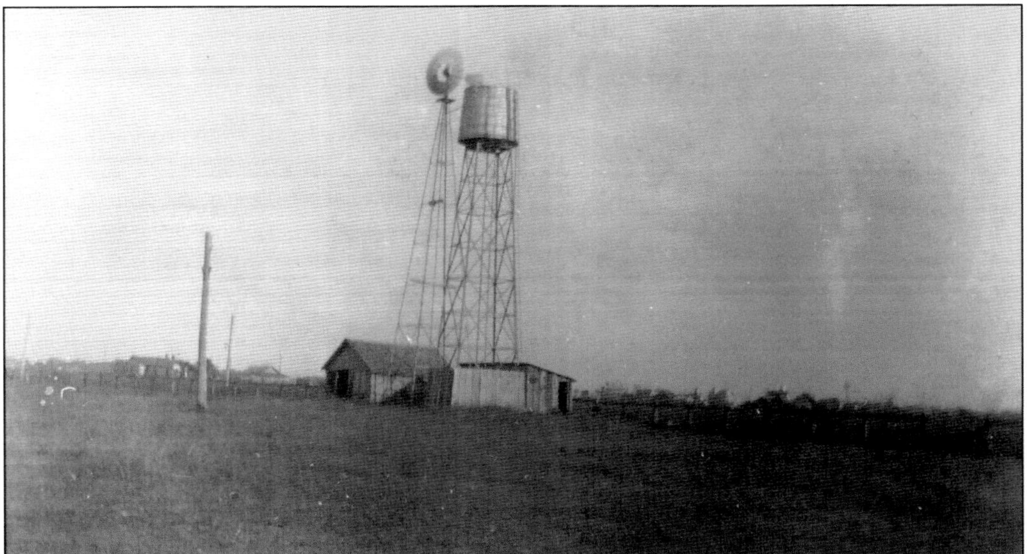

This photograph shows the La Porte High School water well with an attendant tank and windmill to keep the water pumping.

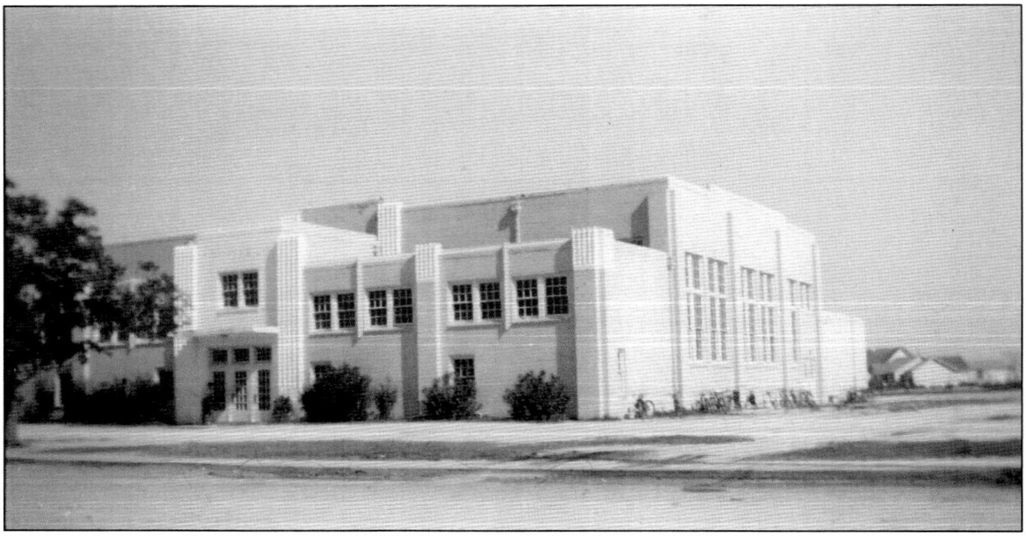

A new elementary school, situated on Broadway Street just south of the existing three-story school, was opened in 1940. Until that time, the three-story building had served as the only school for La Porte, Morgan's Point, Lomax, and Shoreacres.

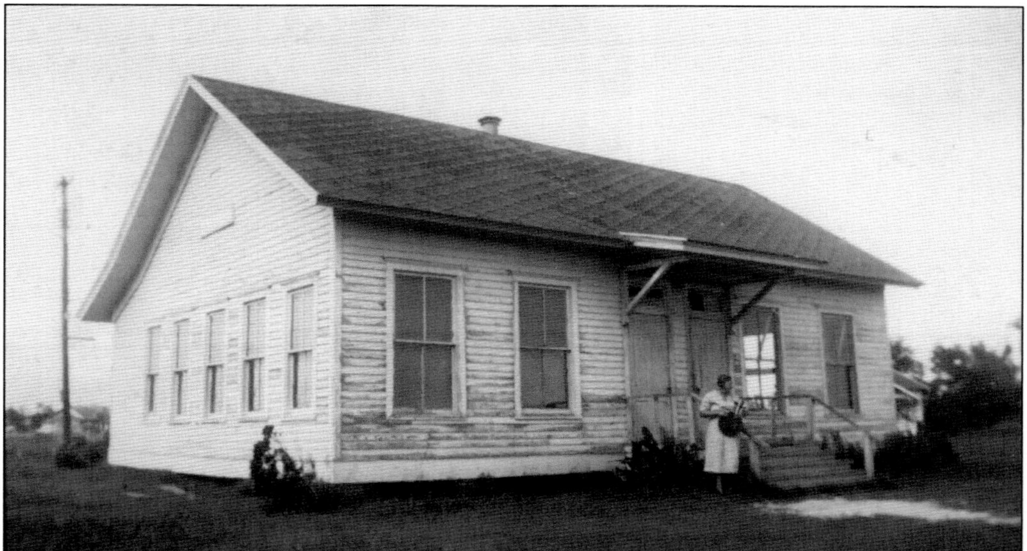

The building shown was the schoolhouse from Morgan's Point. It was moved to La Porte and placed next to the La Porte High School where it served as elementary classrooms and later the band hall. Mr. Norris renovated it into a rental house and moved it to North Fifth Street where it still stands occupied today.

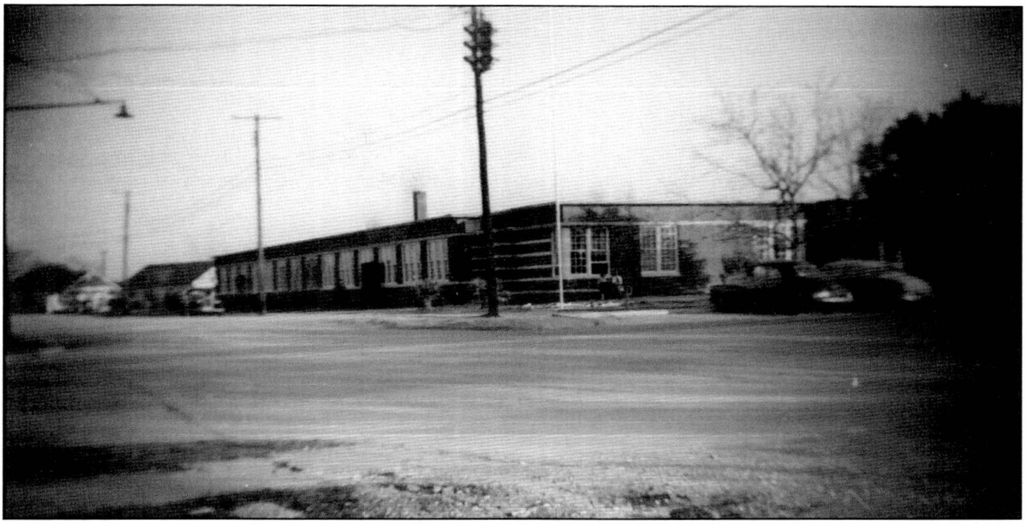

After the hurricane of 1943 destroyed part of the three-story brick school building, it was remodeled into a one-story building. The photograph shows the building after it was remodeled; the small, white structure behind the school is the Morgan's Point school.

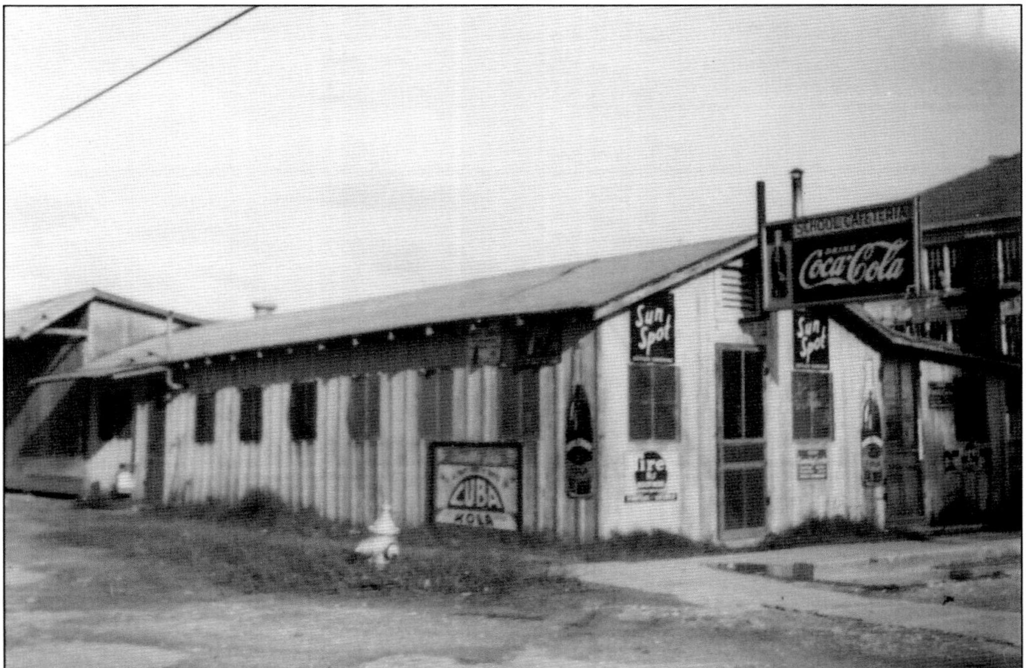

The sign on the front of the building (just above the Coca Cola sign) identifies it as the School Cafeteria. The school can just barely be seen in the background on the right. La Porte resident Jolene Wickel Berkeley remembers that J.W. Canada used to sell hamburgers for students out of his garage (among his many other activities), but it is unclear if this was Canada's operation.

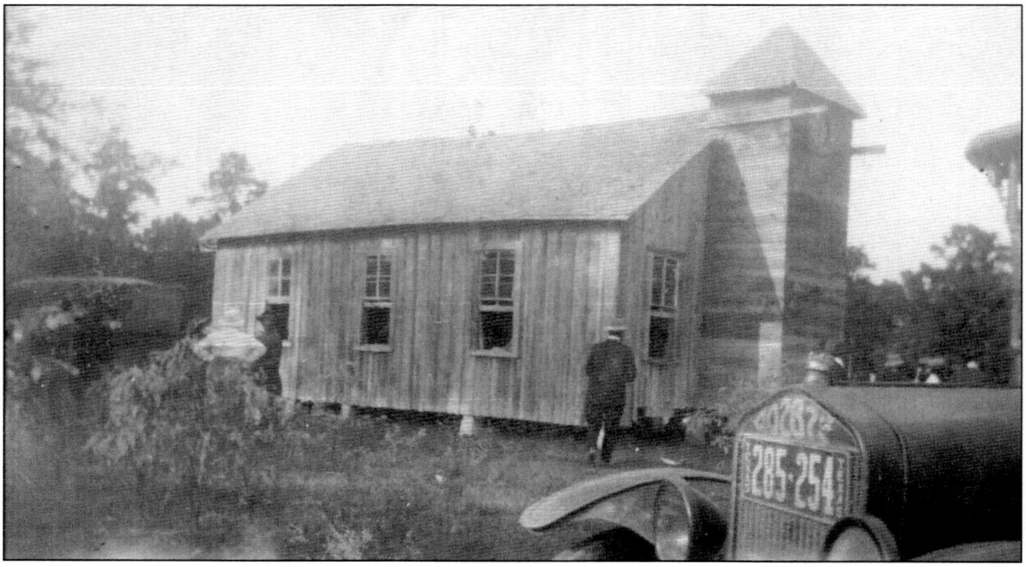

In 1909, a school for black children was organized by the La Porte School District. Classes were first held in this black Baptist church during the week, and church services were held on Sunday. Viola DeWalt was the first teacher of the 10 students that came to the school. Later, they moved to a Methodist Church purchased by the La Porte School District. That building still exists.

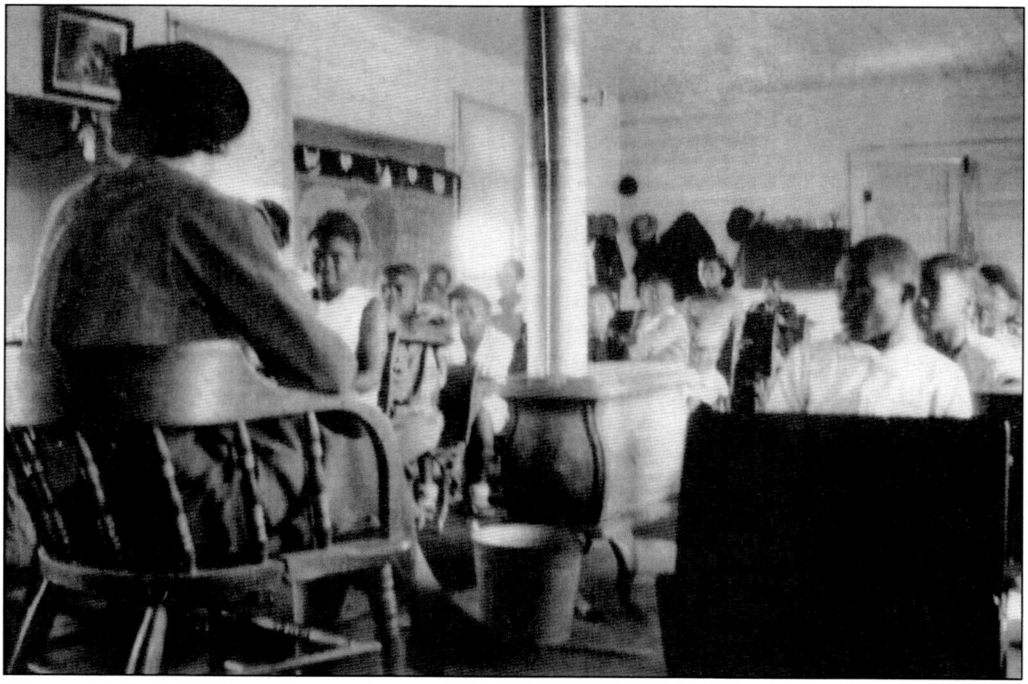

Here is Viola DeWalt reading to her students. She taught in La Porte for over 30 years and is remembered for her outstanding social and religious work. Other teachers who helped in this early endeavor were Marie Curry, Alice McDade, and Sweetie Evans. In 1953, a new school, named in honor of DeWalt, was built to replace the old, one-room Northside Elementary School. (Courtesy of Harris County Public Library Archives.)

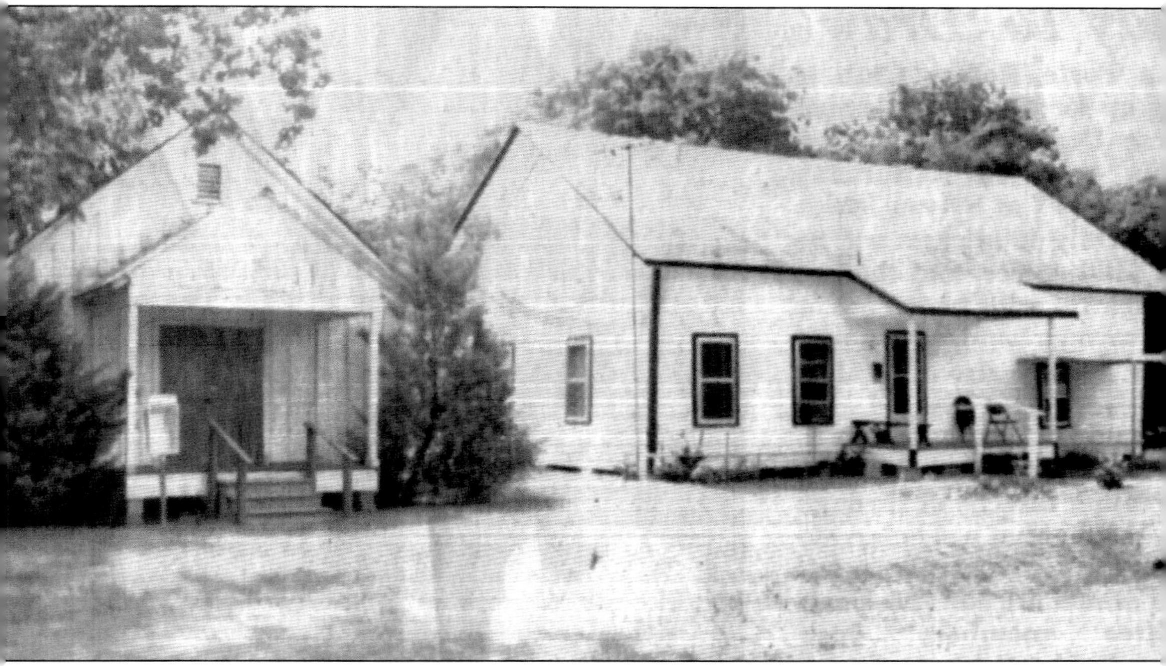

The one-room Methodist church (left) that served as a schoolhouse for black children now belongs to the Eastern Stars Leading Light and is located on North Fifth Street in La Porte. The building next to it is the old Morgan's Point schoolhouse. It is now a rental property. Some noted graduates of La Porte's first black school included Virginia Perry, who taught at Prairie View and Wiley Colleges and became the first black supervisor in Houston schools; John Hunter, who became the president of Virginia State College; Ted Hunter, who established his dental practice in Waco, Texas; and Irma Perry, who formed the first black-owned catering service in Houston, Texas.

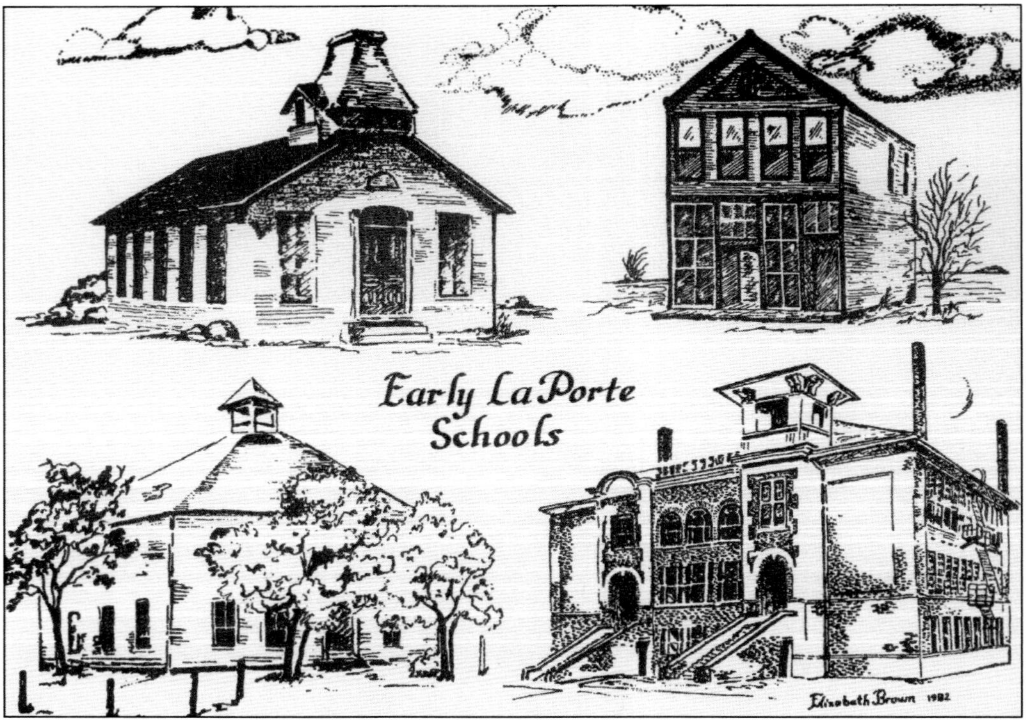

Elizabeth Brown was commissioned by the La Porte Bay Area Heritage Society to draw La Porte's first schools for a 1982 note card series.

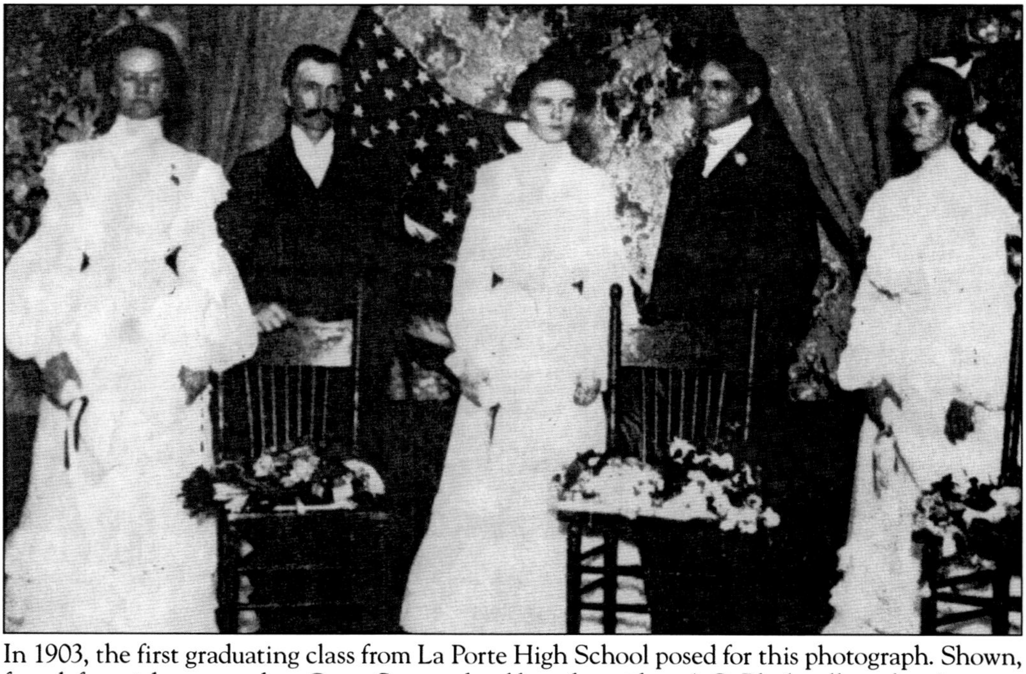

In 1903, the first graduating class from La Porte High School posed for this photograph. Shown, from left to right, are student Grace Stout, school board president A.O. Blackwell, student Laverne McKay, professor W.S. Fry, and student Bessie Shannon.

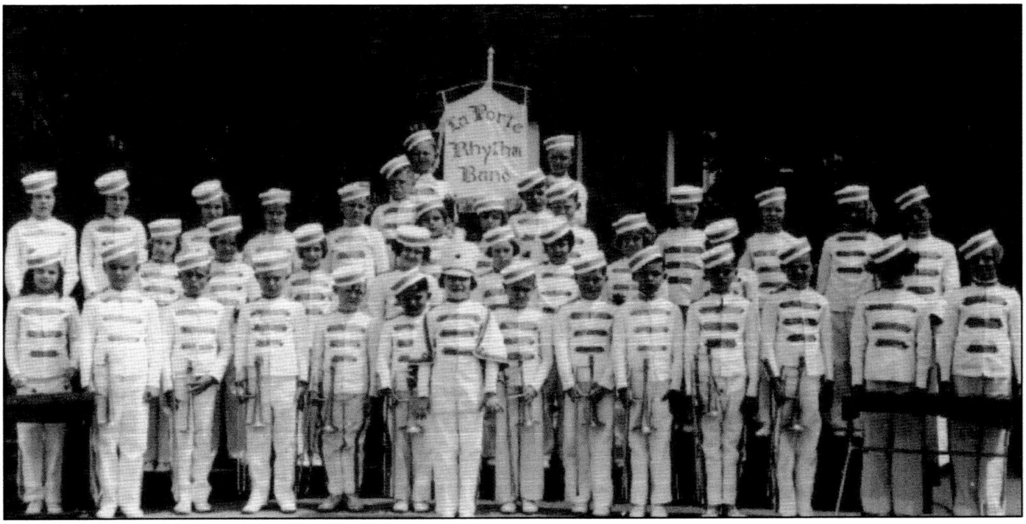

This photograph of the 1935 third-grade rhythm band from La Porte Elementary School was donated to the Heritage Society Museum by Shirley Wood. The last names of these students—Hovey, Aves, Squibb, Knighton, Isensee, Linkhart, McClure, Wilson, and Harrison—are echoes of some of the early settlers' names.

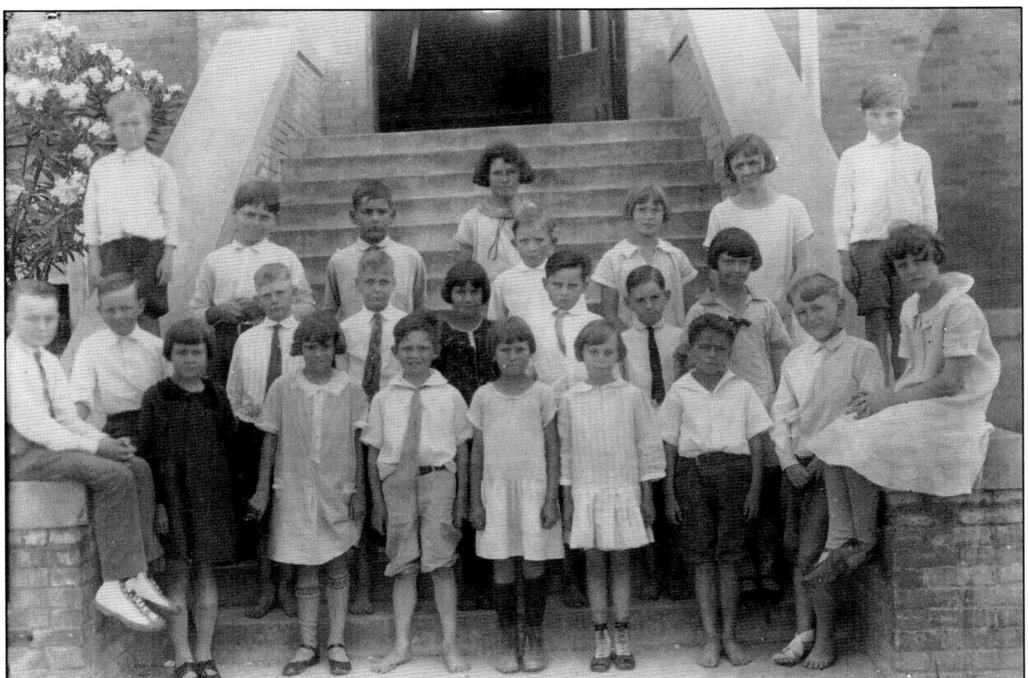

In the 1930s, picture day was a fun day in elementary school—just as it is today. Everyone looks their best for the annual class photograph taken on the steps of the high school. That's not Huck Finn and Tom Sawyer on the front row without their shoes, but it sure could be.

THIRD AND FIFTH GRADES

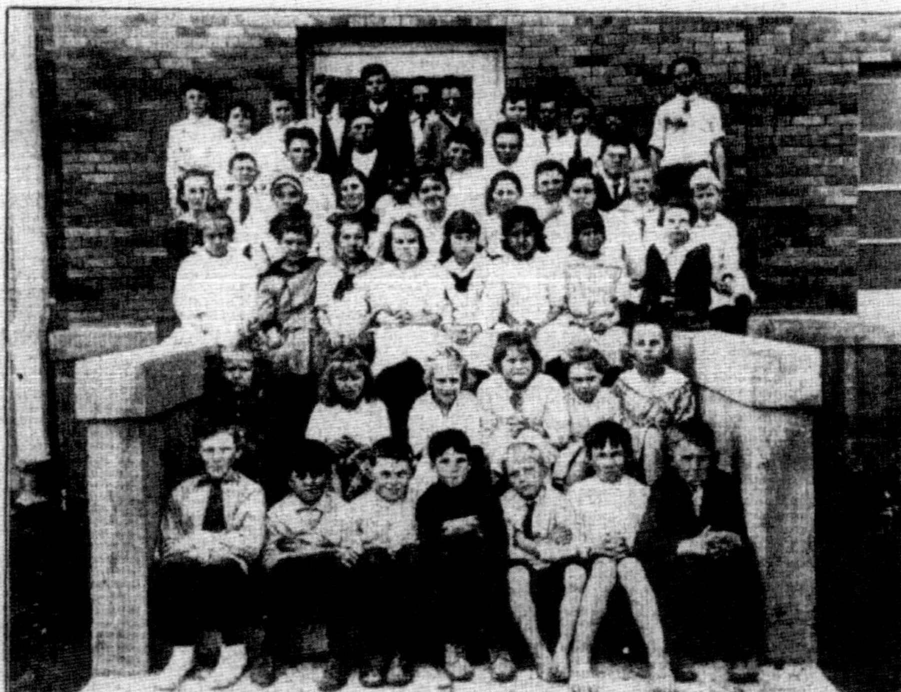

Fifth Grade

Herbert Renfrow, Robert Work, Henry Black, George Hamilton, Wilber McNitt, Rush Temple, Milton Purdy, Orman Kirkpatrick, Ernest Downer, Joe Pizzitola, Harry Murray, Percy Follett, Edison Arthur, Thomas Taylor, Maxwell Higginbotham, Tommie Arthur, Frank Gates, William Monk, Ruth Hershberger, Ruth Tischouser, Edith Muldoon, Louise Ridpath, Frances Burson, Julia Hall, Myrtis Waddell, Lucy Williams, Arlyne Smith, Lena Pizzitola, Jennie Roberts, Georgie Baker, Carol Moody, Genevie Shaw, Marguerite Campbell, E. R. Crook

Third Grade

Eugene Redman, Louis Higginbotham, Kenneth Lawrence, Ruth Renfrow, Emily Ross, Bertha Nickel, Mildred Hamilton, Hila Harris, Helen Curry, Glen Shaw, Julias Politz, Boyce Stewart, Foster Measles, Clyde Newsom, Clarence Roberts

The names printed on this yearbook page are also a reminder of the many families who have settled in the Bay Area through the years.

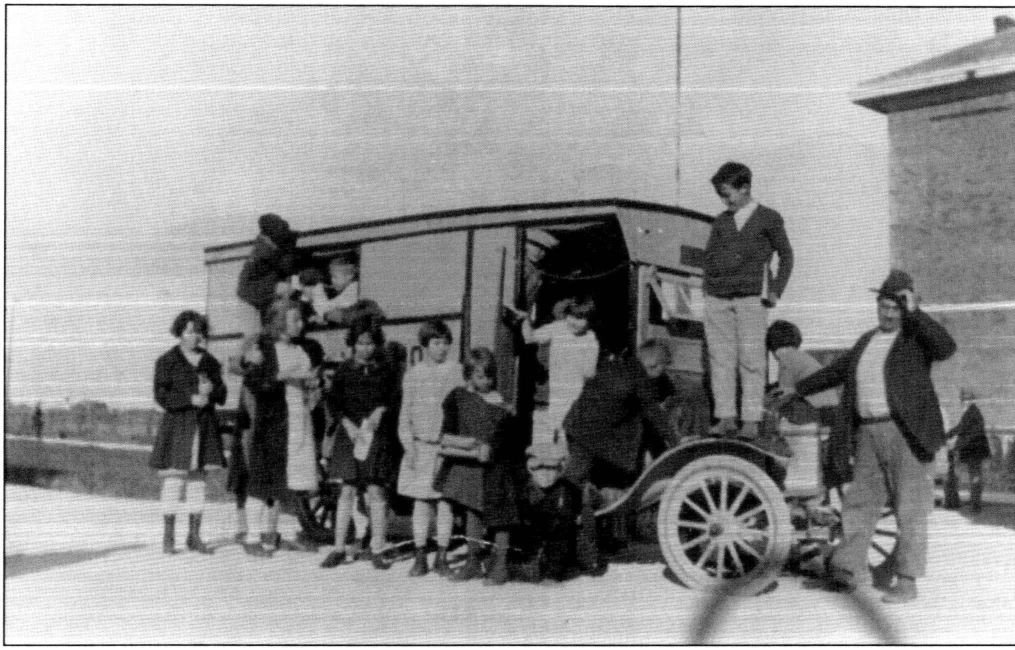

This photograph of a La Porte school bus was taken in the late 1920s. The bus driver, A.O. Taylor, is at the right saying to the girls, "Thank you girls; smile at the camera," and to the boys, "Don't climb on the fenders or throw your classmates out the windows." The busload of Morgan's Point children is on the way to school.

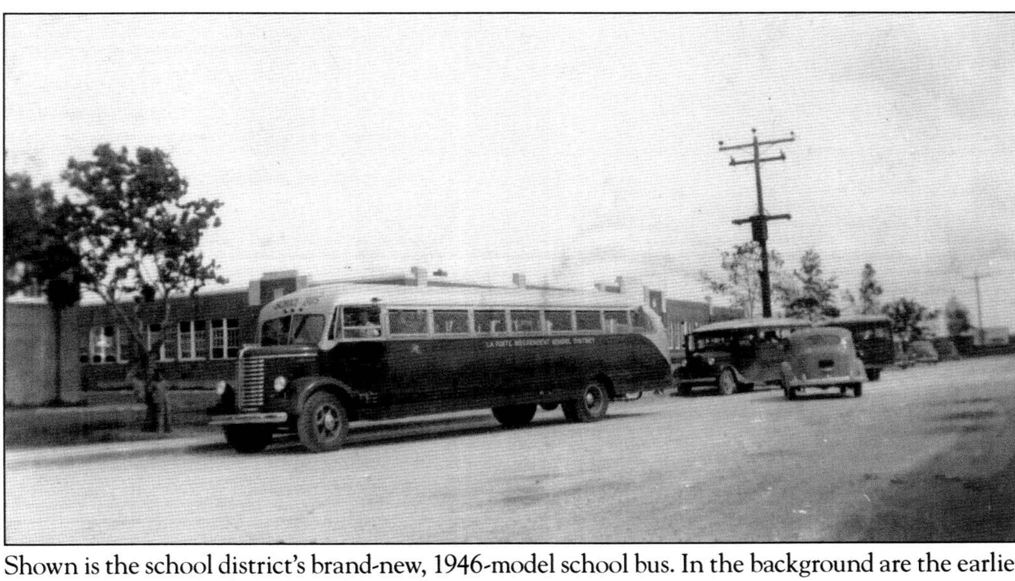

Shown is the school district's brand-new, 1946-model school bus. In the background are the earlier versions of the old school bus.

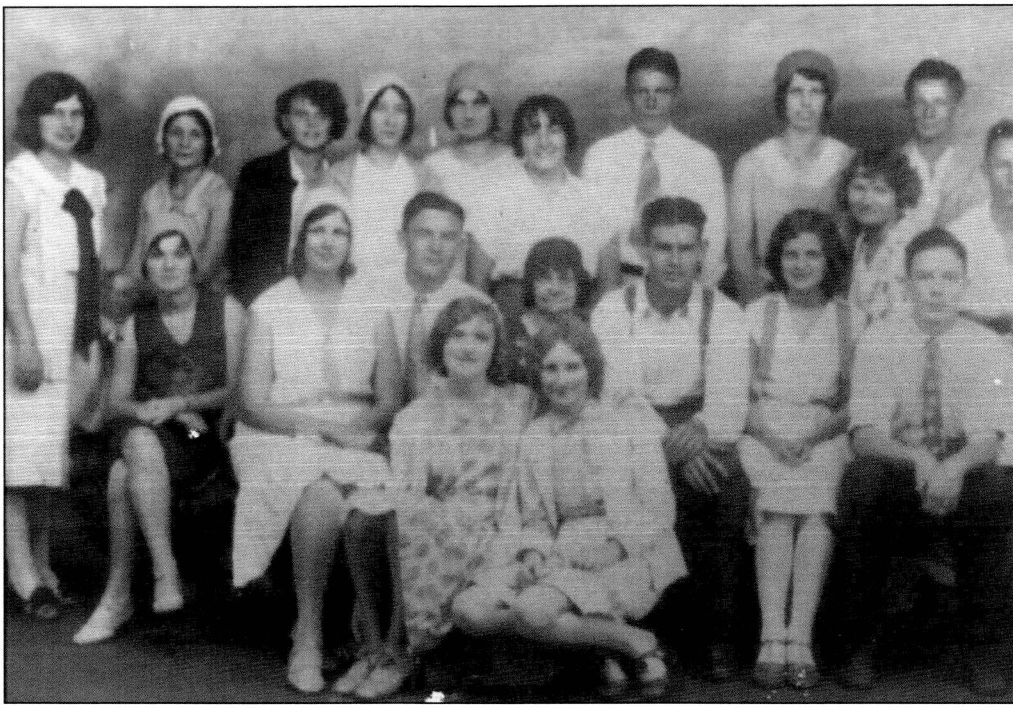

This photograph shows students at La Porte High School in 1920. Erna Beth Seamman Foxworth (mother of Robert Foxworth) is the young lady in suspenders. La Porte did not require students attending high school to be handsome—it just worked out that way.

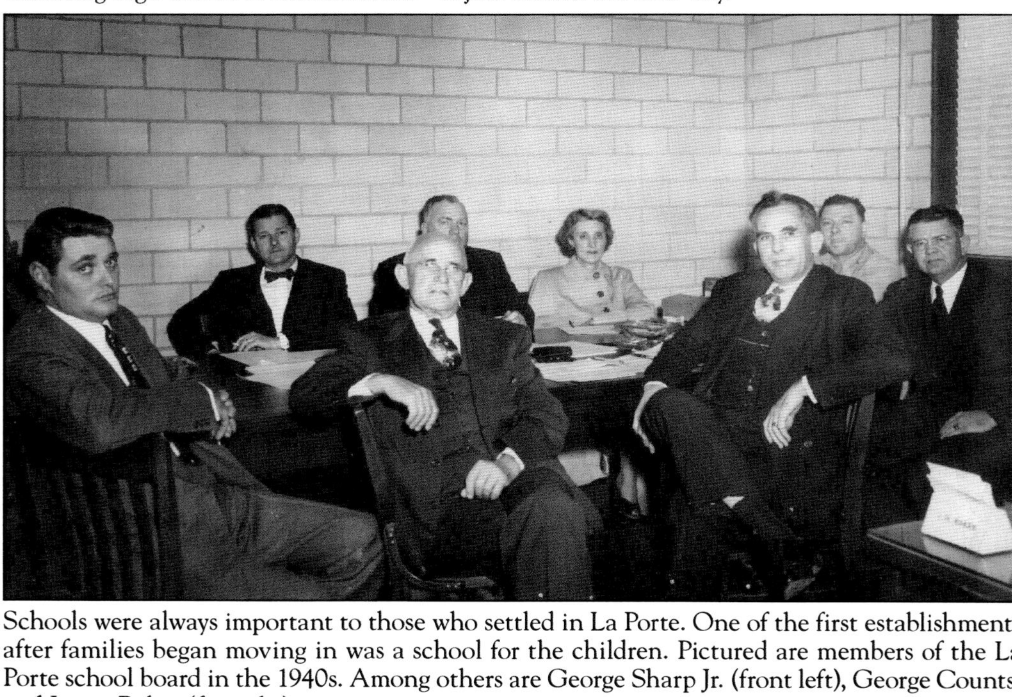

Schools were always important to those who settled in La Porte. One of the first establishments after families began moving in was a school for the children. Pictured are members of the La Porte school board in the 1940s. Among others are George Sharp Jr. (front left), George Counts, and James Baker (far right).

SEVENTH GRADE

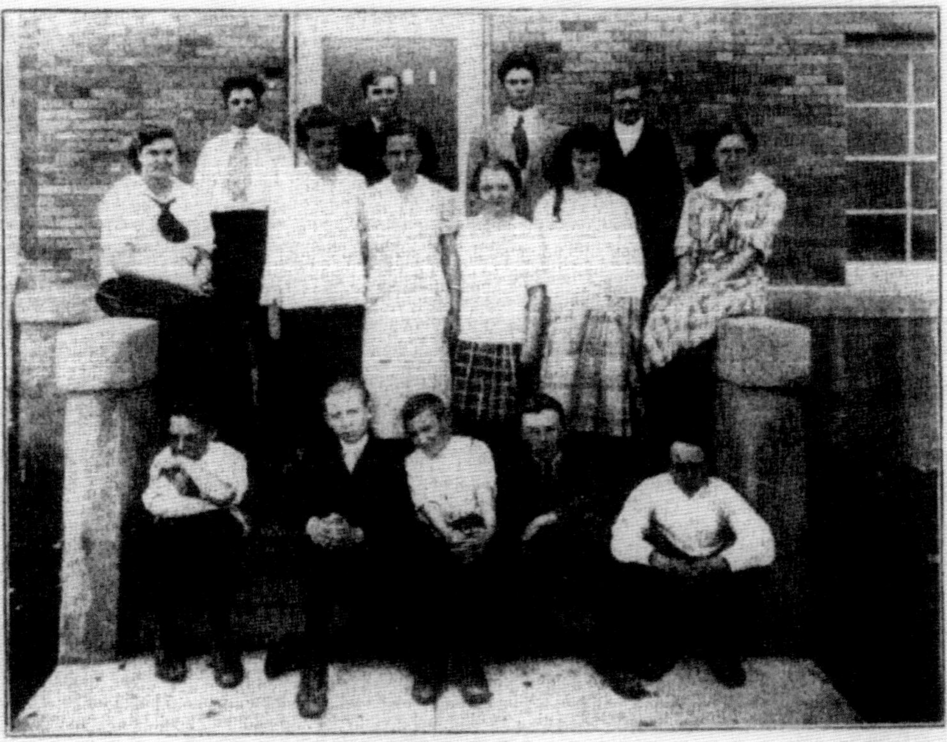

Bessie Workman, Vivian Measles, Rebecca Paschal, Harold Pheiffer, Charlie Williams, Magdalene Woelber, Tiney Bohanan, John Pizzitola, Bertha Sharp, Homer Divan, John Roberts, Arnold Pheiffer, Glenn Seaureau, Cecil Burson, Melville Squibb, Fred Knighton

ETROPAL

This is the seventh-grade class photograph in the school yearbook. They called the book *Etropal* ("La Porte" spelled backwards, which was the thing to do in those days). The names printed under the photograph are the names that contributed to making La Porte what it is today.

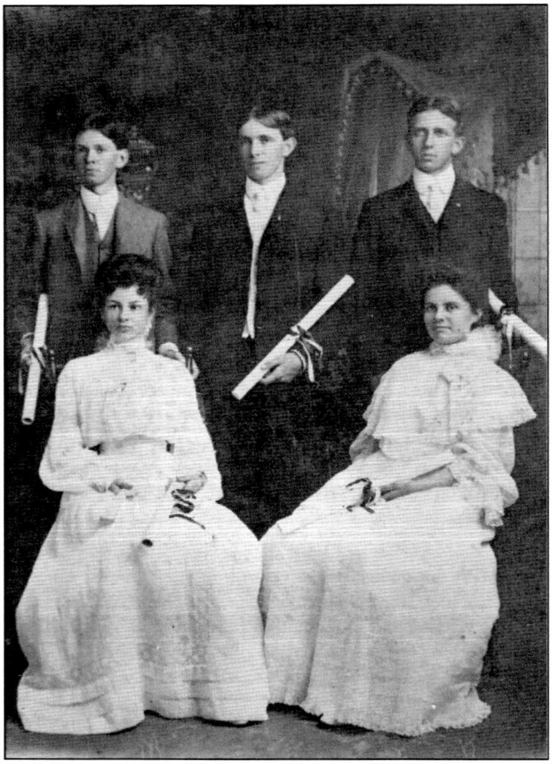

The second commencement class of La Porte was in 1904. Pictured are Jack Beazley, Swan Compton, Ward Figley, and Ella Carr. Beazley's father sold land to the Nebraska Syndicate, early promoters of La Porte. Compton's mother was secretary to the Syndicate and, later, a greeter and hostess to the excursion trains that brought in settlers and investors. Figley's father was a photographer and went on to become mayor of La Porte. From left to right are (first row) Ella Carr and Millie Lamb; (second row) Jack Beazley, Swan Compton, and Ward Figley.

Pictured is the La Porte High School graduating class of 1921. Again the names, Pfeiffer, Williams, Brunson, Diven, Sereau, Seamman, Vickers, Nichel, Workman, Bartel, and Dumeu are the ones that are often heard when speaking of the history of La Porte and its contiguous communities.

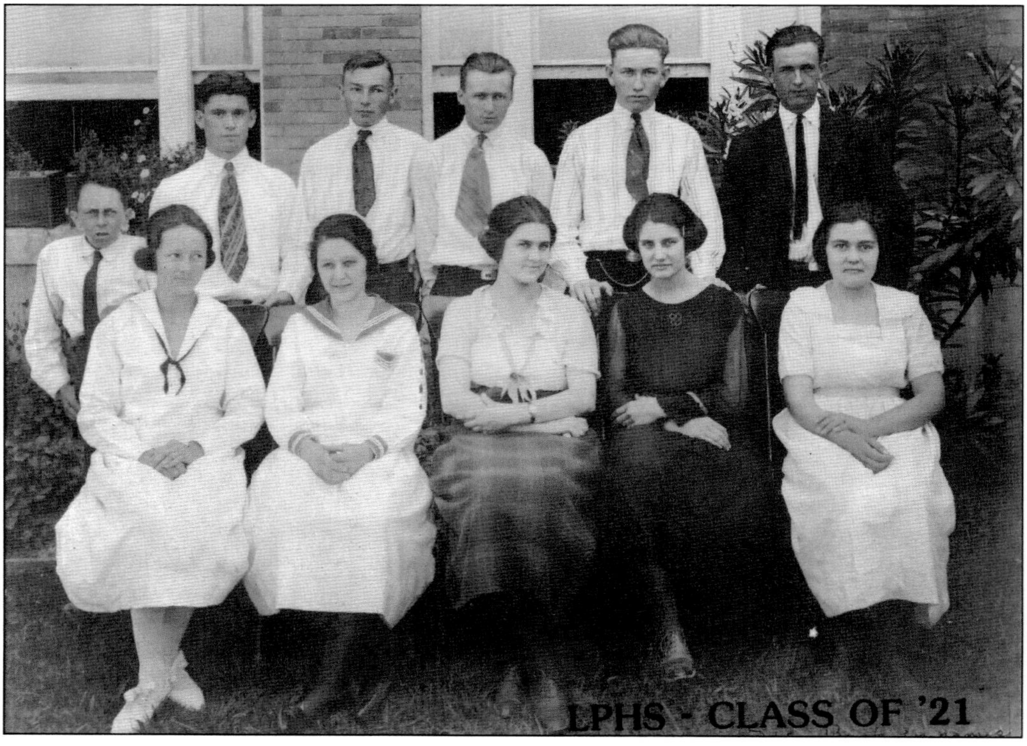

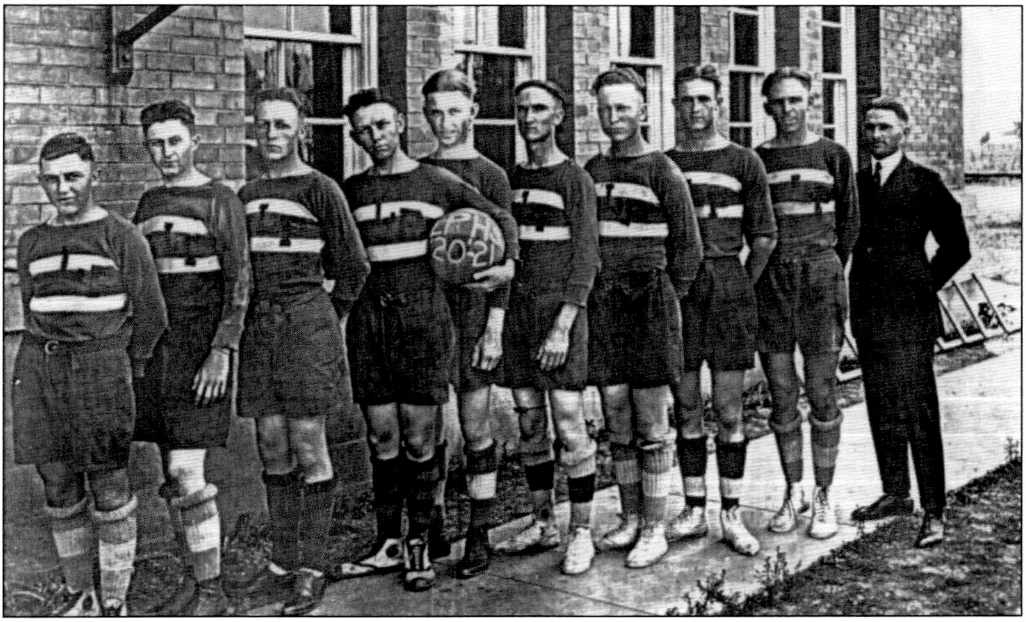

Pictured is La Porte's first basketball team, organized in 1921 by a new principal who wanted to have a physically well-rounded school that could participate in all sports.

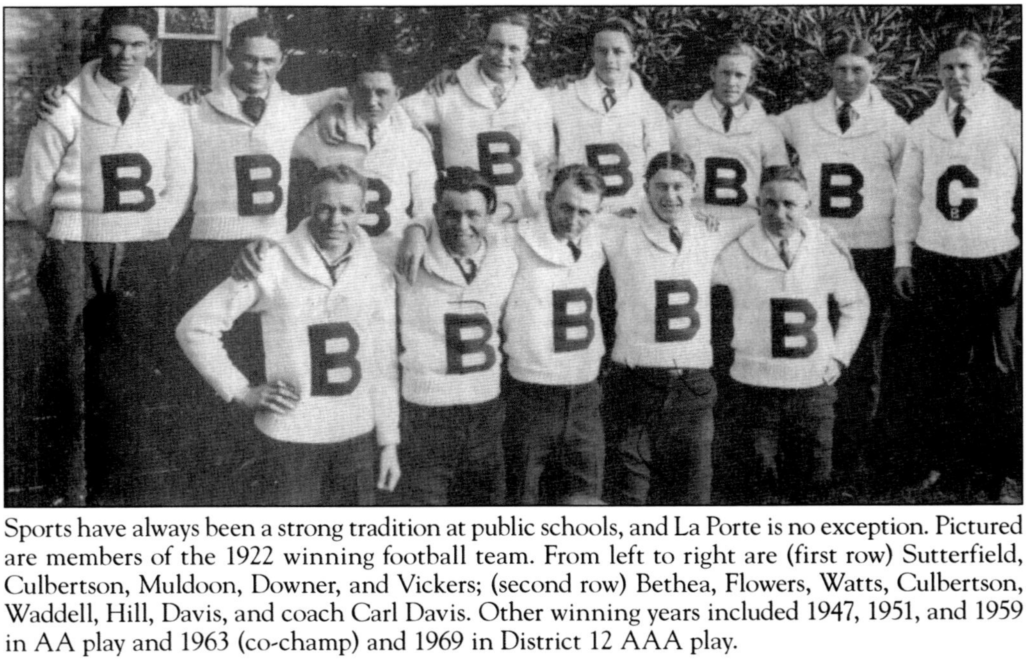

Sports have always been a strong tradition at public schools, and La Porte is no exception. Pictured are members of the 1922 winning football team. From left to right are (first row) Sutterfield, Culbertson, Muldoon, Downer, and Vickers; (second row) Bethea, Flowers, Watts, Culbertson, Waddell, Hill, Davis, and coach Carl Davis. Other winning years included 1947, 1951, and 1959 in AA play and 1963 (co-champ) and 1969 in District 12 AAA play.

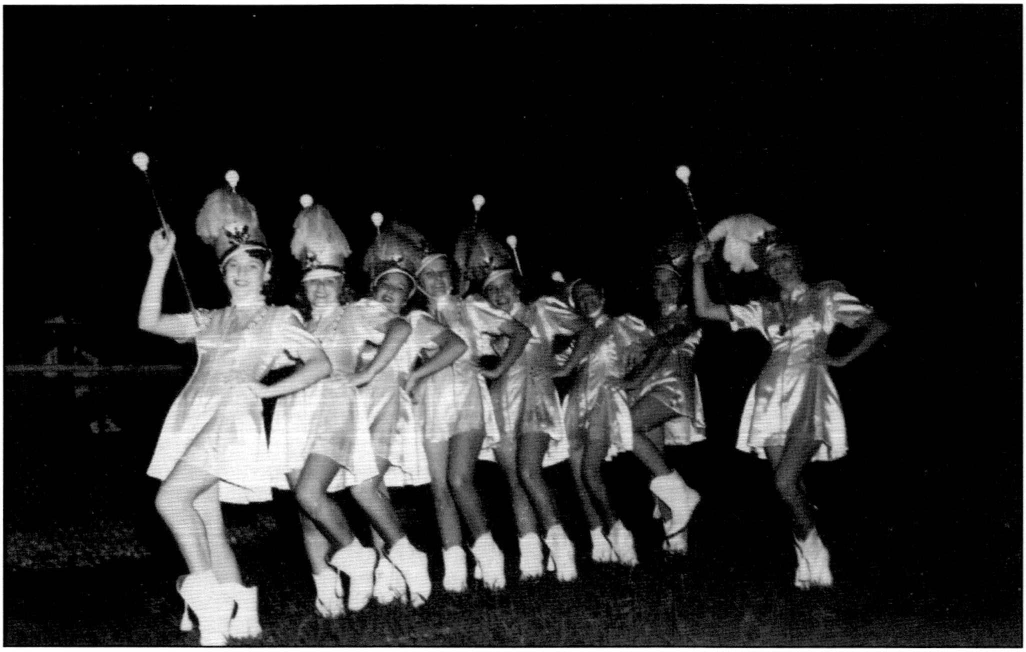

Around 1940, the girls of La Porte High School band strut their stuff before a big football game at the high school stadium on Broadway Street. These were memory-making days.

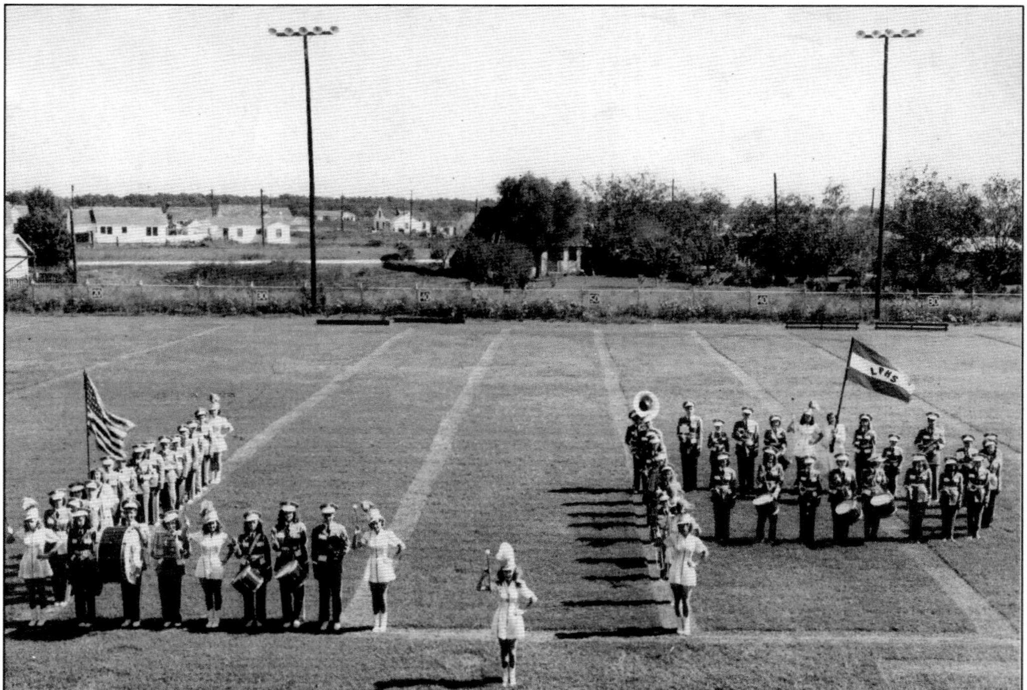

The La Porte High School band has always exited the ball field (and still does) while in the formation of the letters *L* and *P* and playing the school fight song. This stirs the enthusiasm for the football team and school. Also, it is a great way to leave the audience wanting more football and music.

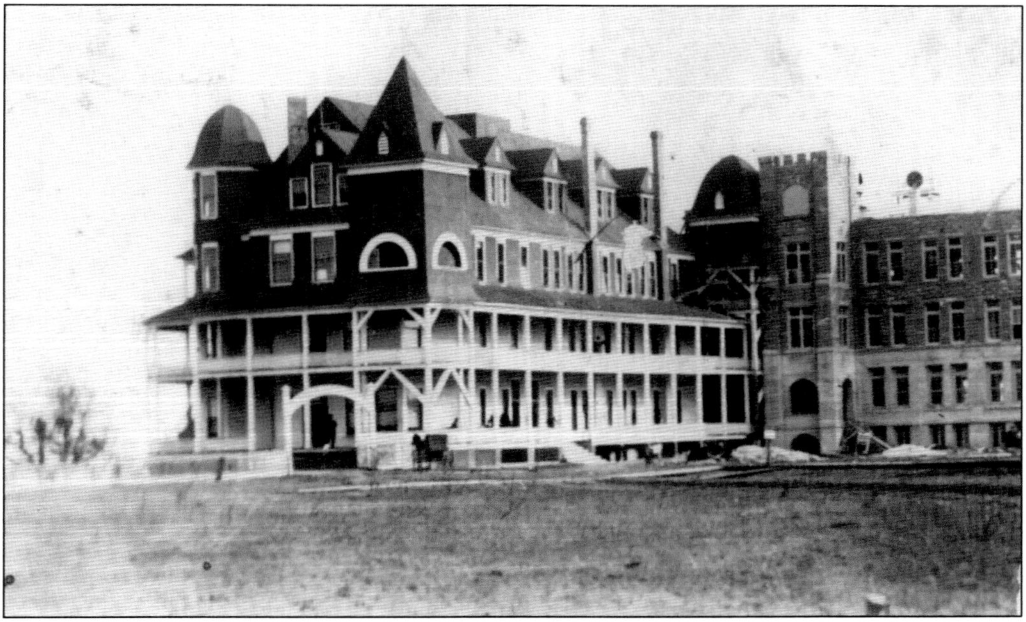

Bishop Nicholas Gallagher wanted to establish a seminary. When the Sylvan Hotel in La Porte became available after being damaged in the 1900 storm, the Catholic Diocese bought it. The diocese restored the building, which became part of St. Mary's Seminary in 1902.

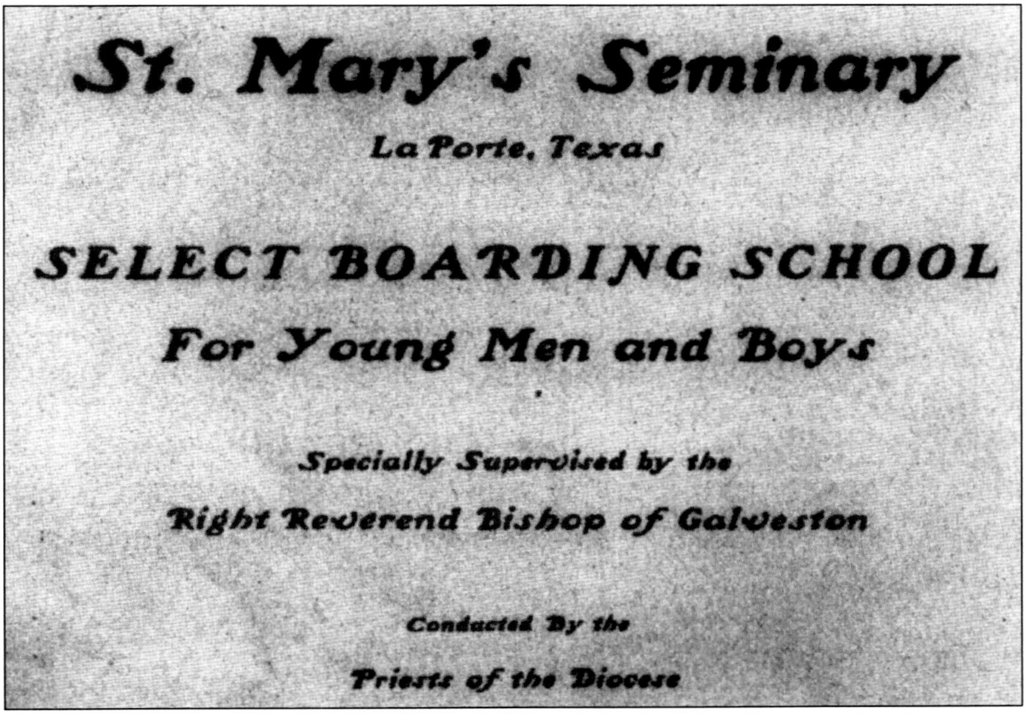

This advertisement encouraging families to send their boys to St. Mary's, a select boarding school for religious education, appeared in many newspapers. In its first year of operation, the school had six seminary students and 30 school-age boys from fifth grade up.

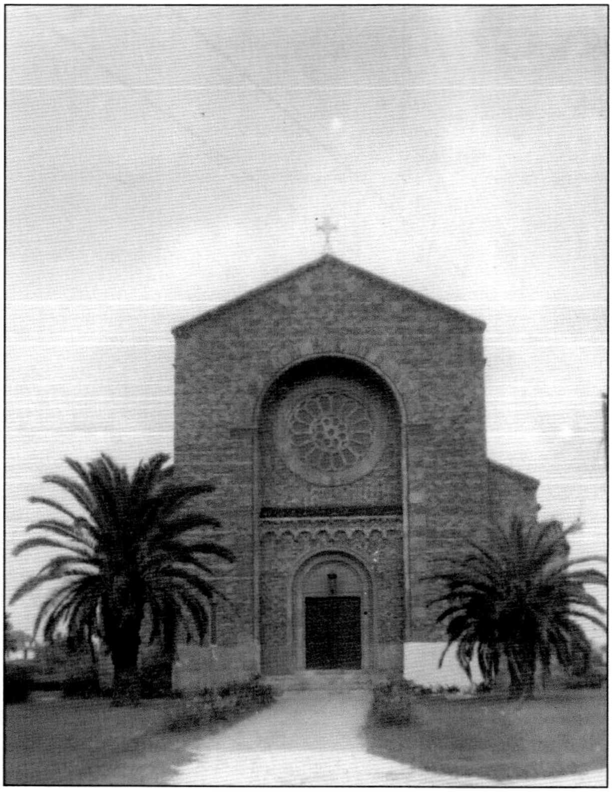

St. Mary's Seminary opened in La Porte in October 1901. The school's bishop, N.A. Gallagher, purchased the Sylvan Beach Hotel to convert it into a dormitory for the seminary. The structure measured 60 feet by 120 feet and included verandas on all sides, 50 rooms, six baths, classrooms, and a library. A second four-story building was constructed to compliment the hotel after its conversion and complete the housing for the new seminary and college. Beautiful St. Mary's Church, looking out over the bay, was completed in 1927. The seminary was moved to Memorial Drive in Houston in 1954. The last priest ordained at St. Mary's in La Porte was Rev. Joseph Fiorenza, (now retired) bishop of the Galveston-Houston Diocese. The photograph below shows the completed buildings as they stood for over 50 years. The seminary building in La Porte burned in December 1973.

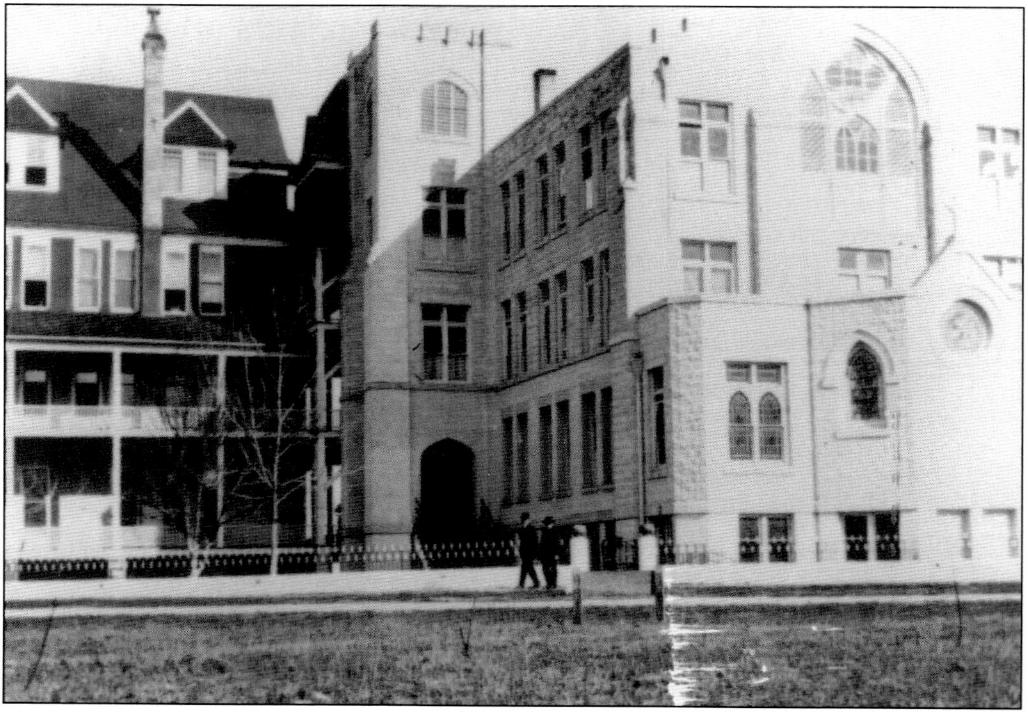

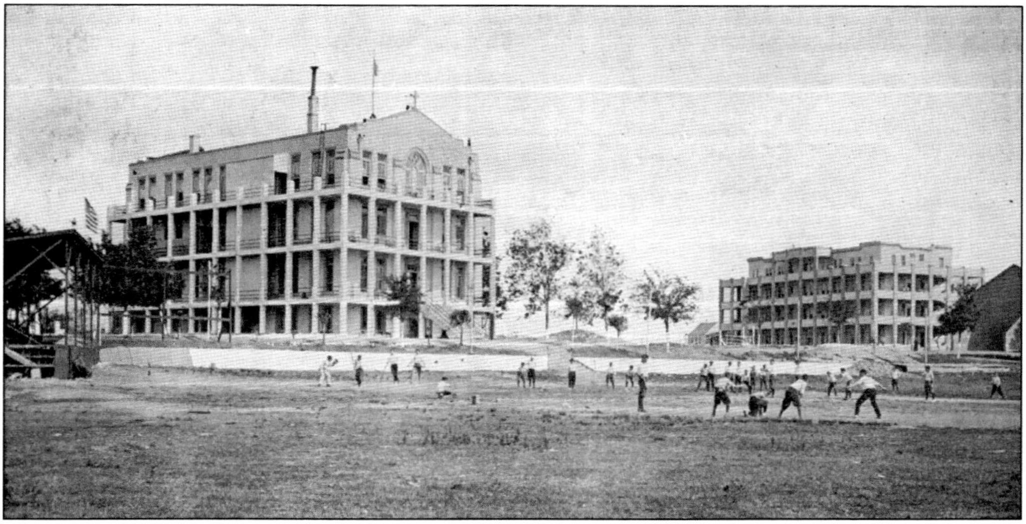

St. Mary's continued to grow, and this is how it looked after completion. The students and the young men of the seminary were encouraged to participate in all sports. Baseball was always prime among the boys, but swimming and boating activities were available also. St. Mary's and its students were a vital part of La Porte's way of life for many years.

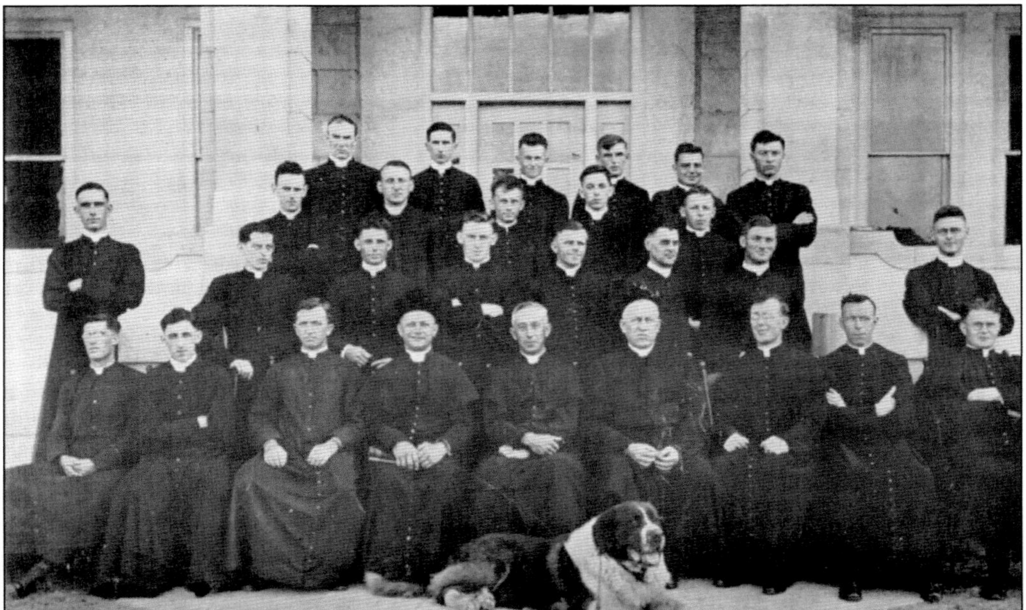

As St. Mary's grew, so did the teaching staff. This photograph shows the diocesan priests who taught there. St. Mary's Seminary remained in La Porte until 1954 when it was moved to Houston. Bishop Joseph Fiorenza, archbishop of Houston-Galveston Archdiocese attended St. Mary's.

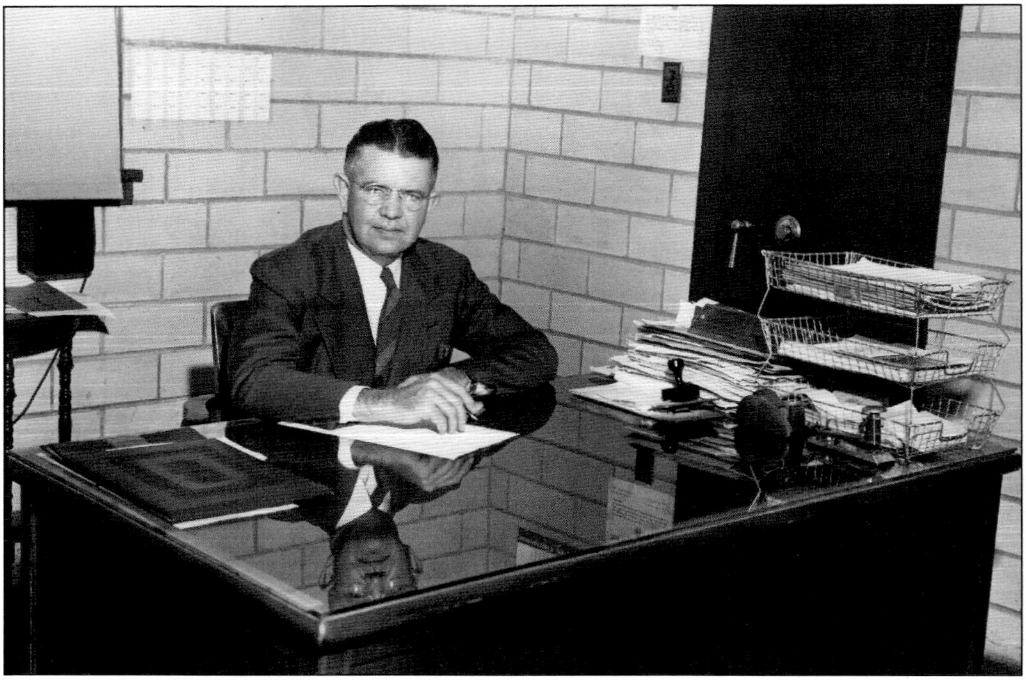

James Baker was one of La Porte's leading citizens. This teacher and principal was involved in many activities over the years and was always a great supporter of the city. This photograph shows Baker in the 1940s when he was superintendent of the La Porte School District.

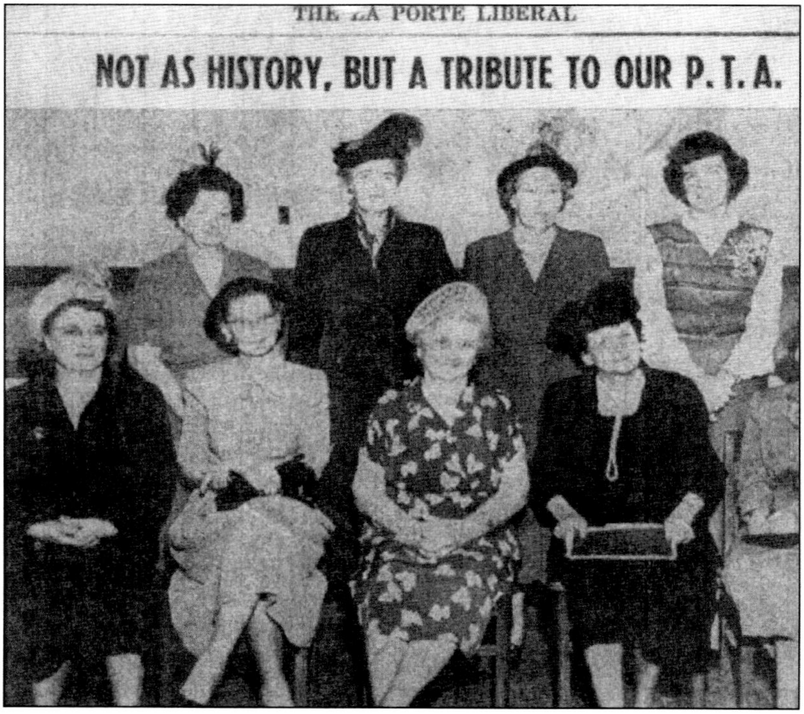

The school Parent Teacher Association (PTA) has always been a large supporter of education. Ladies of the community involved in the PTA included, from left to right, Mesdames (first row) H.M. Ralston, J. Crate, Gertrude Akerly, E.E. Seamman, and M.O. Burgin (face not visible); (second row) E.S. Lyne, A.L. Hershberger, Otis Harrison, and D. Kennedy.

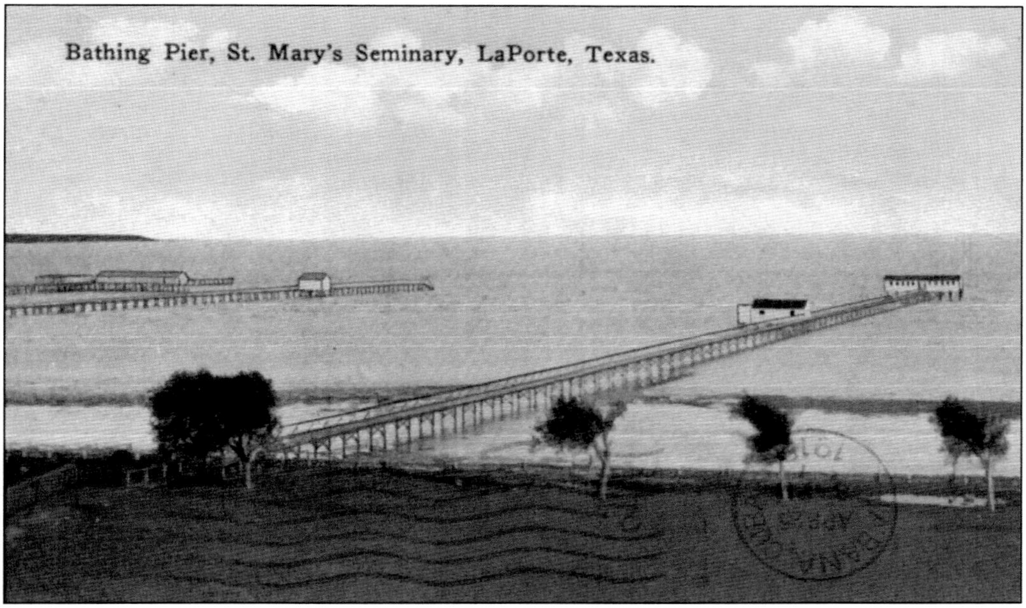

This postcard shows the St. Mary's pier around 1910. The seminary's campus covered 10 acres and had space for sports fields, gardens, oak groves, and a dairy maintained by the Dominican Sisters and Basillian Fathers who ran the campus. The school included two separate departments: a seminary open to young men even if they did not wish to enter the priesthood and a school offering preparatory and college classes in classics and business.

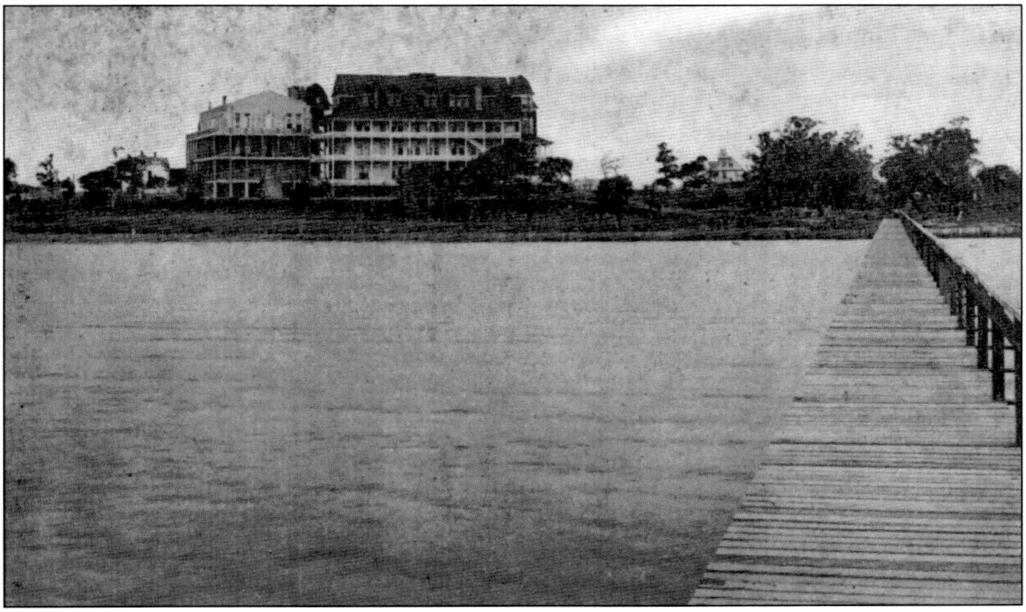

This is the view of the main structures at St. Mary's, as seen from the pier shown above. The building on the left opened in 1906 and was constructed entirely of steel and concrete. The building on the right is the old Sylvan Beach Hotel, purchased by the Catholic Diocese shortly after the seminary opened in the fall of 1901 and adopted for use as dormitories, classrooms, and halls for students.

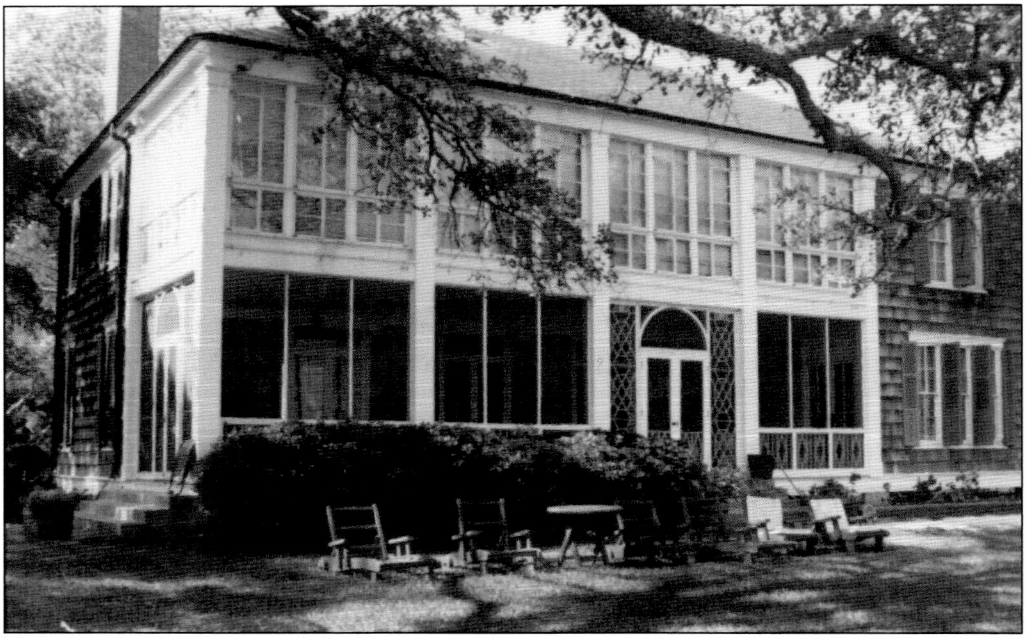

Around the end of the 19th century, wealthy businessmen from Houston found Morgan's Point to be the perfect place for summer and year-round residences. Some noted residents of Morgan's Point have included Glenn McCarthy, oilman and owner of the Shamrock Hotel; Judge Roy Hofheinz of the Astrodome fame; and others. In 1917, Gov. Ross Sterling built his home on Galveston Bay. He is said to have pulled out a $20 bill and told his architect he wanted his house to look like the one on the bill. Whether this is true or not, the structure does resemble the White House. At the time it was built, the Sterling mansion had 34 rooms and was the largest private residence on the Texas coast. The mansion and the rest of these wonderful homes are a tribute to the history of Morgan's Point.

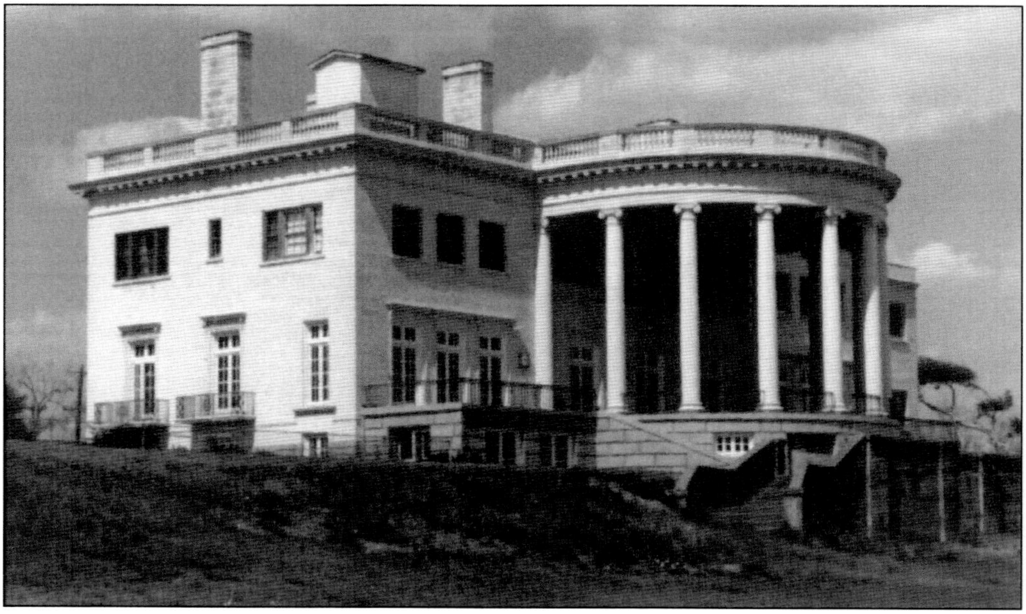

Four

Around La Porte

Adjacent to the city of La Porte are Morgan's Point, Shoreacres, and Lomax. Morgan's Point is located east of La Porte and has a long and interesting history connected to the legend of "The Yellow Rose of Texas." This area has been known as Rightor's Point, Hunter's Point, and Clopper's Point. Now Morgan's Point, it has served as the summer stopping point and year-round residence of wealthy families from Houston for many years. Gov. Ross Sterling built his mansion there in 1927 (modeled after the White House), and it still stands today. In 1931, Morgan's Point was the home of the first ferry connection to Baytown, Texas, which was home to busy oil fields. Morgan's Point incorporated in 1949 and today it is primarily a bedroom community but stands as a reminder of the early commercial history of Harris County.

Shoreacres is a small village south of La Porte. For many years, it was a popular vacation spot owned by M.E. Tracy, but by the beginning of World War I, Tracy sold the property to Shoreacres, Incorporated. Developers viewed Shoreacres as the perfect place for suburbia, mainly because it was only 45 minutes from downtown Houston. Thus Shoreacres was born and dedicated in 1925. The city has a size of 1.9 square miles, was incorporated in 1949, and is primarily a bedroom community. The Houston Yacht Club chose this area to establish its headquarters.

In 1895, R.A. Lomax, a businessman from Illinois, purchased several hundred acres just west of La Porte. Lomax divided this land into 10-acre plots to sell to farmers and cattlemen who ventured down from the North. He also set aside several acres for a school. Lomax has traditionally been rural and most of the individual homes are built on several acres. Lomax was annexed by La Porte in 1940, but was de-annexed in 1952. At that time, it became a city and remained so until 1980 when once again it was annexed by La Porte. Telephone service has been available in Lomax since 1905, electricity came in 1929, and roads were paved in the 1950s.

Names of some of the earliest settlers of Shoreacres, Morgan's Point, and Lomax still appear in the area and include Pizzatola, Rizzuto, Riggs, Wakefield, Black, Hershberger, Wall, Sharp, Lemon, Sullivan, McClure, Clingin, Rosenbalm, Waters, and Malone, to name a few.

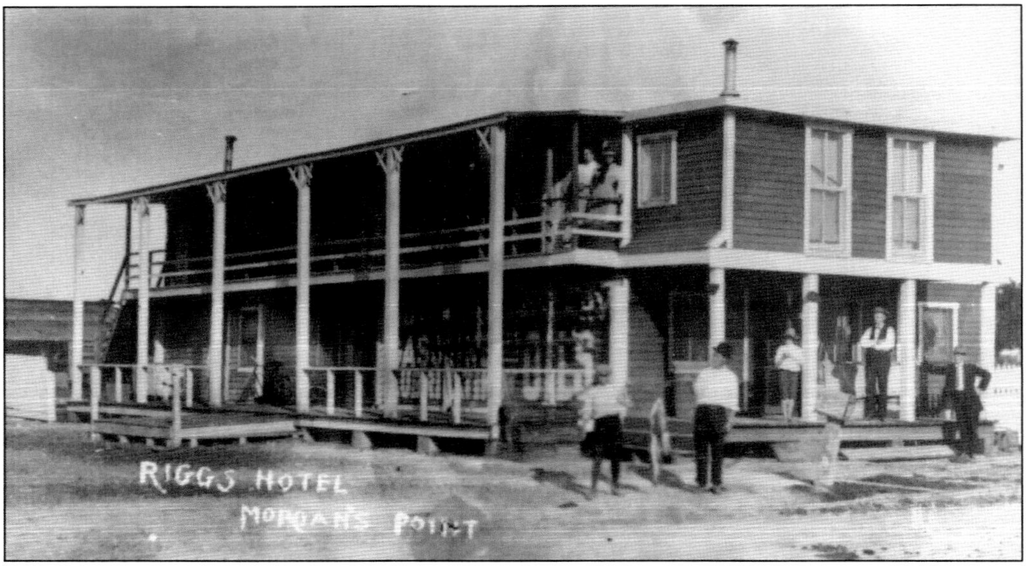

Fishermen, hunters, and excursionists and pleasure parties on the ship channel find Morgan's Point a favorite resort. A stay at the Riggs Hotel is convenient as a starting point for fishing and hunting in the area. Mrs. Riggs, the welcoming hostess and supervisor of the hotel, sees that the food and other amenities are unsurpassed.

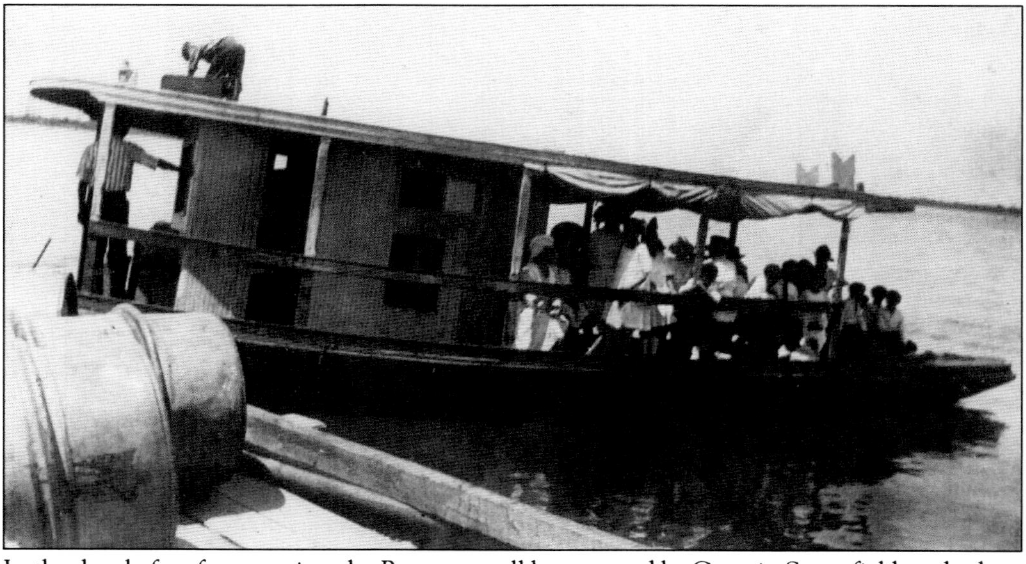

In the days before ferry service, the *Pansy*, a small boat owned by Captain Sutterfield, and others like it, ferried workers to the oil fields in Baytown and on trips down Buffalo Bayou to Houston and other points. Many people chose to live in La Porte and commuted daily. The oil boom began in 1911 and drew hundreds to the area.

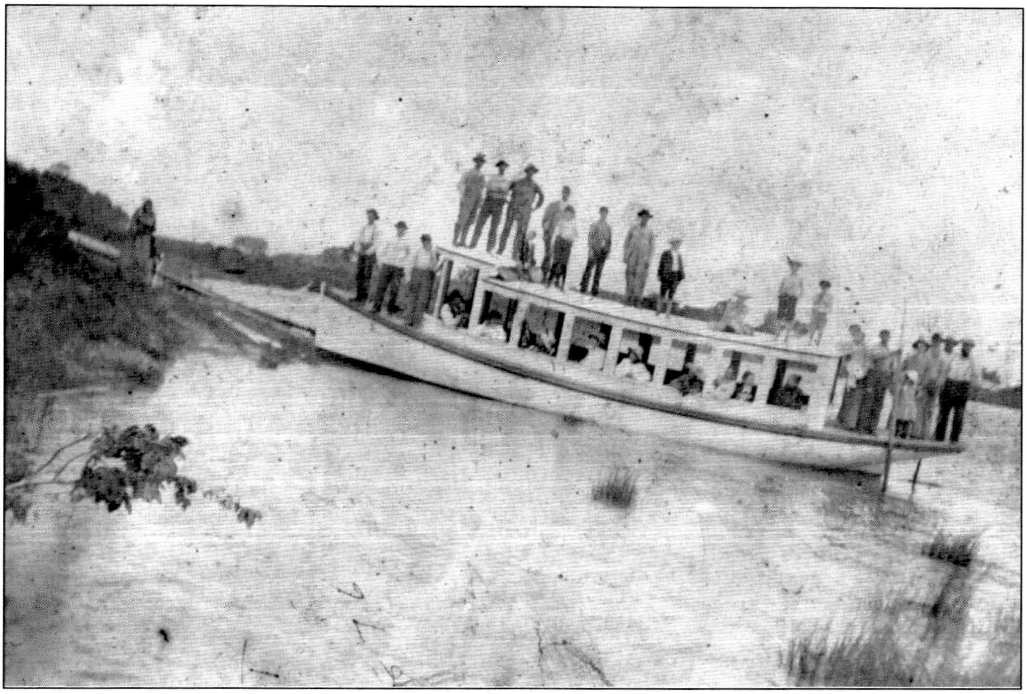

This boat, filled with passengers, has been caught on a sandbar at low tide or blown off course by bad weather. This occurred occasionally, making boat travel precarious at times. The passengers are waiting for high tide to float them free so they may continue on their way.

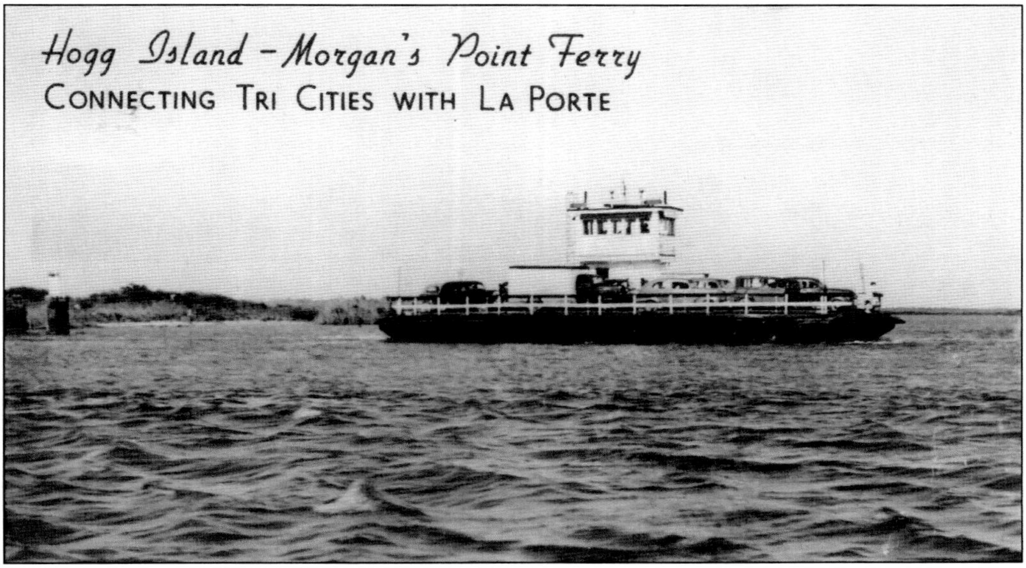

The Charles D. Massey ferry opened service to Morgan's Point, La Porte, and Baytown in 1933. It ran between Morgan's Point and Hogg Island and was the longest ferry ride in Harris County; from Hogg Island, vehicles could then take the Tabbs Bay causeway to Baytown and access the Tri-City area. Ferry service was discontinued in 1953 when the Baytown–La Porte Tunnel was opened. Hurricane Carla destroyed the remains of the causeway in 1964.

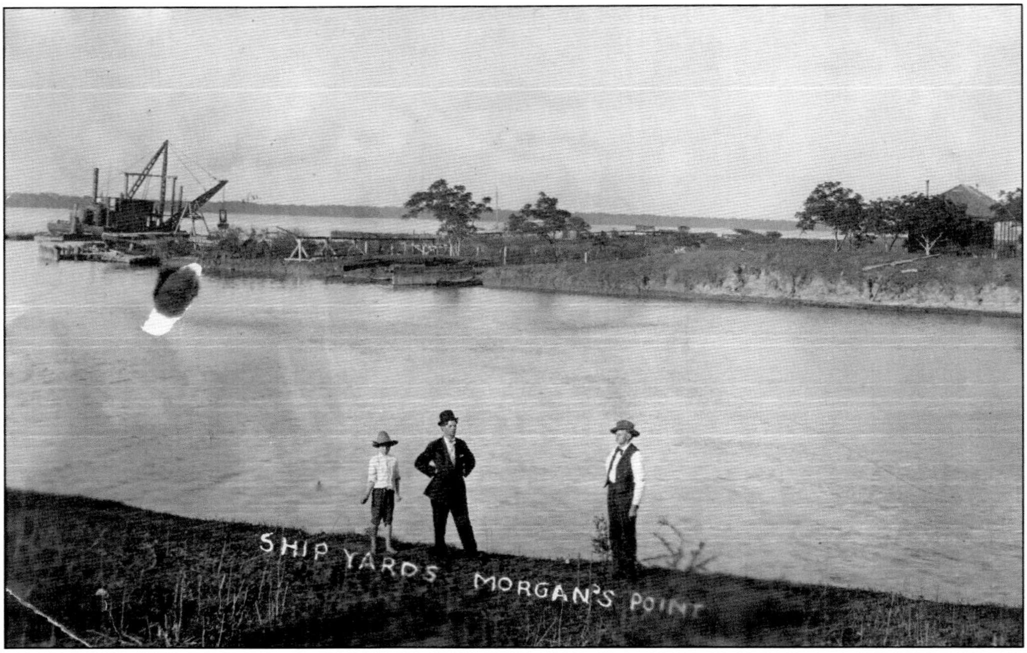

This photograph shows the Morgan's Point shipyard, which started in the area very early. Morgan's Point has been home to many businesses such as Jim Black's restaurant, the Ferry Fish Market, Pizzatola's grocery, Sanders' grocery, Fusulla's service station, and many other large and small ventures. Zeisig's restaurant came later and became a well-known stop in Morgan's Point and the Houston area.

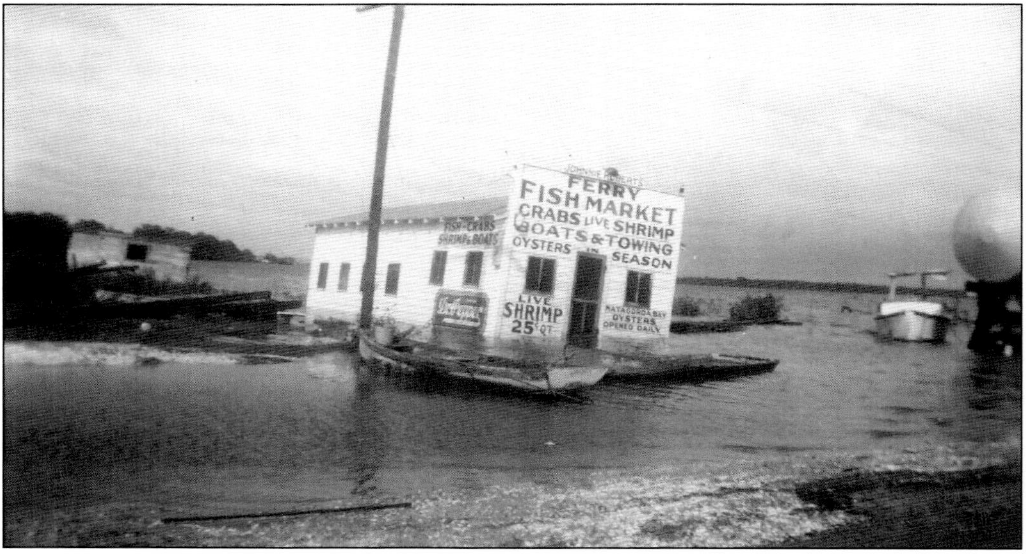

The Ferry Fish Market was damaged in the 1941 hurricane that came without warning. World War II was on the horizon. For security reasons, not everything was broadcast; and the same thing happened in 1943 when another unannounced hurricane appeared and created even more havoc.

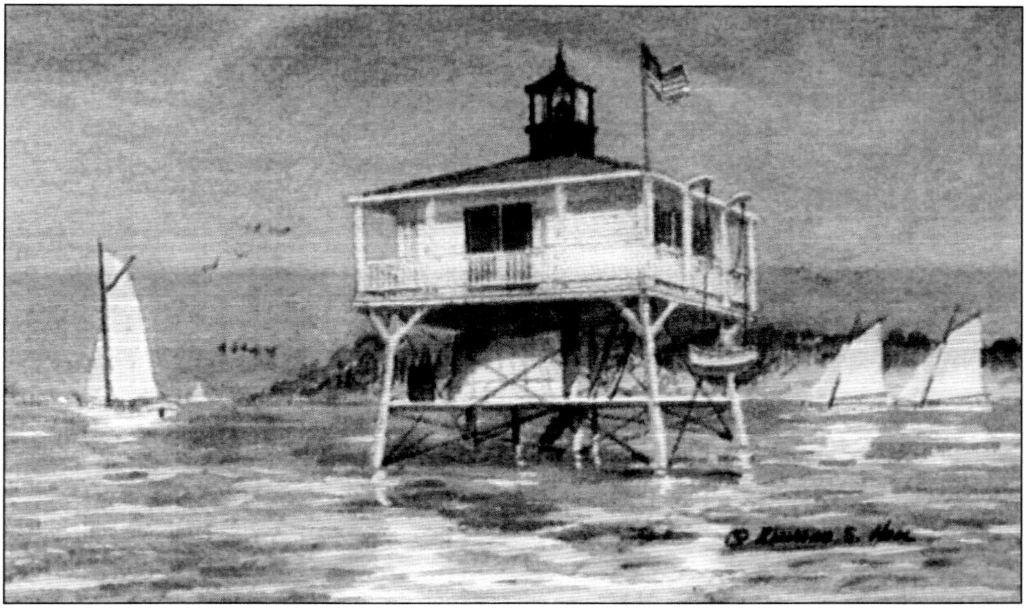

The lighthouse at Clopper's Bar marked the treacherously shallow oyster reef and mud flat between Morgan's Point and Cedar Point where the San Jacinto River enters Upper Galveston Bay. It was built in 1854 and served the area until 1880 when it became a day mark for ships. After the ship channel was dredged, the lighthouse was not needed for navigation purposes. The Clopper's Bar Lighthouse no longer exists.

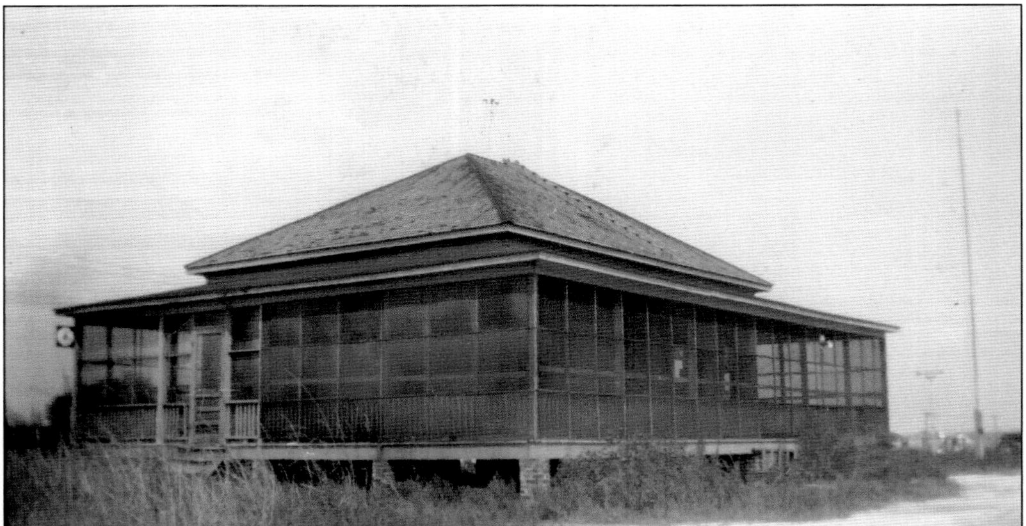

The Maritime Station at Morgan's Point was established in November 1923 because of increased boat traffic. Will Black was hired to manage traffic, a position he held for 30 years. The first building became obsolete, was sold, moved, and renovated by Joe Fusulla as a service station. The old Pillot summer home was purchased and used as the Maritime Station until 1953.

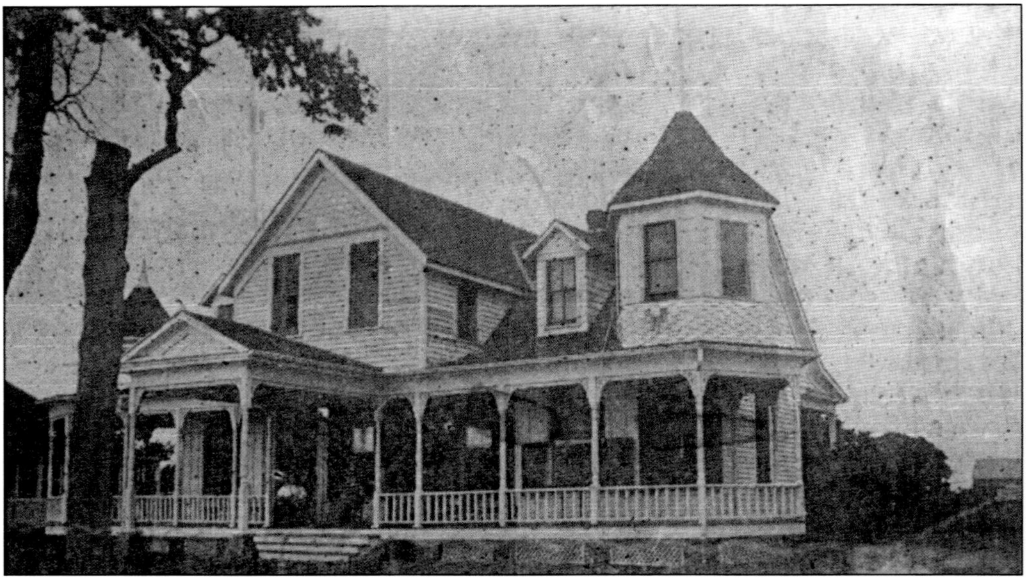

Bayridge was a residential company started by wealthy Houstonians in 1898; a group of 12 homeowners, led by H.F. Ring, owned 50 acres. Two Bayridge homes are shown on this page, Jonelle Bryan's home is above and E.P. Hamblen's home (an attorney and later a judge) is below. Neither Bryan nor Hamblen were among the original property owners.

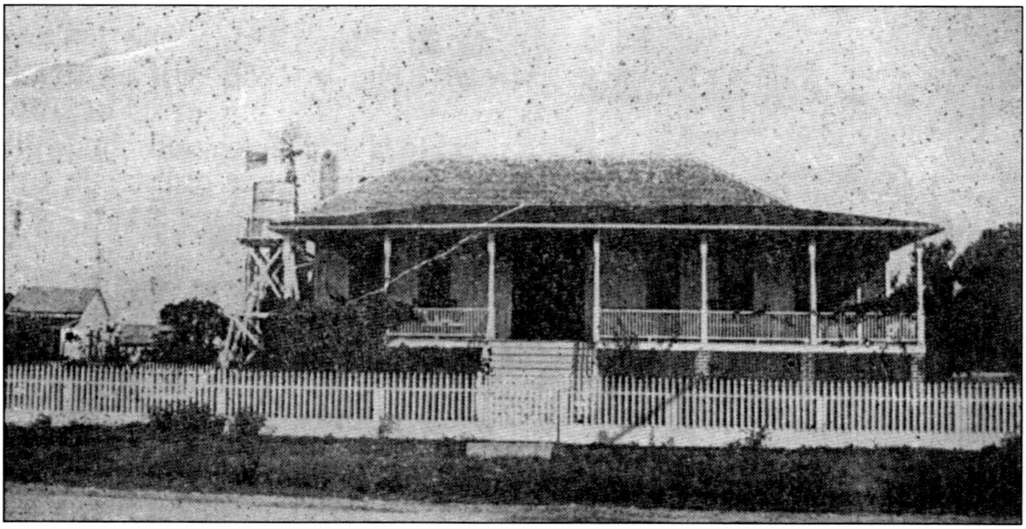

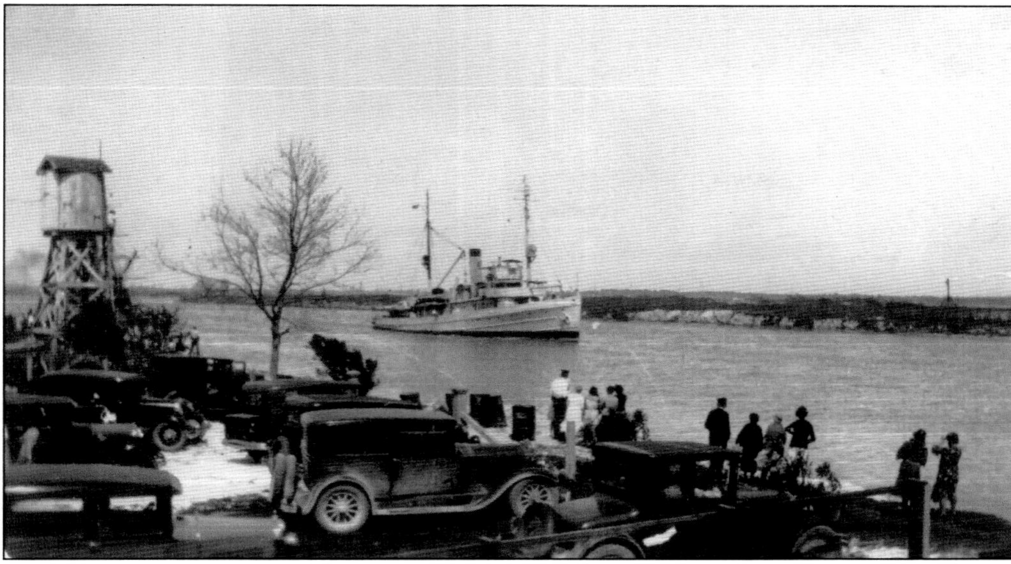

Morgan's Point was and is the perfect place to see great ships traverse the waterway to their final destinations. As seen in this photograph, the channel is not very wide at this point, and an excellent view of the ships is possible. Julia Green Dautriel, a native of Morgan's Point, remembers seeing or being told about Old Ironsides, the Battleship *Texas*, USS *Houston*, and others that have come this way.

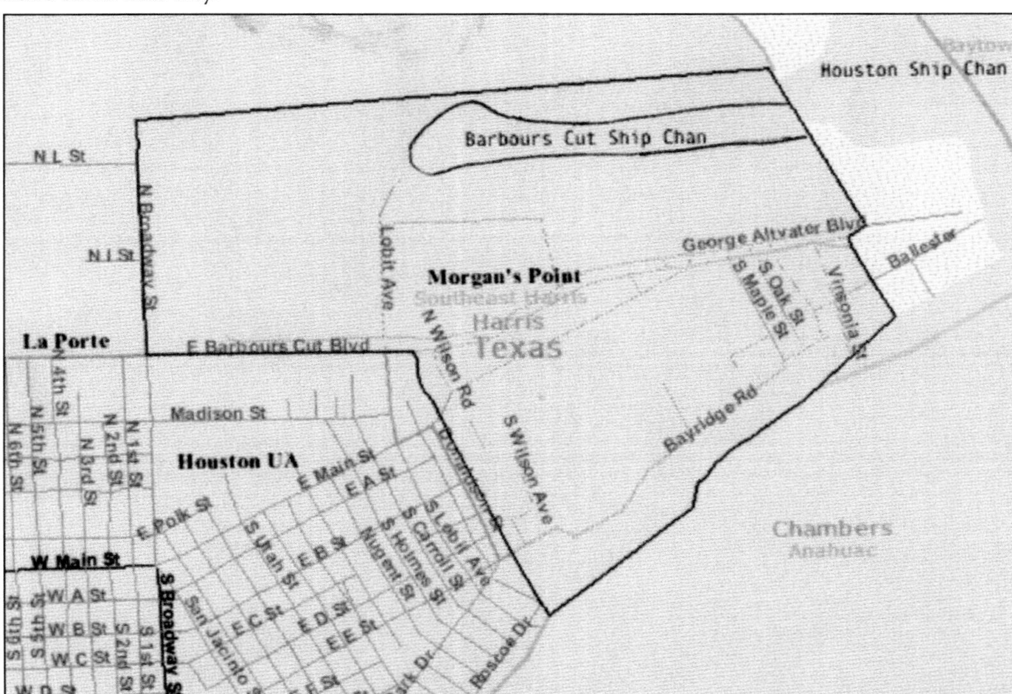

This is a map of Morgan's Point, Texas. Morgan's Point is small in population, but rich in history and home of the yellow rose of Texas. Morgan's Point is situated in Harris County, but the bay is claimed by Chambers County.

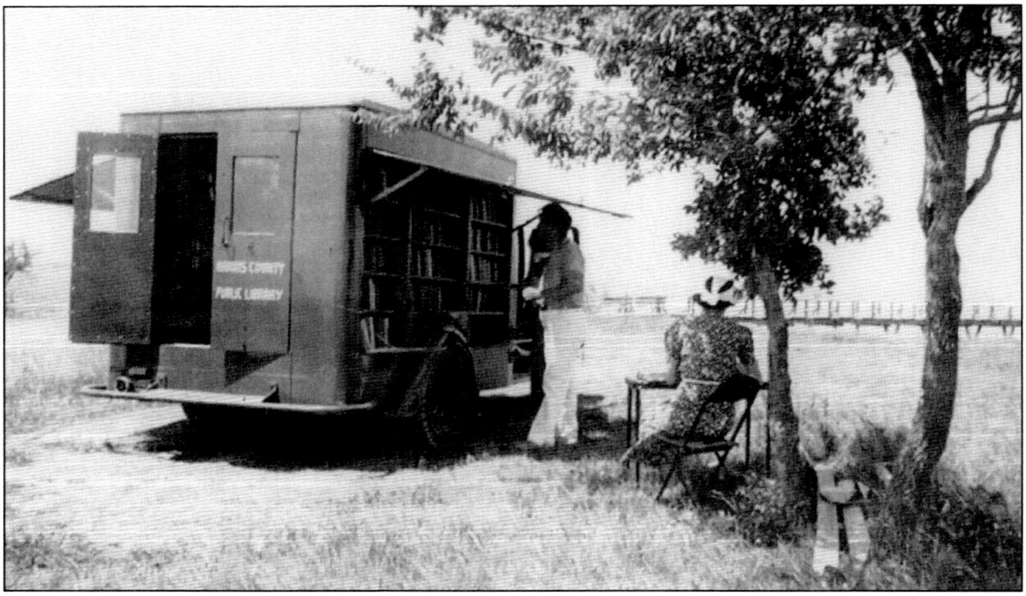

Shoreacres: Invented in 1905, the earliest bookmobiles were horse-drawn carriages with homemade shelves. The idea of mobile libraries spread quickly across the country and, by 1937, bookmobile production in the United States was on the increase. In this photograph, a bookmobile stands on the shores at Shoreacres ready to provide a mobile library for the citizens of the area. (Courtesy of the Harris County Public Library Archives.)

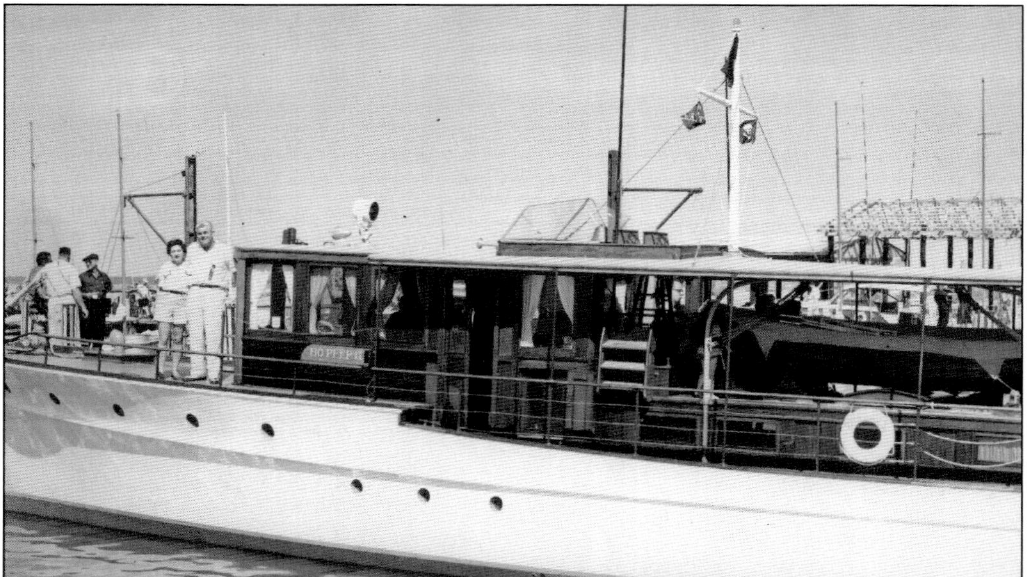

Shoreacres: Louis and Edna Bonner stand atop the deck of their yacht, the *Bo Peep II*. This vessel could sleep seven people and had a full galley as well as two heads. The Bonners were known to sail as far as Key West at any given time. Once docked in the harbor of the Houston Yacht Club, this boat would crowd with friends and family ready to enjoy festive celebrations. (Courtesy of Buck Bonner.)

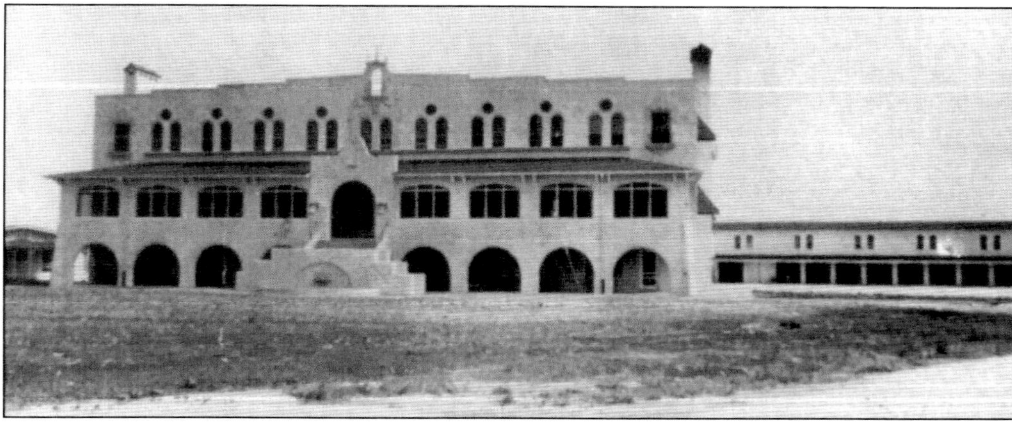

The Houston Yacht Club, shown above, was built in the present location in Shoreacres between 1926 and 1931. It had existed at other locations, mostly in Harrisburg, and had merged with the Houston Yacht and Power Boat Club and the Houston Launch Club. At one time, the Houston Yacht Club had its own golf course and airfield. Shown below is Camille Pillot's yacht, the *Augusta*. A Houston resident and partner in the business of Henke and Pillot (which is know known as Kroger), he was an avid water sportsman and involved with the development of the Houston Ship Channel. Because of his work with the Houston Ship Channel, Pillot became interested in water recreation. The Navy leased the *Augusta* in August 1917, and after the armistice, the Augusta was returned to Pillot, who enjoyed it until his death in 1953 at age 92.

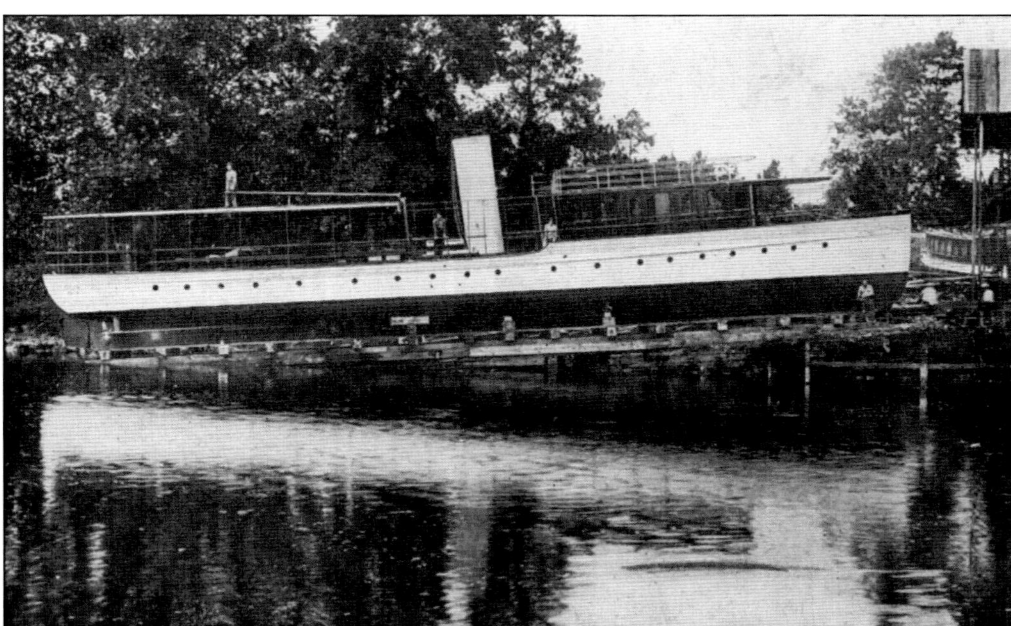

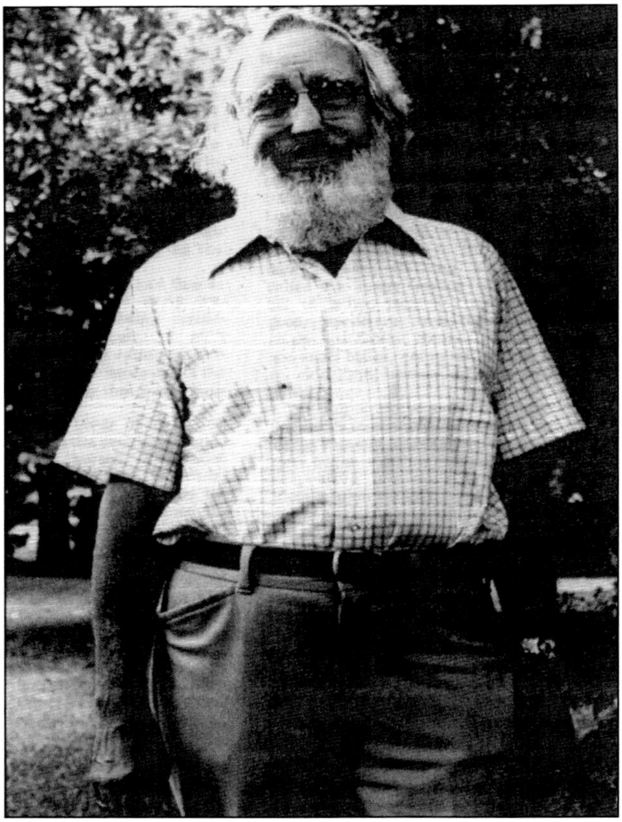

John Harkness was the first mayor of Shoreacres in 1949. He and his wife, Elizabeth, were the first full-time residents and the 42nd residents overall in 1948 when they moved to Shoreacres. Harkness, who served three terms, says Shoreacres was started in the 1920s as a private company by a family named Carter and that 242 people voted in the 1949 referendum on incorporating Shoreacres. The third mayor of Shoreacres was Ben Johnson, who won by way of write-in votes.

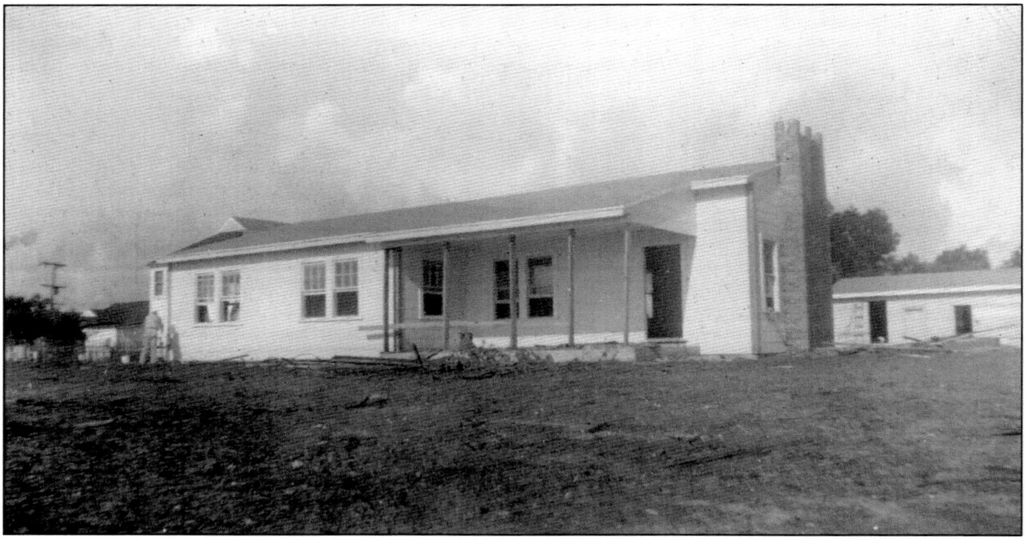

The Rothermels built their home near La Porte (or what would become Shoreacres) in 1947. William G. Rothermel Sr., shown here was, along with brother Louis, a founding partner in the Maritime Oil Company. In his early career, Rothermel was an architect, so this summer home in the La Porte area was not only a relaxing getaway for him and his four children, but also a creative return to his architectural roots. (Courtesy of Louis F. Rothermel II.)

Marquerite "Madlin" and Joseph Donald were the children of Joe and Mary Emma MacDonald Stevenson, who were married in Houston in 1880. Madlin was born in 1904, and brother Joseph Donald in 1910. Joe Stevenson was an accomplished architect and businessman who built a summer home in Shoreacres in 1928. The Stevenson family spent holidays and summers at the bay, where they sailed the *Gypsy Queen*. This picture of a 1930s-model roadster filled with smiling youngsters is evidence of their summer fun. Madlin Stevenson was a generous woman whose legacy lives on with the endowment of Texas A&M University's Stevenson Companion Animal Life-Care Center. As one reporter described, the facility "could come straight from a 19th-century painter's vision of the 'peaceable kingdom'—lions, lambs, babes and bulls all lolling in blissful communion." Madlin was a dedicated benefactor to this cause. (Courtesy of the Houston Yacht Club Archives Stevenson Collection.)

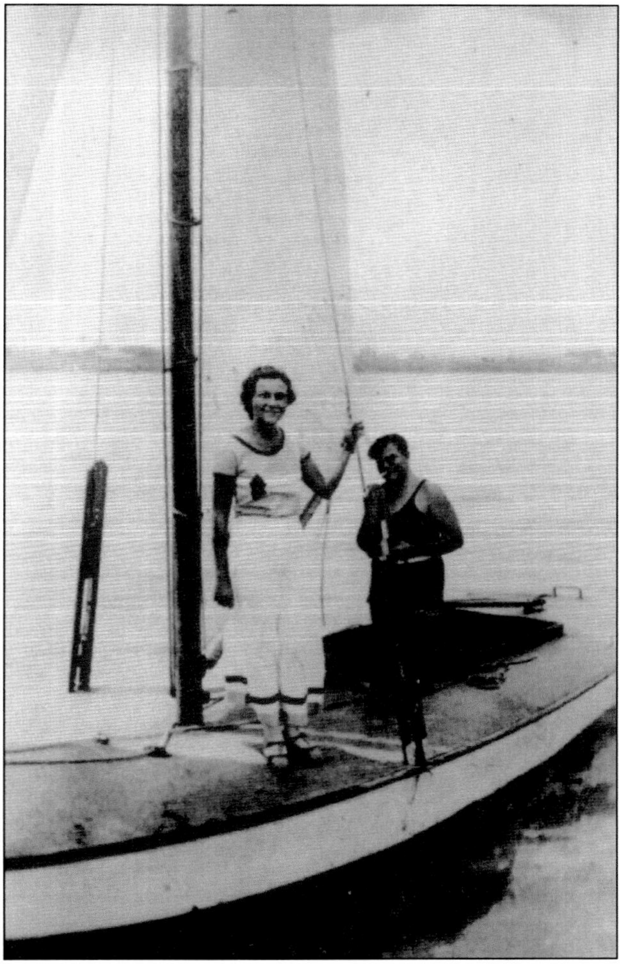

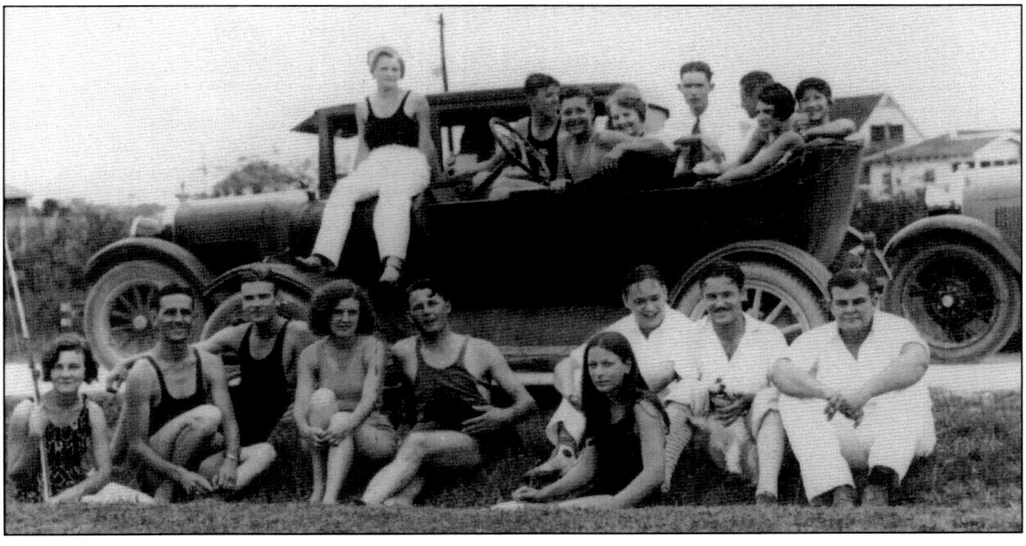

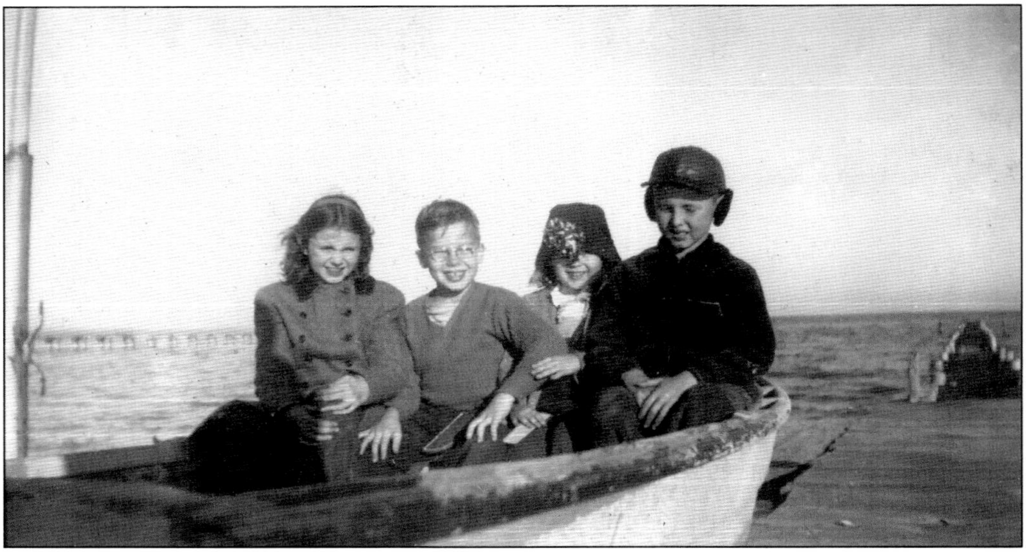

This picture shows the children of two so-called summer-folk families. As soon as school let out, many families packed up and moved to the bay for the summer. It was common for the entire family to live around La Porte all summer with the father returning to his office in Houston during the day. Pictured, from left to right, are Sarah Rothermel, Billy Sellers, and Ellen and Louis Rothermel in a skiff. (Courtesy of Sarah Duncan and Ellen Stuart.)

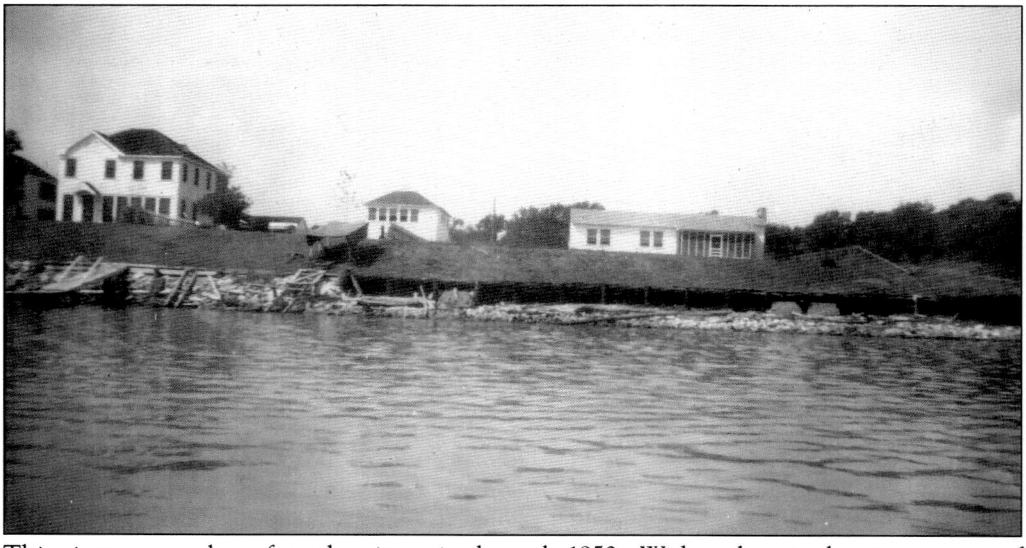

This picture was taken after a hurricane in the early 1950s. With each major hurricane, most of the piers are washed away and driftwood can be found everywhere. One pier association paints the ends of their planks blue, so that after a storm they are able to gather their lumber and put the structure together again more easily. (Courtesy of Louis F, Rothermel II.)

In 1893, Isaac "Ike" Shireman, came to Lomax and bought 102 acres on what is now L Street. In 1894, he brought his family to join him, and upon their arrival, his wife commented that the weather looked like snow. Ike's reply was, "It doesn't snow here," but the next day Texas had one of its worst snowstorms in history. Regardless, the Shiremans stayed.

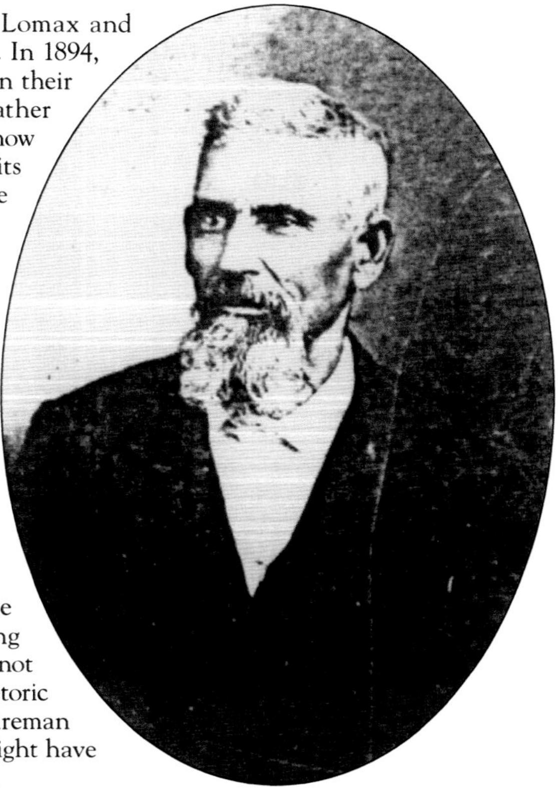

Like most of the farmers in Lomax, Ike Shireman tried to raise fruit orchards along with his crops and cattle, but the weather did not cooperate as well as the promotional sales rhetoric suggested it would. This photograph of Shireman and his granddaughter Lucy shows what might have been had the weather been more agreeable.

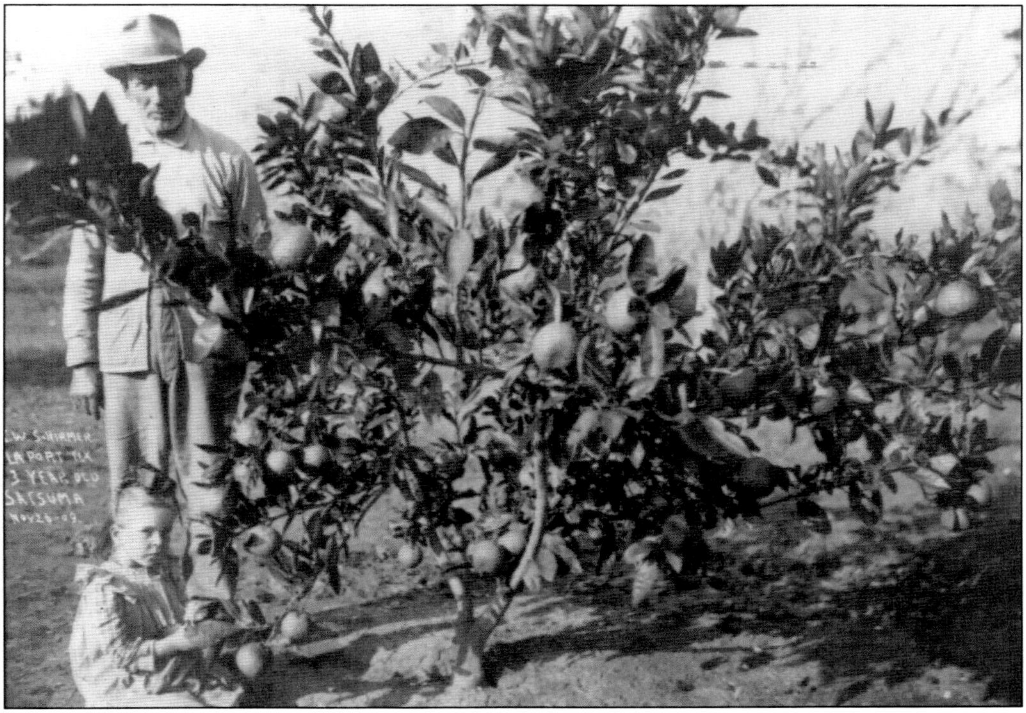

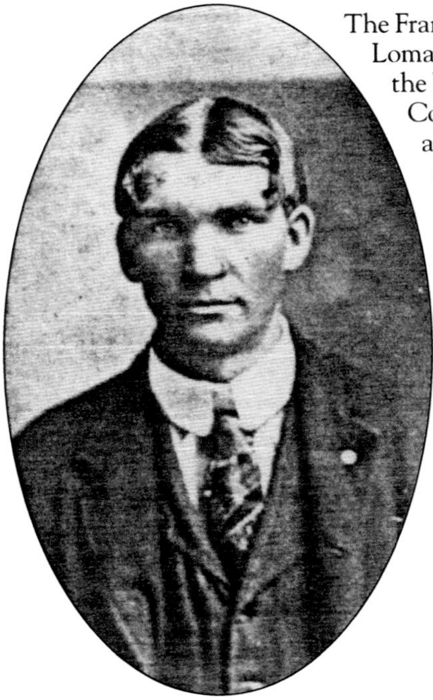

The Frank Gates family from Montgomery County, Texas, came to Lomax in 1903. Gates was a prominent cotton farmer, but after the boll weevil scourge, he traded his 200 acres in Montgomery County for 20 acres in Lomax. He bought an existing house and raised his family there. In 1917, he built a small grocery store behind his house and ran it for 10 years.

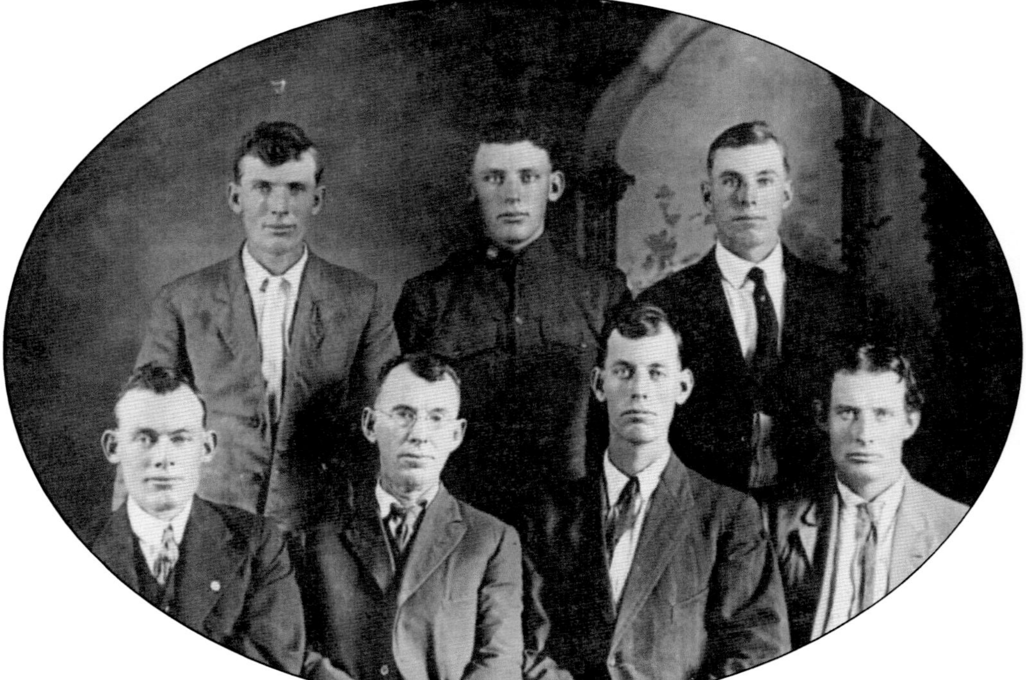

The Browning family arrived from Granger, Texas, in 1903. They came by wagon and had two mules. The family's destination was Pelly, near Baytown, but Mrs. Browning wanted a farm. And so they came across San Jacinto Bay to Lomax. The Brownings had five sons as well as daughters, and relatives of this founding Lomax family still live in the area.

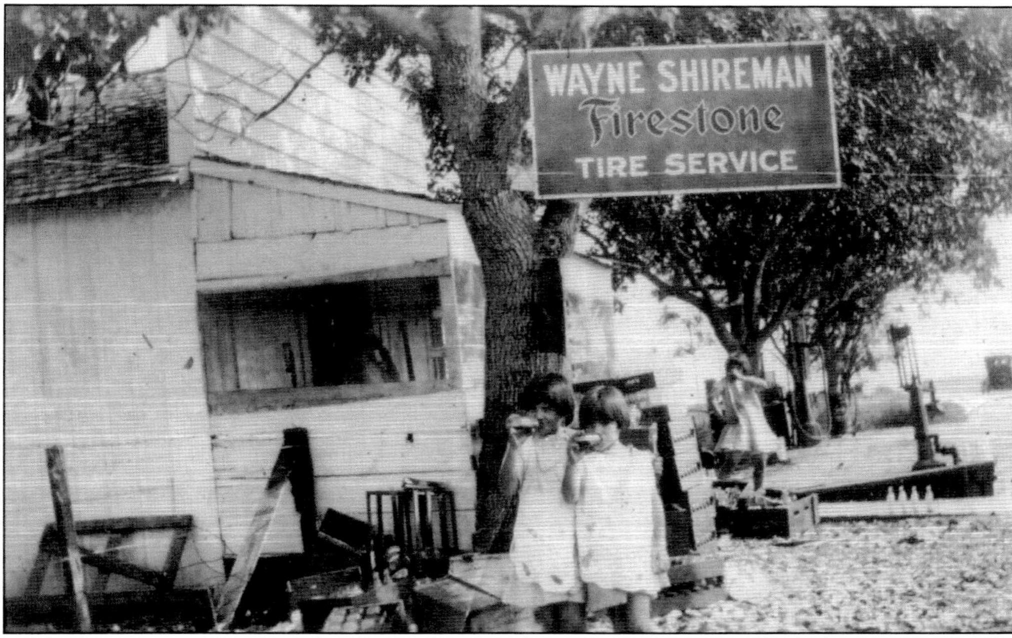

Wayne Shireman came to Lomax in the 1900s and eventually married Lidie Gates, one of the daughters of Frank Gates. In 1927, Wayne and Lidie bought the grocery store and house from Lidie's father. Wayne was very involved in the communities of Lomax and La Porte. He was the first mayor of Lomax and served on the La Porte school board. For years, the Shireman store was a gathering place for the community.

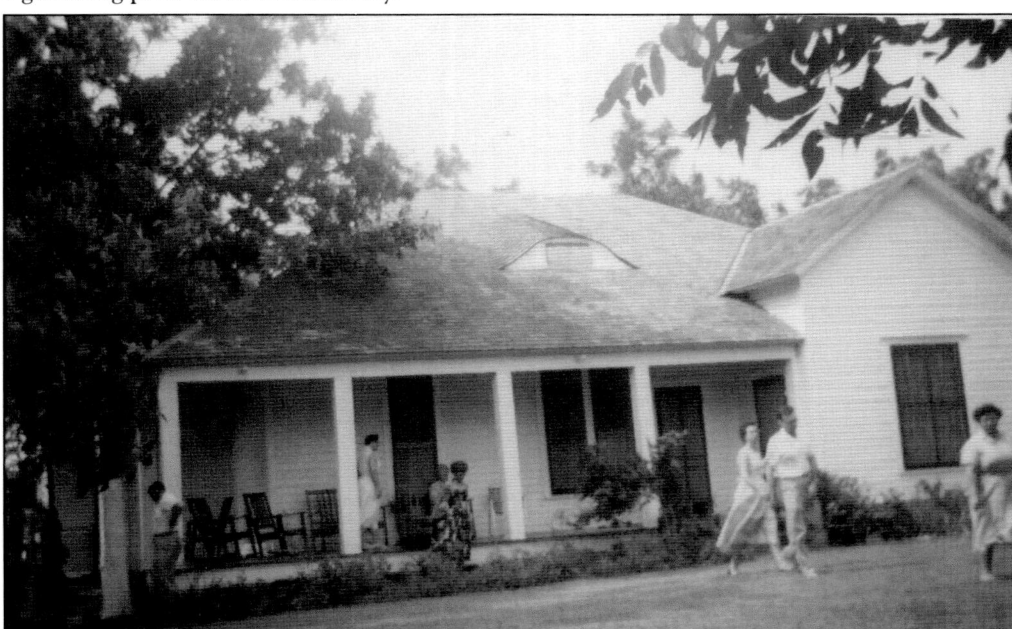

This is a photograph of the old Gates-Shireman home in Lomax. Judy Berry, the Shiremans' daughter, had invited the La Porte Bay Area Heritage Society out for the day. The house and store stood for many years in their original locations, but were both recently moved.

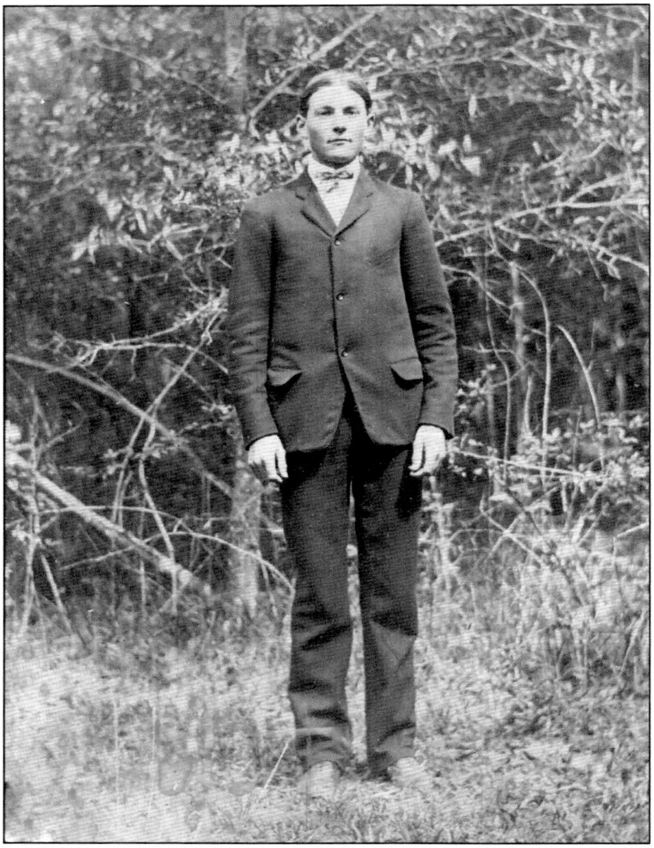

Andy Womack, pictured here, was a member of another prominent family in Lomax. The Womacks came by wagon to Lomax in 1902 from Montgomery County, Texas. They had six children, and the two oldest boys herded the cattle the entire trip. Descendants of the Womacks still live in and support the Lomax and La Porte areas.

Lomax and La Porte young people always had a bit of rivalry—the country boys versus the city boys. A group of young men from Lomax formed the P Street Reds for fun and to make sure the city folks did not forget their country cousins.

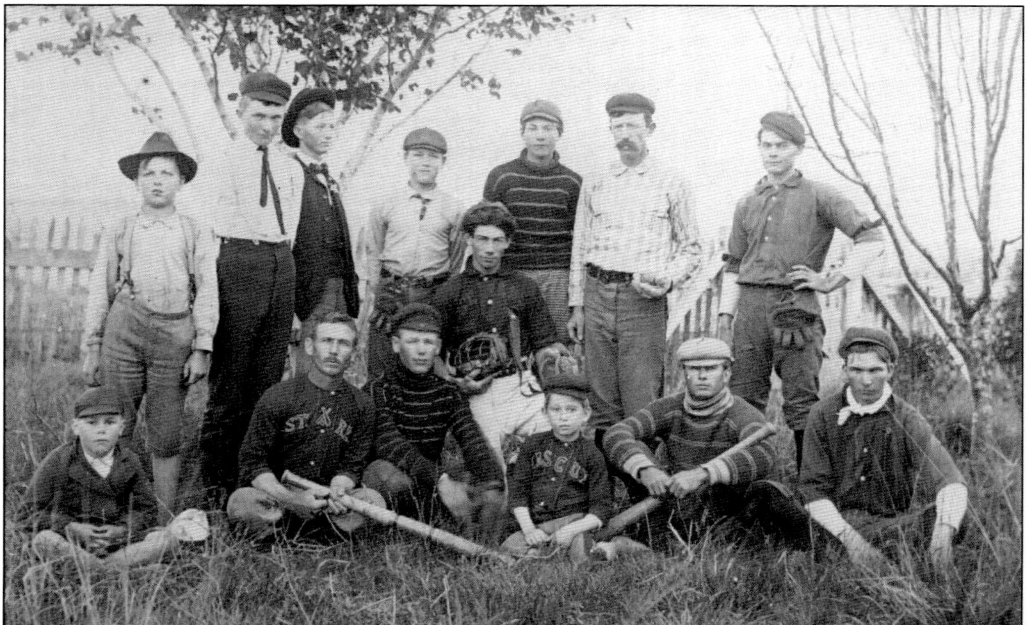

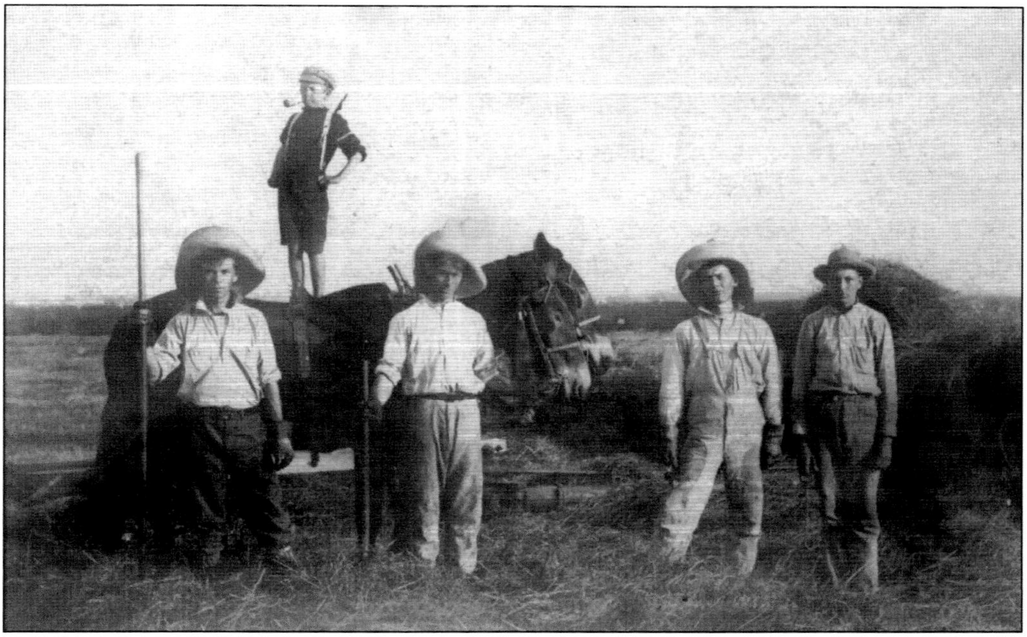

Ike Shireman, along with the Browning boys, baled the prairie grass, which was good quality and easy to sell. This proved to be a very good crop for industrious farmers in Lomax, as did figs. The fig tree was the only fruit tree to survive the weather on a consistent basis.

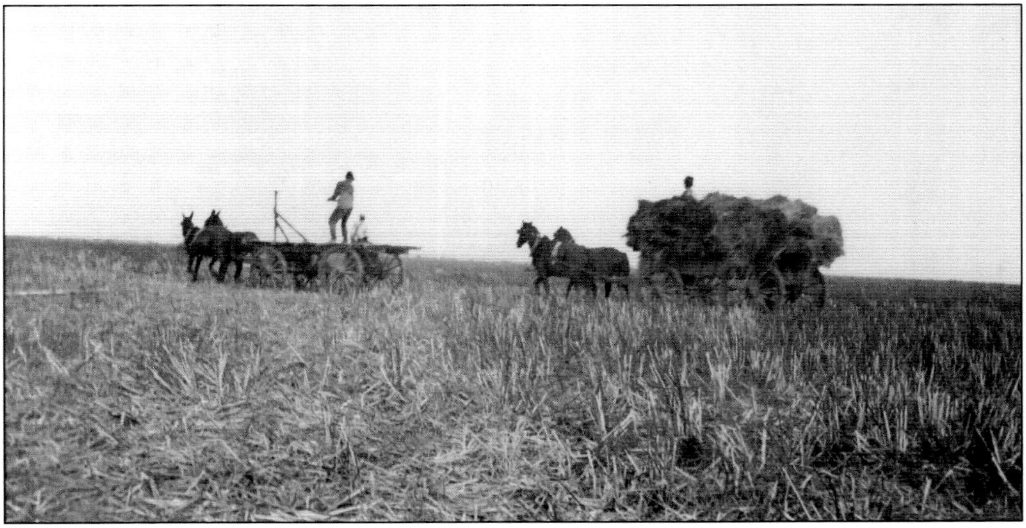

Crops are being taken to the barn after a long, hard day of work. This scene was typical for many years on the prairie that is Lomax. The people who settled there were a very hardworking group.

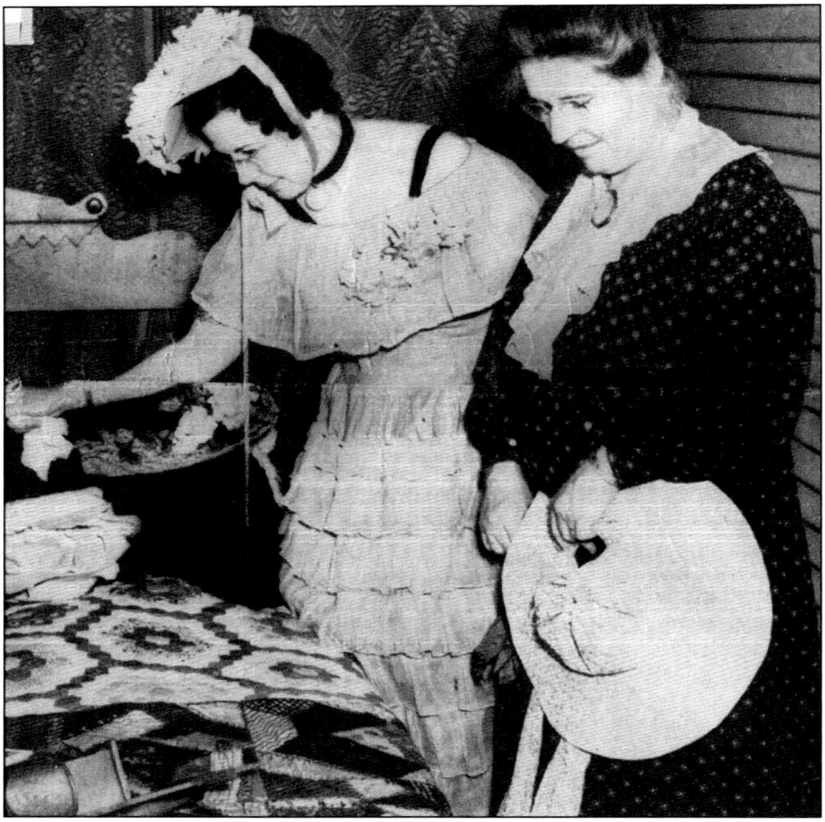

Mrs. Aves (left) and Mrs. Sandel of the La Porte Reading Club are dressed in vintage clothing. The club met at the home of Mrs. Anderson in Lomax for a costume luncheon and to enjoy looking at historical items.

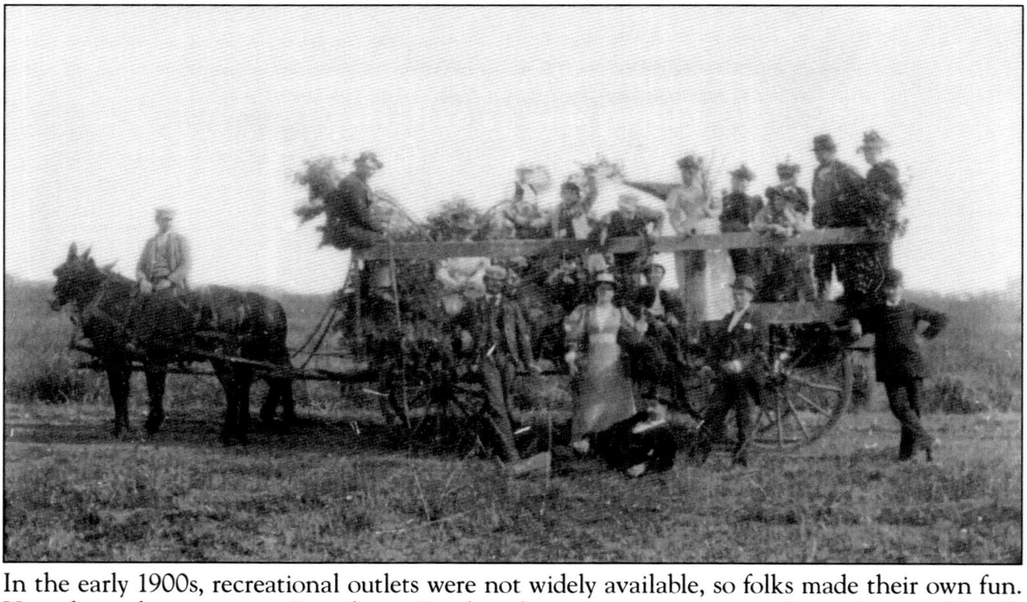

In the early 1900s, recreational outlets were not widely available, so folks made their own fun. Hayrides and picnics on a Saturday or Sunday afternoon were quite popular and enjoyed by all. The folks in this photograph are enjoying a hayride on the Lomax prairie. A picnic was probably also included.

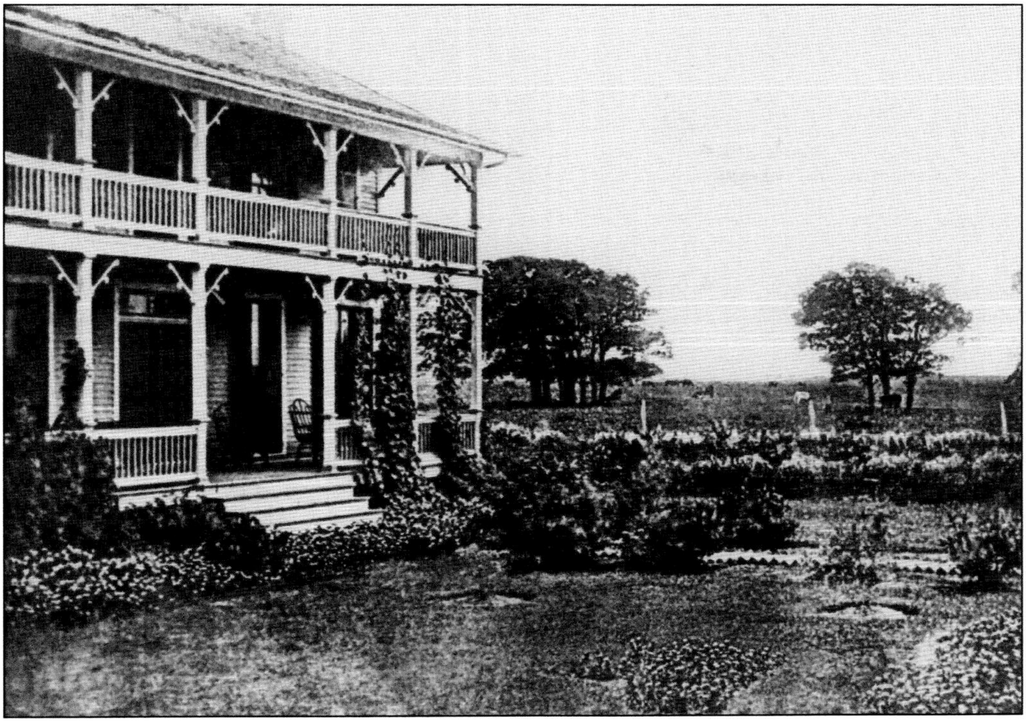

Houses large and small dot the Lomax prairie. The area has never been densely populated because most settlers own acreage. This is an example of one of the larger homes in Lomax.

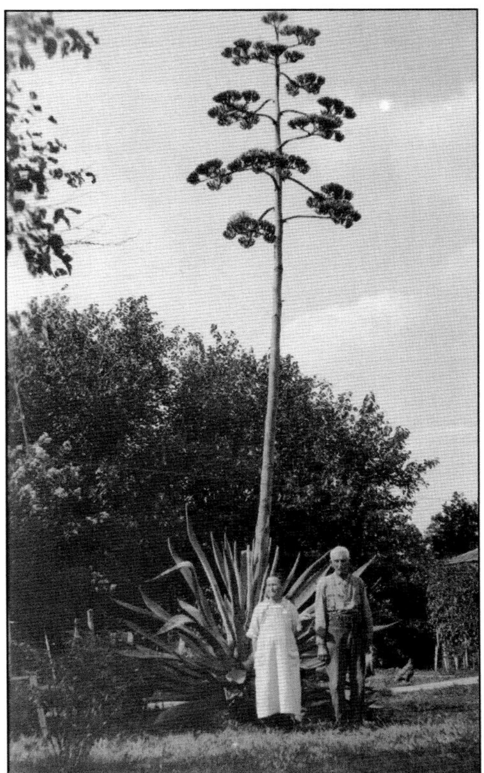

This photograph is of Mr. and Mrs. Ike Shireman standing in front of a century plant they planted when they first arrived in Lomax. In the background are trees that have also grown up over time.

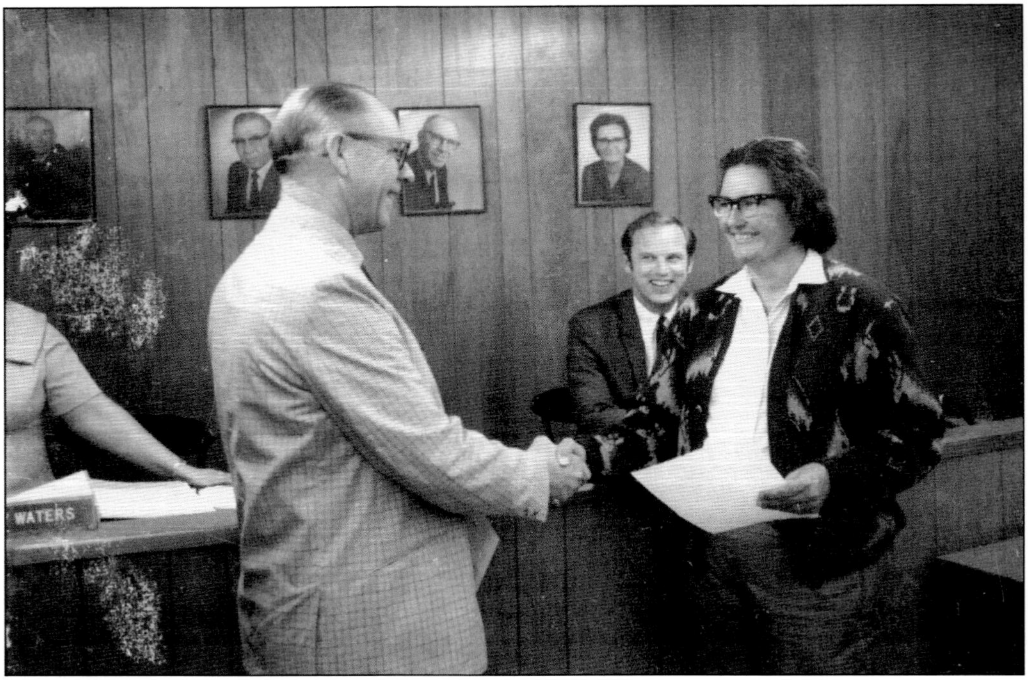

Ann Stevenson was one of the first women to be elected mayor of a city in Harris County. This photograph shows her swearing in and congratulating her successor, Ed Lemon.

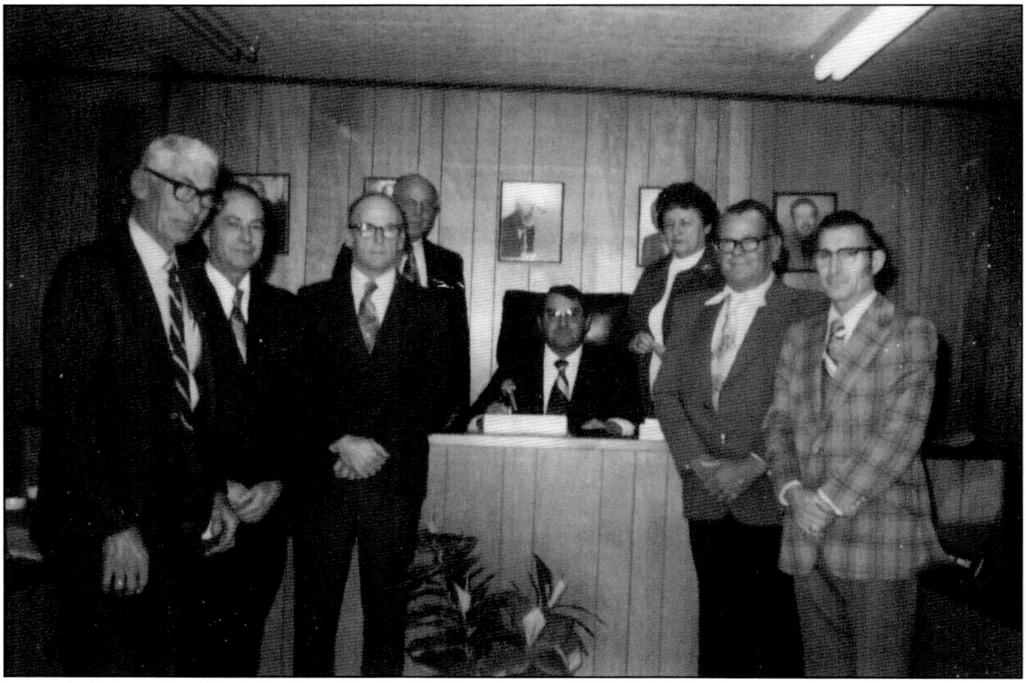

From left to right, the following made up the city government of Lomax before annexation by La Porte: Ralph Mace, J.B. Womack, Doyle Kuehl, attorney Walter Queen, mayor Norman Malone, city secretary Betty Waters, Buck Medlin, and Carl McManners.

Five

People around La Porte

The quality of any city is determined by the quality of its residents. La Porte and the neighboring communities of Morgan's Point, Lomax, and Shoreacres are no exception. Moreover, the beauty of Sylvan Beach and the communities around La Porte beckoned many from Houston and around Texas to come down and make a summer home by the bay. Many fell in love with it, and many went back. Texans as diverse as Ross Sterling, novelist David Westheimer, and heart surgeon Denton Cooley have all come down to the bay to live or work or write, and contribute to the culture and lifestyle of the community.

When John Beazley's home on Sylvan Beach burned in 1928, the *Houston Chronicle* reported that after the Beazleys bought the home in 1892, the "wide veranda became the social center for Galveston Bay, and it was on this porch that General Sam Houston, Mirabeau Lamar and General Sidney Sherman used to sit and watch the sailboat races out in the Bay."

Although this chapter pictures many of the area's finest residents, many have also been left out. The authors beg the indulgence and forgiveness of readers who would have loved to see a picture or mention of someone left out. It was due to the weakness of our memories and the shortness of time and space allotted, and not due to any lack of pride in the memory of any who were omitted.

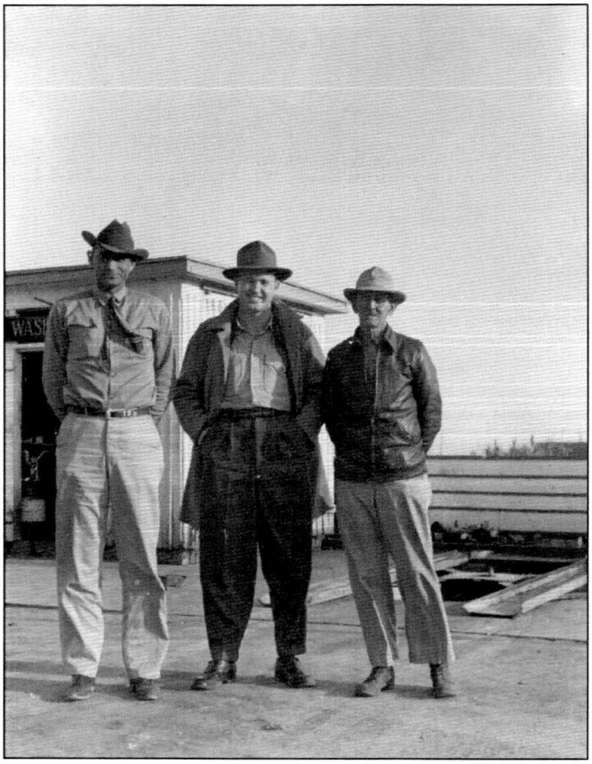

On the left was one of the best-liked and most respected lawmen in La Porte. Jake Bussey, who was county constable for 30 years, is shown with the infamous Dale Richardson (center) and Calder Ewing, who was justice of the peace. Bussey always had a good story to tell and never carried a gun to get his point across. According to Bussey, there was once a casino and brothel in La Porte. Richardson was elected county constable and quickly became noticed. His claim to fame was getting rid of illegal gambling in his and other precincts. Ol' Dale, as he was known, did so by smashing slot machines with a baseball bat, among other things, and thus made a name for himself all over the country.

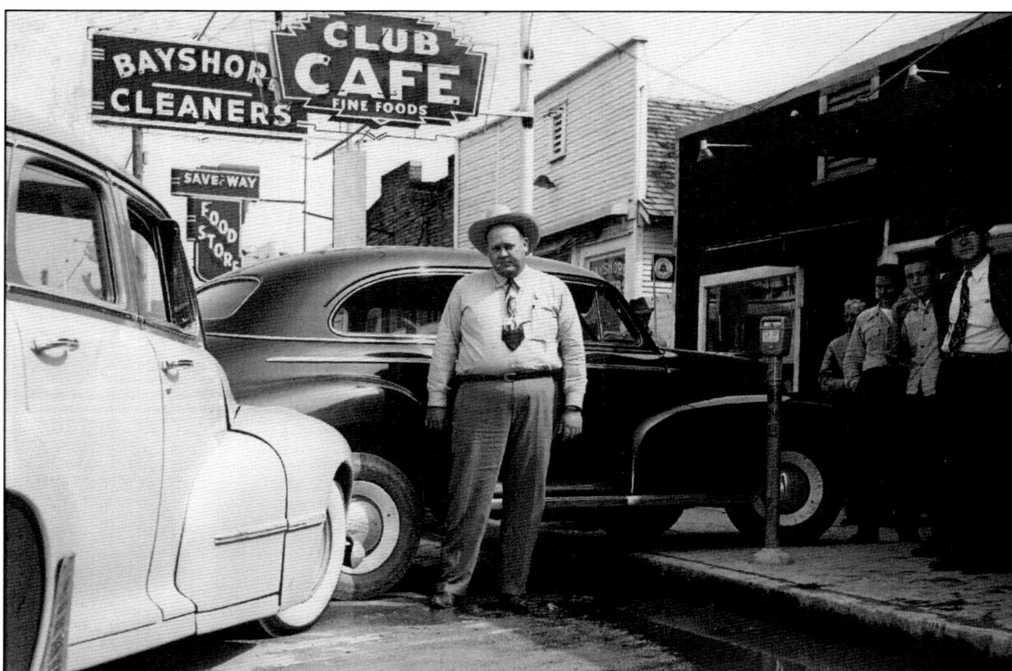

In this photograph, police chief Walter "Heavy" Robertson is trying to keep the peace on Main Street and settle a problem as curious folks look on. Some things never change.

Rudell Phillips was the first black police officer to become part of the La Porte Police Department. He served with them for 20 years. In 1942, Phillips and wife Ruby moved to La Porte from Winona, Texas. He first worked at the shipyards during World War II and then for the Keyser family as caretaker at Big Water on the bay. Phillips family members still live in La Porte. (Courtesy of Lola and Marvin Phillips.)

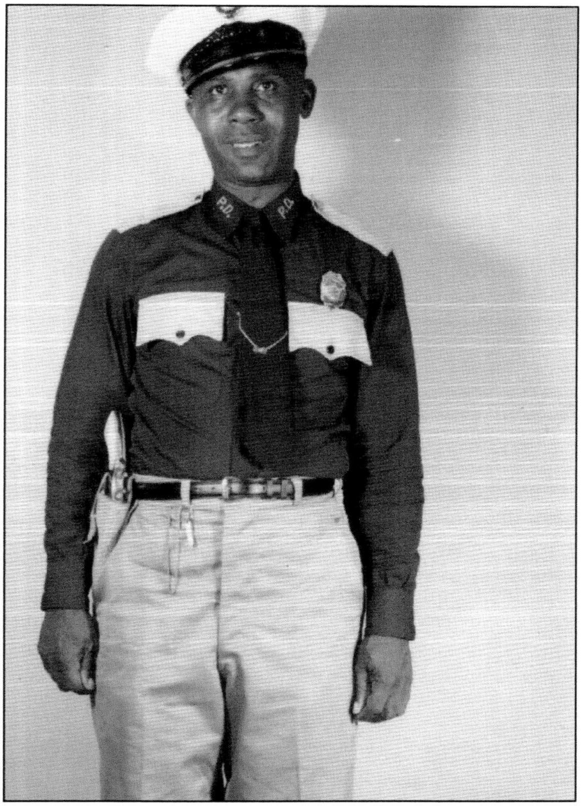

Mr. and Mrs. Weaver were the first couple to be married in La Porte. As a wedding gift from the city, they received a completely furnished house on Second Street.

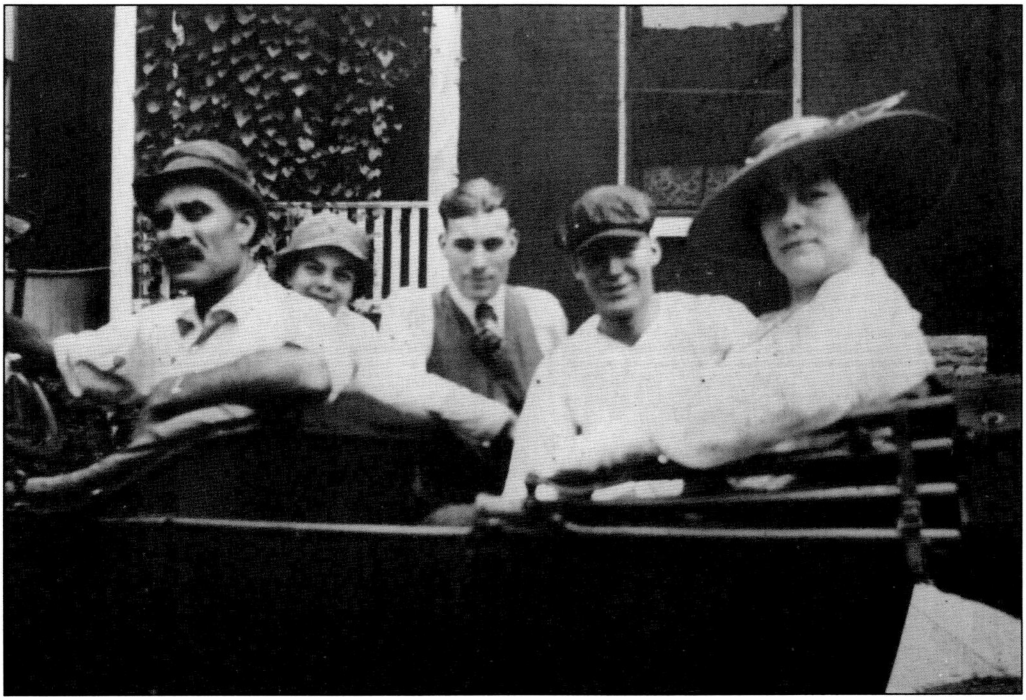

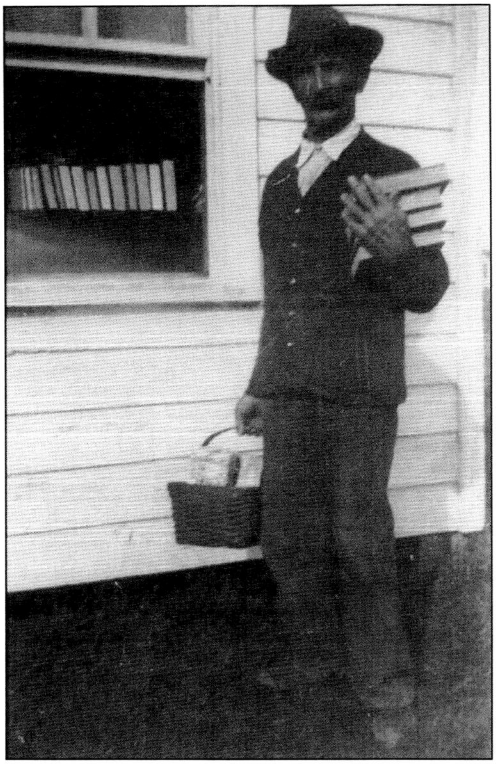

Pictured is A.O. Blackwell, an early La Porte founder. He chose to live out his life in the city he helped found. I.R. Holmes, another early promoter, also stayed. The rest moved on to other ventures.

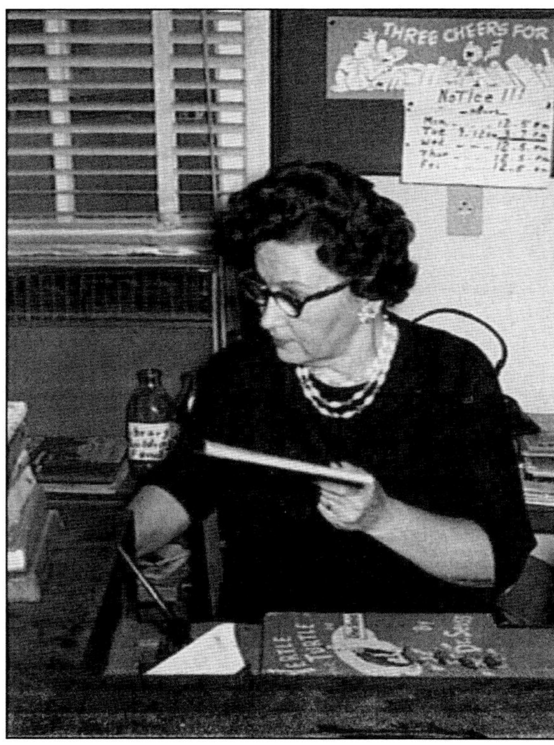

Edith Wilson was a librarian in La Porte for many years. She started in the city's first one-room library and then moved to the new library, which was named in her honor. Many remember Wilson fondly.

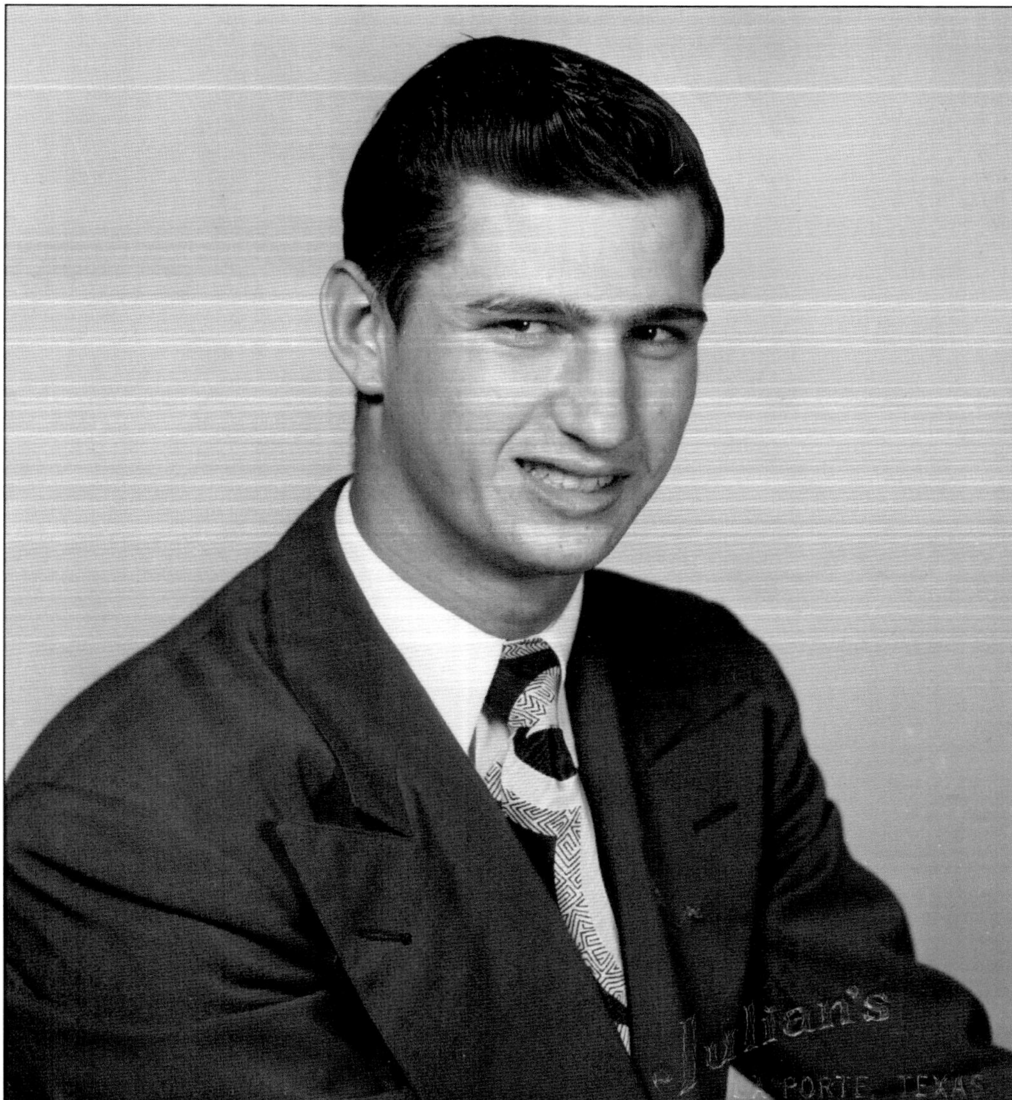

Here is La Porte's historian as a young man. Gordon Black has spent countless hours researching and collecting the stories and history of this town. The people of La Porte are greatly indebted to him for his diligence and for following in the footsteps of his grandmother, Gertrude Ackerly, who meticulously recorded the early history of the city. Cheri, Black's wife, still resides in La Porte.

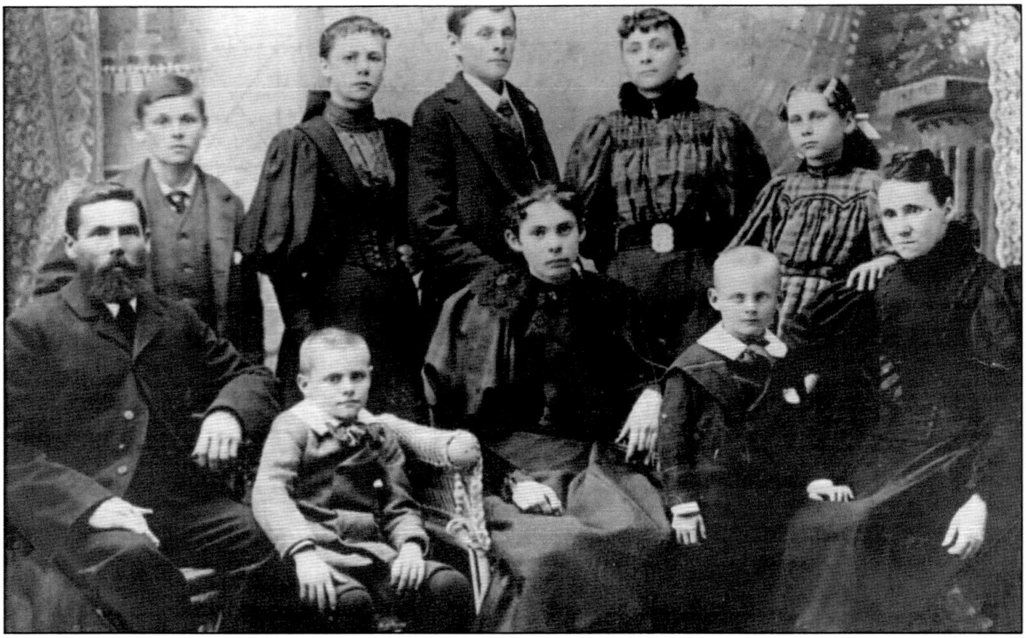

The Norris family came to La Porte in 1900 with eight children and quickly found their place in the business, civic, and social life of the new city. Through marriage, they are related to the Knighton, Hamilton, and Shepherd families.

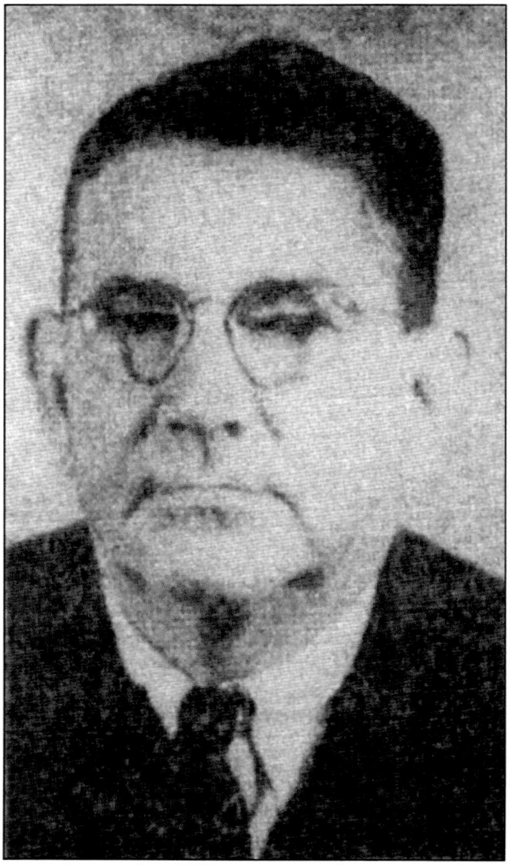

Dr. D.R. Aves was one of the most remembered and respected doctors to practice in La Porte. Many of his patients praised his ability as a healer and the purple medicine he would put on children's scrapes.

J.J. Meza was mayor of the city of La Porte for six years and was the first Hispanic to be elected mayor in Harris County. He received recognition of this fact from Pres. George H.W. Bush. Meza and his wife, Patsy Wells Meza, have lived and worked in the area for many years and are still active in the civic affairs of La Porte. (Courtesy of Patsy and J.J. Meza.)

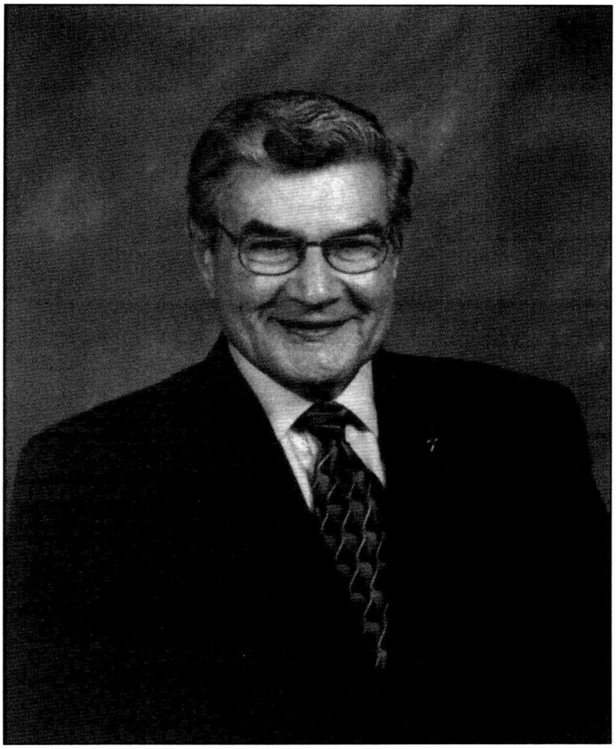

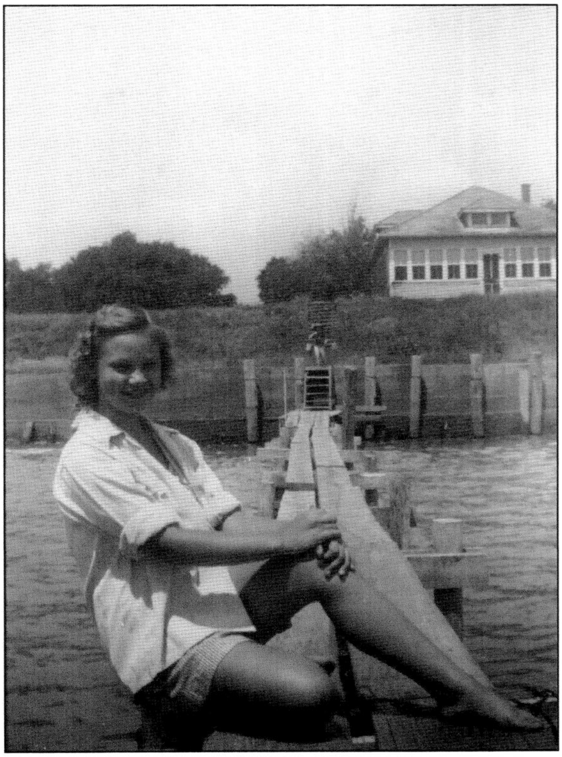

Rose Westerman Hall is relaxing on the pier near her grandparent's bay home. She and her friends spent many wonderful summer days on the bay in La Porte as did others. Hall is now employed by the city and works at city hall. (Courtesy of Rose Hall.)

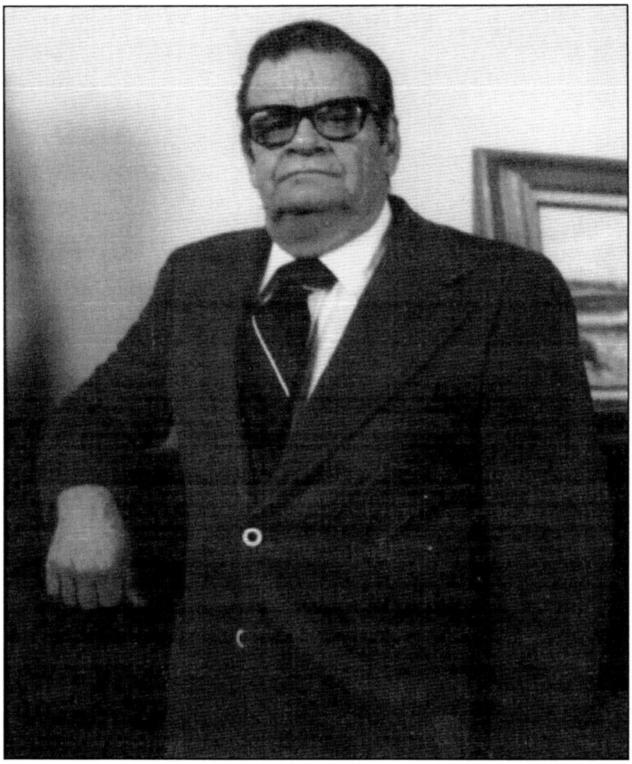

When thoughts of the Port Theater come to mind, local residents immediately think of Doodle Rigby. To every child in La Porte, he was known as Mr. Rigby. He didn't just manage the theater, but was also involved in city activities. He was city commissioner, mayor pro tem, and even filled in as mayor of the city for a short while. His son Louis is now mayor of La Porte. (Courtesy of the Rigby family.)

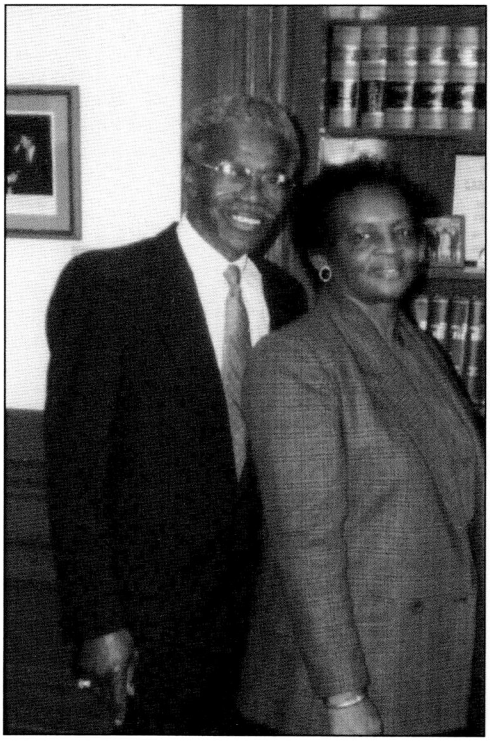

Deotis Gay served on La Porte's City Council for 20 years. He arrived with his family in 1940. Councilman Gay and his wife, Mary, raised a family in La Porte, and they both have been continuously involved in civic affairs and are a driving force in the community. (Courtesy of Mary Gay.)

Daisy La Porte Ballentine had the honor of being the first baby born in La Porte, Texas, in 1892. Her father was McElroy Ballentine, who built a small hotel in the new city. Daisy eventually married a Mallen and resided in Kansas City, Kansas, but kept up with her hometown.

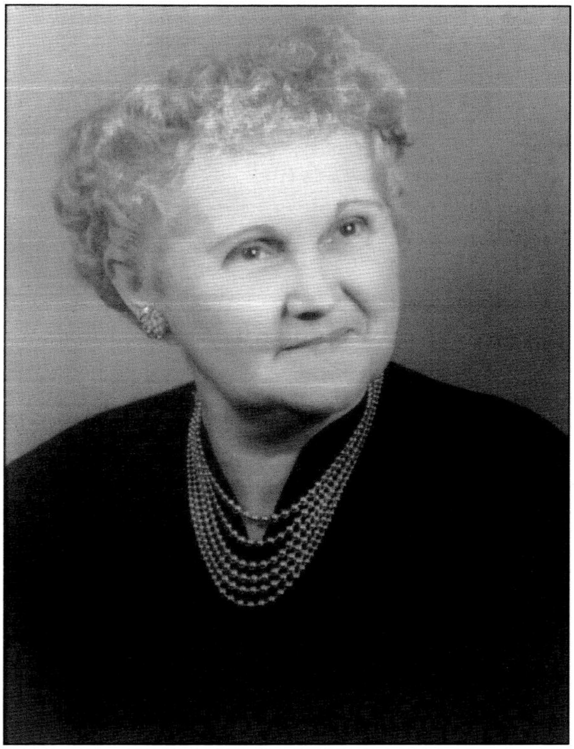

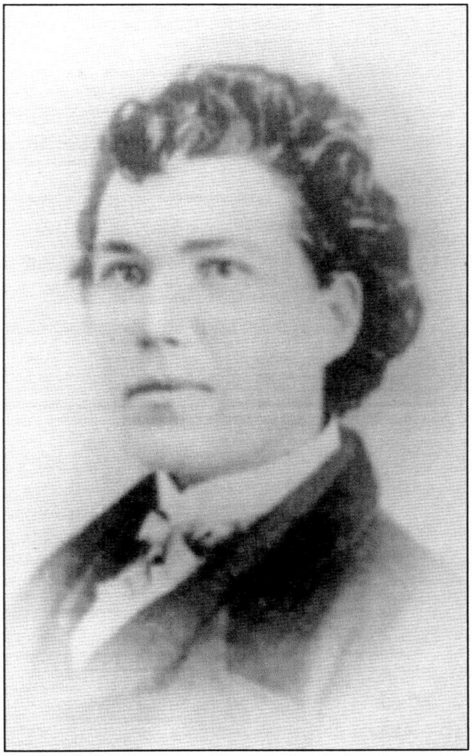

This lady was known in La Porte as Emma Seelye, but during the Civil War she was Pvt. Frank Thompson, who joined the Union army and became a spy. After an honorable discharge from the army, she lived and died in a house on Main Street. The same house is rumored also to be the home of Juliet Marchant, a female doctor who worked during a time when women did not practice medicine.

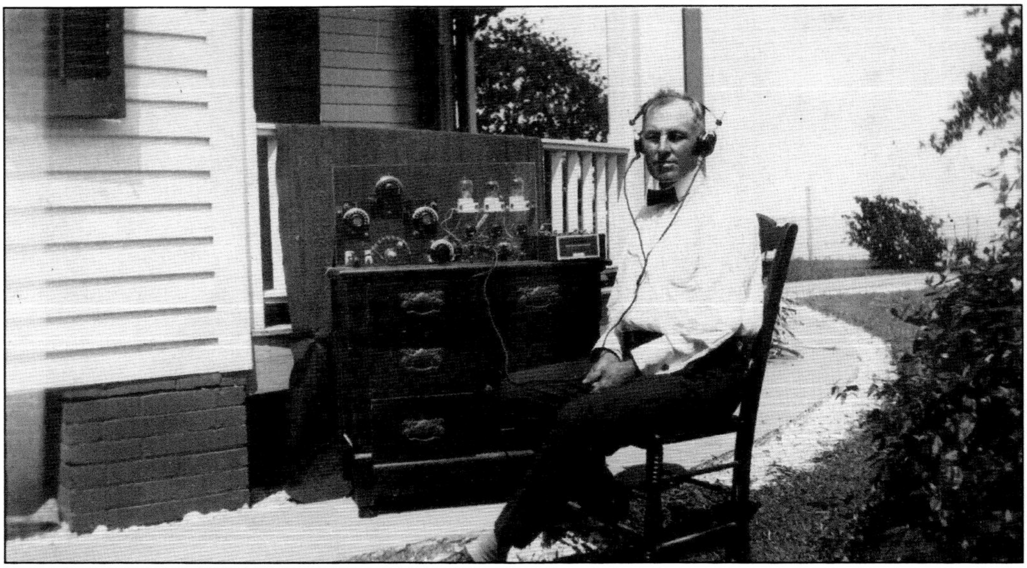

Charles Ashton was a prominent businessman of Morgan's Point. In the early days, he had a thriving tugboat business. After retirement, he continued in other ventures. He is shown with a short wave radio, the first in the city.

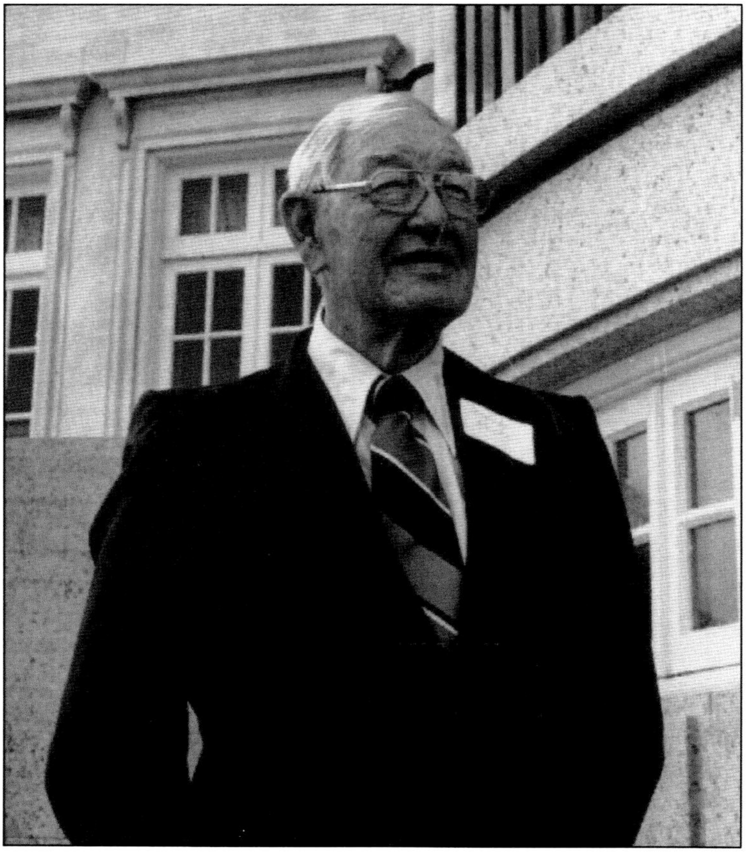

Frank Baker, born in La Porte in 1899, was continuously active in civic affairs and one of La Porte's biggest boosters. He was involved in many businesses and he and his wife, Dell Stephens, were instrumental in starting the Episcopal church in La Porte. His daughter Helen Arthur Crowder still lives in La Porte and has followed in Frank's footsteps as an avid La Porte booster.

Florence Counts was the matriarch of the Counts family. She and her husband, George, were continually involved in making La Porte a better place to live. George was a businessman, judge, and civic leader. Counts family members still live in La Porte.

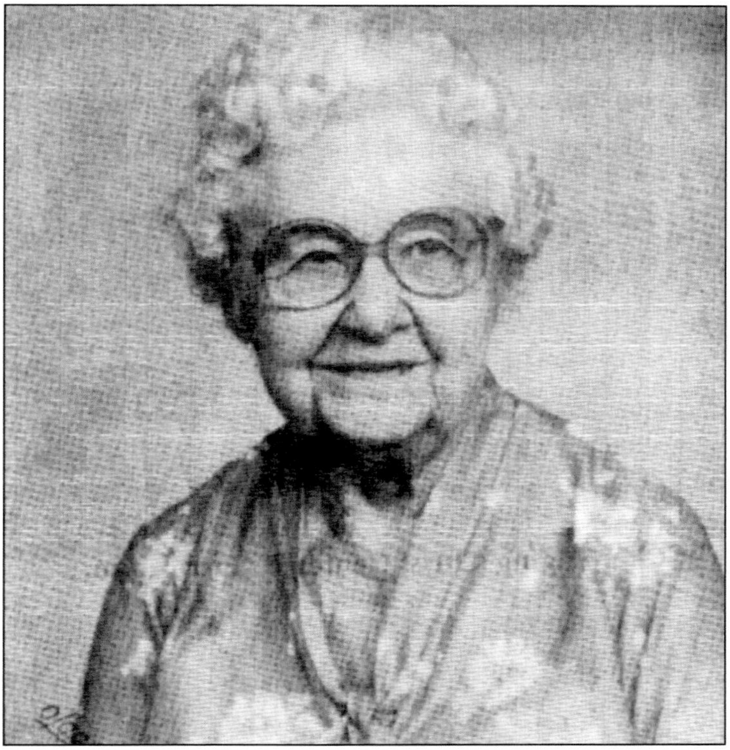

The group pictured below worked diligently for Lomax when it was a small city. From left to right are tax assessor Norma Hutchins, city secretary Betty Waters, office clerk Barbara Womack, mayor Norman Malone, maintenance worker William Owens, and city inspector Lester Butler.

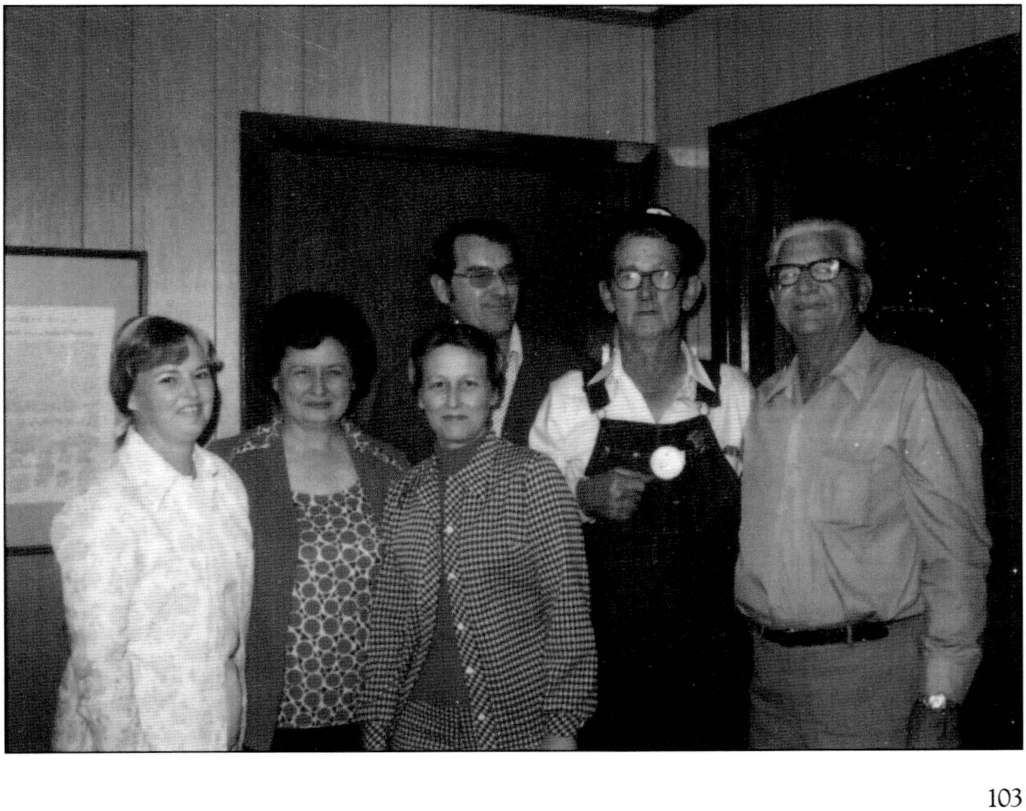

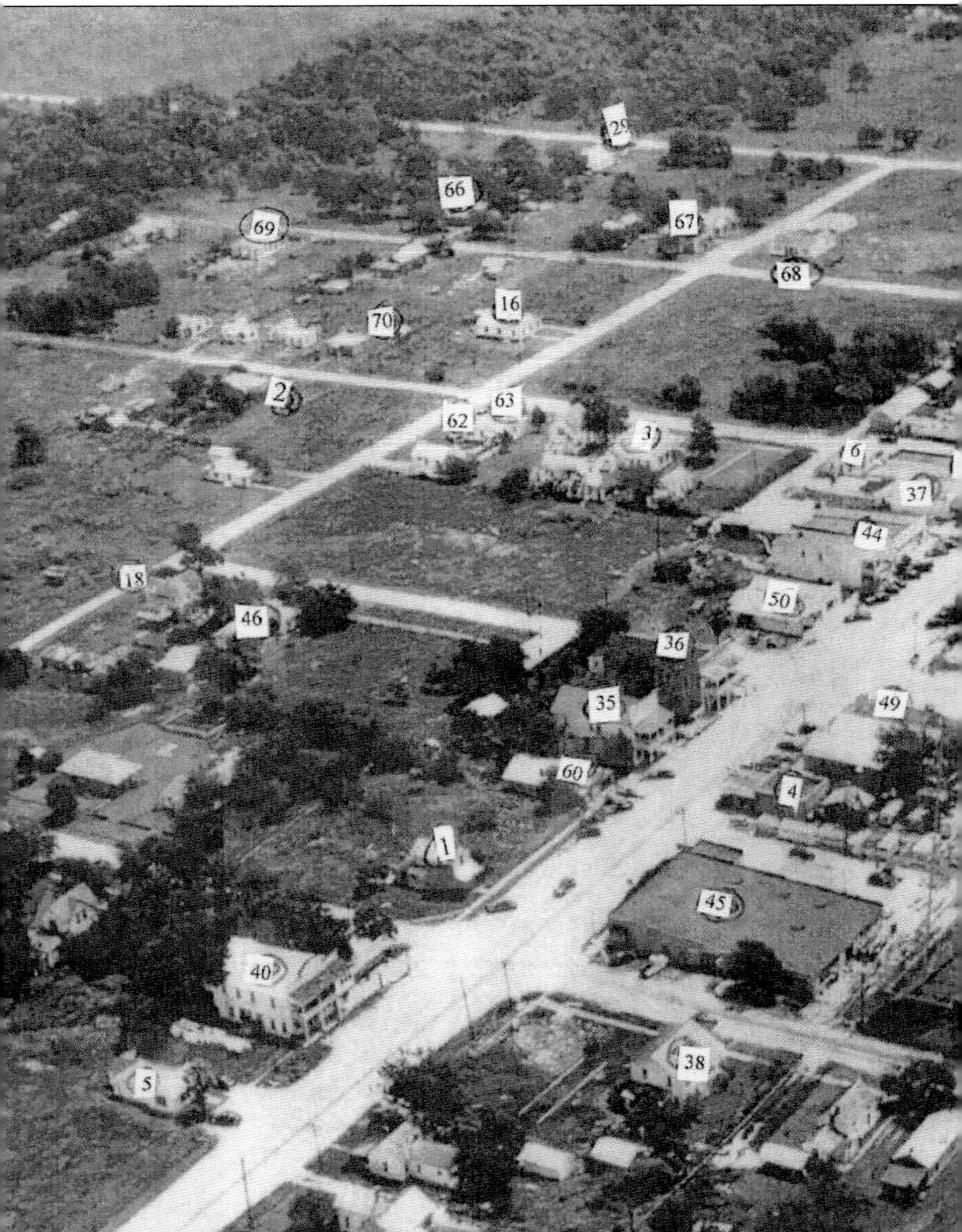
29
66
69
67
68
16
70
2
63
62
3
6
37
44
18
46
50
36
49
35
60
4
1
45
40
38
5

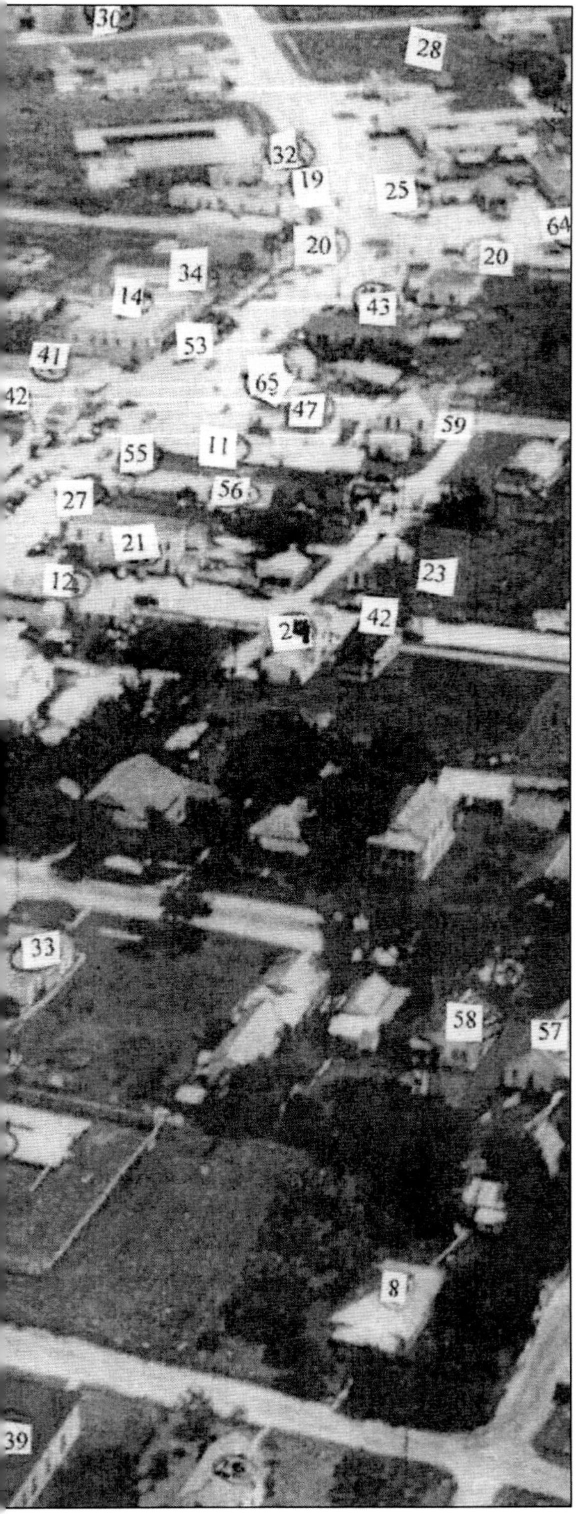

This aerial photograph was taken around 1946. Important landmarks are labeled as follows: (1) house where Dennis Dunham was born, (2) Dunham homestead, (3) George Sharp home, (4) Charlie Williams Liquor-Gas, (5) office of Dr. Aves, (6) Dr. P.J. Mock's office, (7) Picture Show, (8) George Counts house, (9) Agee Drug Store, (10) Hovey Hardware, (11) Thomas Hardware, (12) McDonalds or Rogers Cleaners, (13) Boone Barber Shop, (14) Johnson Hotel, (15) La Porte Water Works, (16) Assembly of God Church, (17) Isensee Grocery (IGA), (18) the Cooling home, (19) Five Points Cafe, (20) La Porte State Bank, (21) Sharp Drug Store, (22) Horlock Ice House, 23) American Legion BSA Troop 90, 24) the John Kiibler home and office, (25) Humble Service Station (26) Shell Service Station, (27) US post office, (28) the Hamilton home, (29) the DeWalt School, (30) Huweiler Lumber Company, (31) Sharp Grain, (32) dentist office of Dr. Sandell, (33) the Crenshaw home, (34) Red and White Grocery, (35) Guy Hamilton Grocery, (36) Sereau Dry Goods, (37) the Counts/Pfeiffer home, (38) Methodist parsonage, (39) Old McKay Bank building, (40) Nelson building (apartments), (41) Hovey's apartments, (42) L.B. & Opal's Cafe, (43) White Kitchen Cafe, (44) Panama Grocery, (45) unidentified, (46) the Ralston/Black home, (47) Gulf Station, (48) the Dick Osborne home and beauty parlor, (49) Blair Garage, (50) Sullivan building, (51) La Porte Hotel, (52) Gibbs Dress Shop, (53) Pugh's Five & Dime, (54) Workman building, (55) Safeway Grocery, (56) Kennerly Cleaners, (57) W.O. Childs, (58) Sally Anderson, (59) Bill and Nadine Jones, (60) *La Porte Reporter* newspaper, (61) George and Fran Sharp, (62) Pop Warren, (63) Hershell and Ruth Childress, (64) McMillan Chevrolet, (65) Bill Jones Insurance, (66) Marks home, (67) Grady Parker, (68) Polly Johnson, (69) Jesse Brown, (70) Roy and France Ferguson, and (71) Dennis Kiibler Insurance.

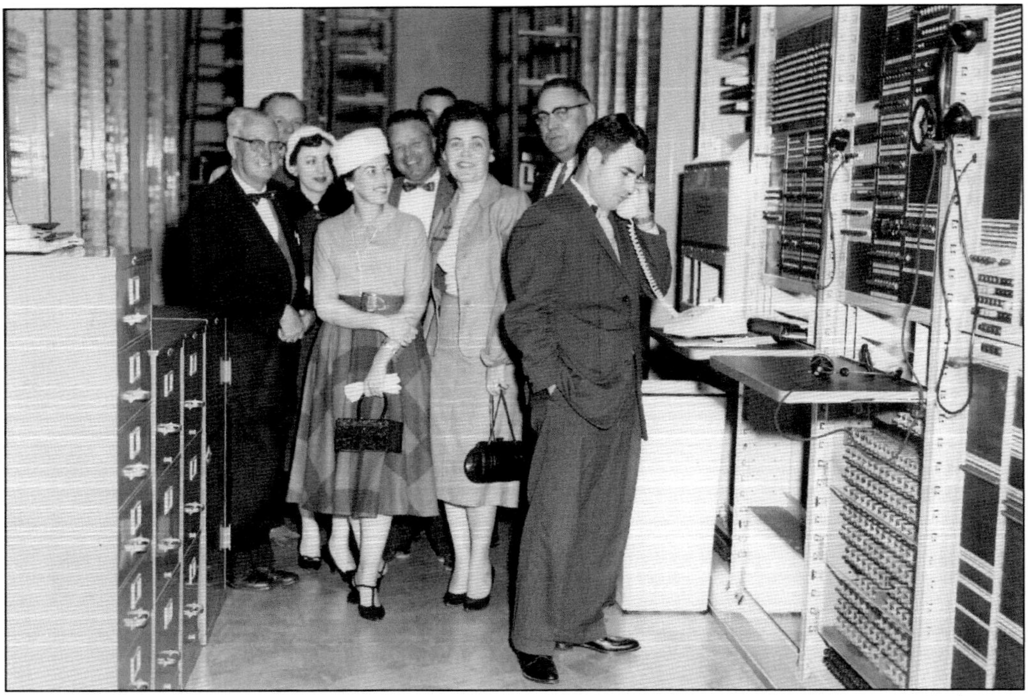

Mayor Harold Pfeiffer is making a telephone call on a new system that has been installed in La Porte, while Frank Boyle, Lou and Jack Lawler, and others look on. Mayor Pfeiffer and Mayor Malone are La Porte's longest serving mayors. Both still have family living in the area.

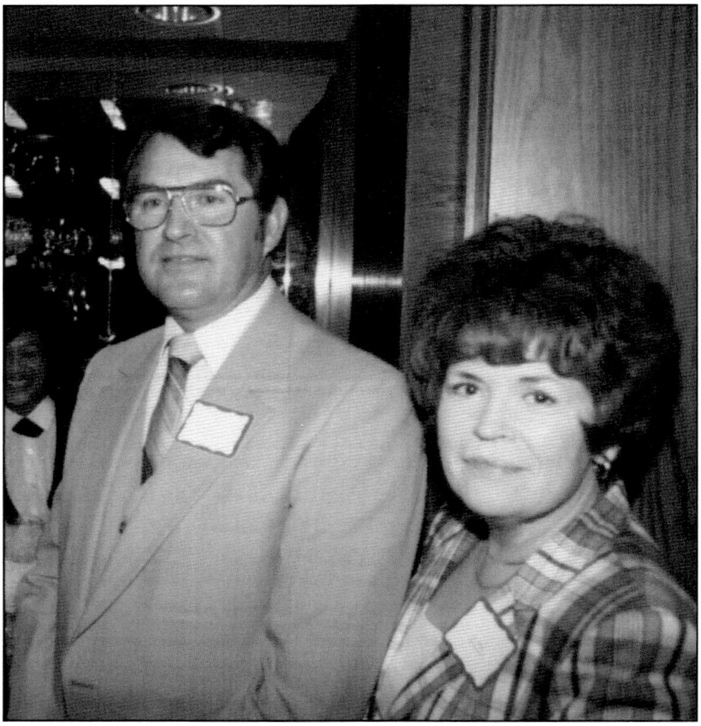

Norman Malone was active in politics for over 20 years. He enjoyed being involved, and, next to his family, he loved his city the best. His daughter Georgia Malone followed him into politics. He is pictured here with his wife, Ann, at one of the many functions they attended.

Six

Sylvan Beach

The founders of La Porte set aside 22 acres of the land bought from John Beazley for a park. A year after the city was incorporated, the community threw its first collective party, the 1893 Fourth of July celebration. Folks were invited to Sylvan Grove to dance, picnic, and make merry. Sylvan Beach is now well over 100 years old; Frank Lloyd Wright once said, "It is foolish to ignore beauty; you'll soon find yourself without it. Your life will be impoverished. But if you wisely invest in beauty, it will remain with you all the days of your life."

Looking at Sylvan Beach through the lens of Wright's words provides a visual personification of his proscription. The beauty, peace, and grace evident at Sylvan Beach once stretched up and down the inner Galveston Bay and up the shores of Buffalo Bayou towards Wharf Number One (now Allen's Landing). The people who founded La Porte and the early residents and settlers of La Porte had the foresight to set aside some of this land and beauty, and the men and women of the La Porte community who came generations after had the fortune and wisdom to see the land placed in public trust as a county park.

Sylvan Beach has seen many changes, many different dance pavilions and piers, and differences in the beaches and the purposes to which they were put. The ships at which visitors gaze have changed their size, their frequency, and their destinations. The fish and game that the sportsmen seek have changed. But the beauty of the vistas, the good will of the visitors, and the community from which they sprang have been and remain constant.

All over America, communities have possessed fond memories of such little enclaves of beauty and goodwill. Too often, they have been lost to progress, pragmatism, or profit. La Porte is truly blessed to still possess Sylvan Beach, as the images that follow testify.

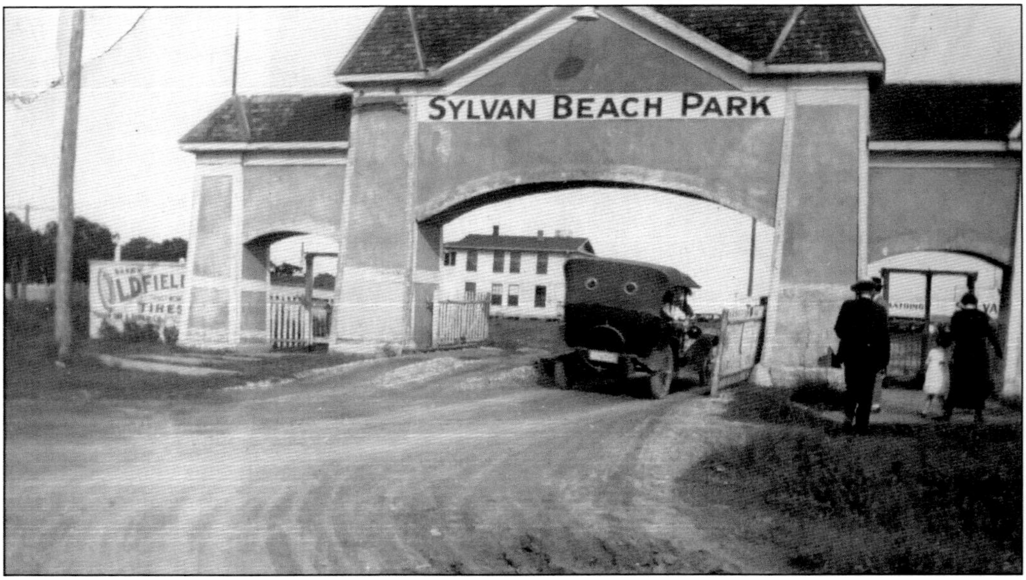

Although Sylvan Beach Park was in existence since 1892, the park's first owner, G.D. Samuels, built this gate in the early 1900s. It was the first of many, but they all served as the entrance to Sylvan Beach. This gate and many other park features were destroyed by the Great Storm of 1915. The park has seen many changes over the last 100 years.

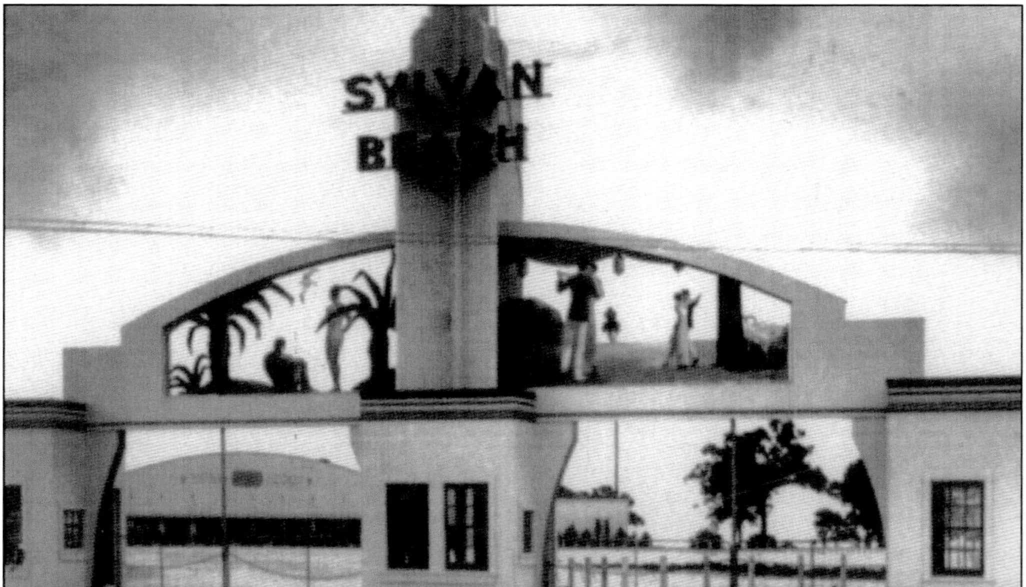

The last great gateway to Sylvan Beach was constructed during the Art Deco period. E.L. Crain had purchased the park and set about changing everything. Cottages that had stood in the park for years were removed, a beautiful glass-front restaurant was built, and the dance floor and arcades were remodeled. Along with Sylvan Beach's thousands of visitors, many of the greatest bands of the era also passed through this gate.

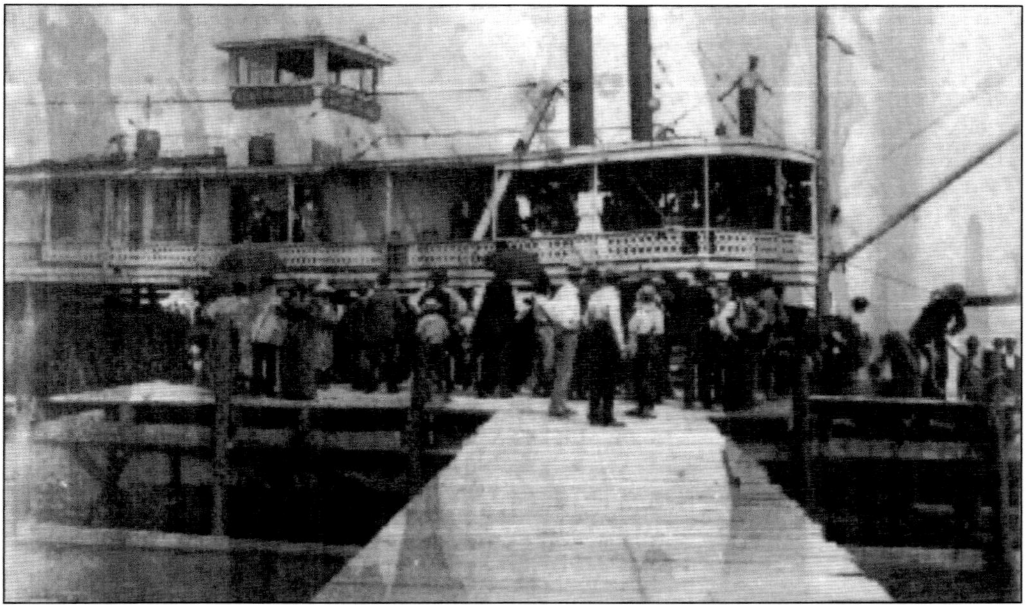

Getting to La Porte in the early days could prove challenging. There were no roads—just rough trails and paths. Buffalo Bayou became our main road with flat-bottom boats plying the waters from Houston and other points to Morgan's Point, using horses and buggies to reach their final destinations. Trains came as far as Deer Park, but passengers still had to take buggies into La Porte and Sylvan Beach.

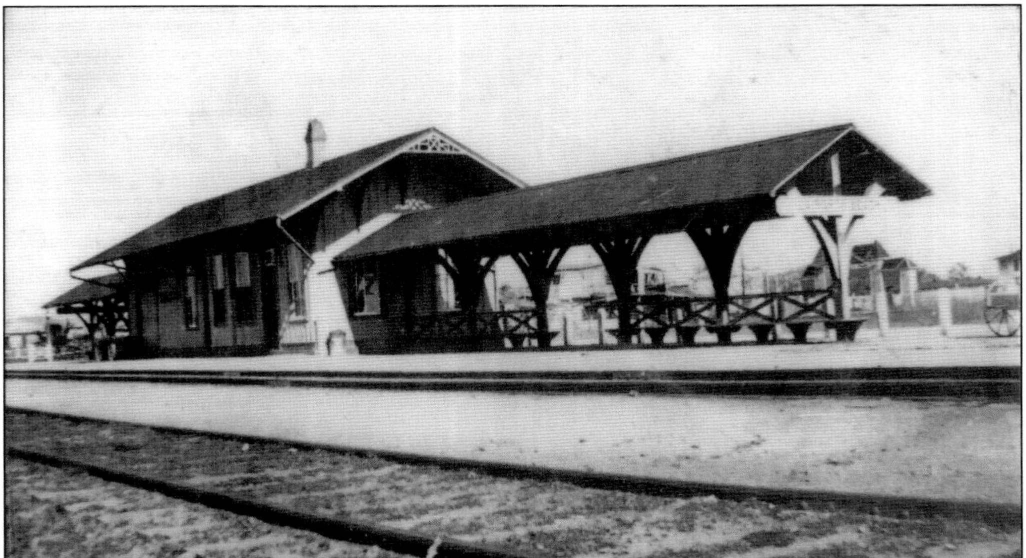

Trains finally began to run to the East La Porte Depot in 1905. This depot, which was first on East Main Street, was eventually moved to Sylvan Beach to better serve the passengers, as the preferred destination for most was Sylvan Beach. The first original gate is visible in the background.

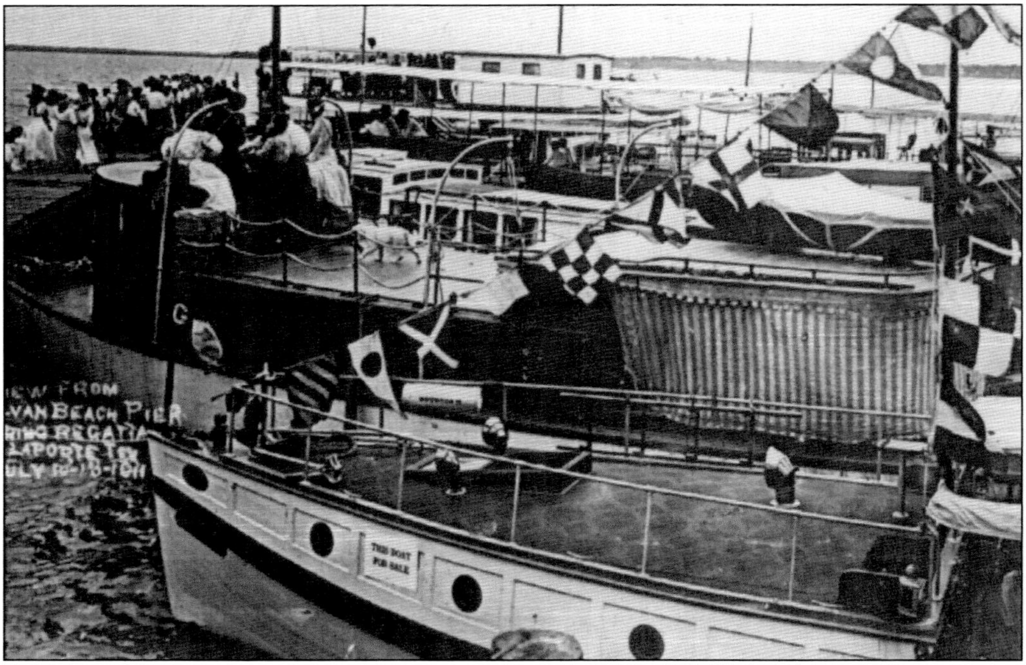

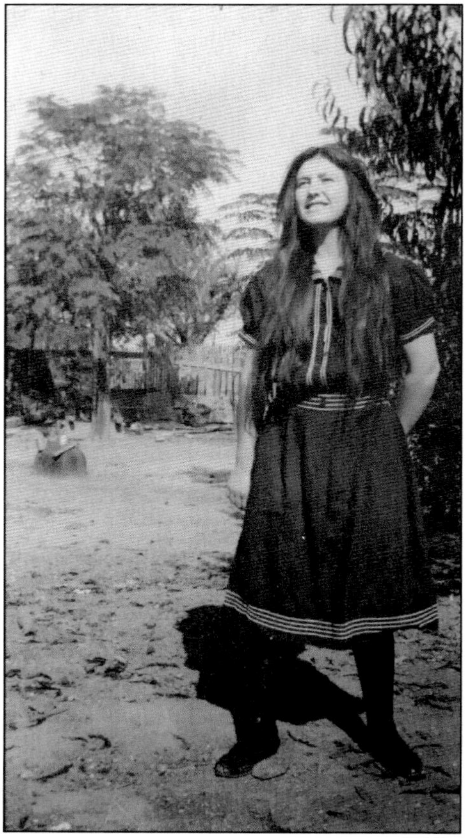

People in the La Porte area have always been boating enthusiasts. In 1911, a large boating regatta was held. This photograph shows the boats tied up at the Sylvan Beach Pier and almost ready to go. The earliest regatta on Galveston Bay was held in 1895.

A bathing costume of the early days insured a young lady would be properly covered for a walk on the beach and a dip in the bay waters.

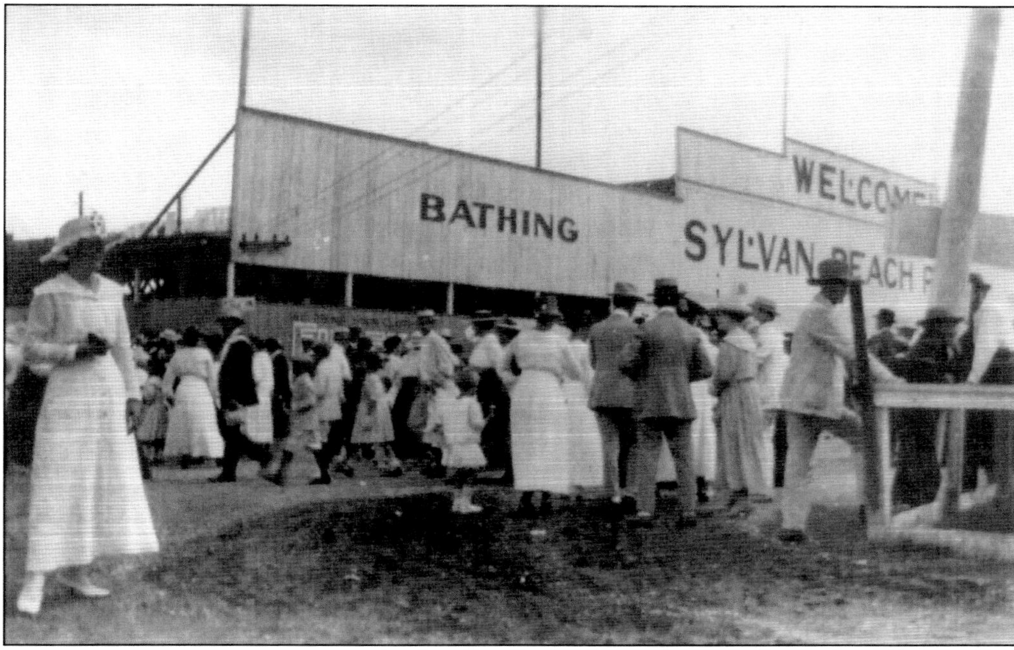

Crowds at Sylvan Beach became the norm for many seasons. Visitors came in the thousands by train, car, and boat to enjoy all that Sylvan Beach had to offer.

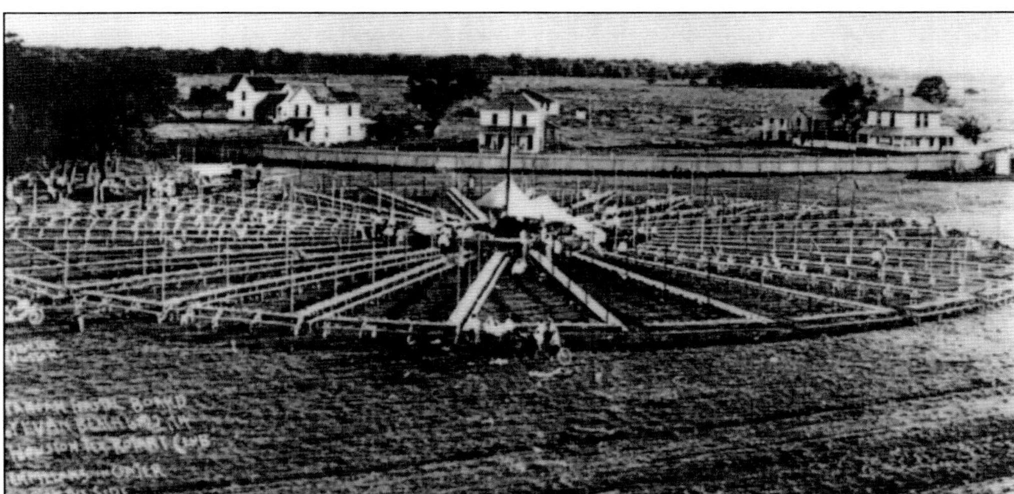

Large picnics have always taken place in Sylvan Beach Park. The symbol of Rotary International was built for the hundreds of Rotarians that were invited to their barbecue. Later, the wood was used to build fences and cottages. Large parties such as this enjoyed the park on a regular basis.

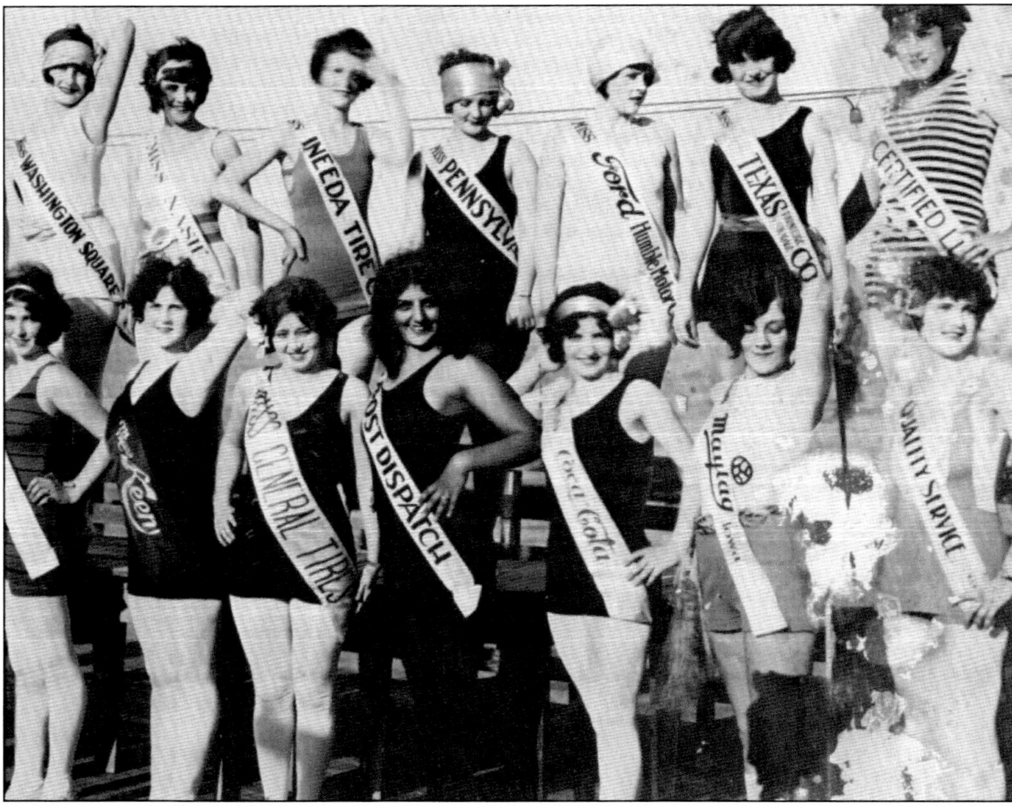

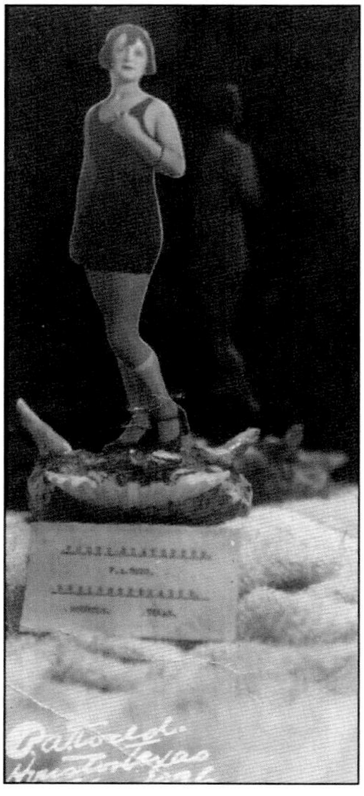

The Bathing Beauty Revues, which began in 1924, were the most popular events at Sylvan Beach. A long, wooden ramp was built on which the ladies paraded back and forth. Most of the contestants were from out of town, and Foley Brothers Department Store in Houston furnished the bathing suits. Here are the first ladies to walk the ramp.

Mildred "Millie" Young was a contestant in the Bathing Beauty Revue at Sylvan Beach in 1926. Her sponsor for this event was the Magnolia Paper Company from Houston, Texas. Rose Hall, her daughter, is a longtime resident of La Porte. (Courtesy of Rose Hall.)

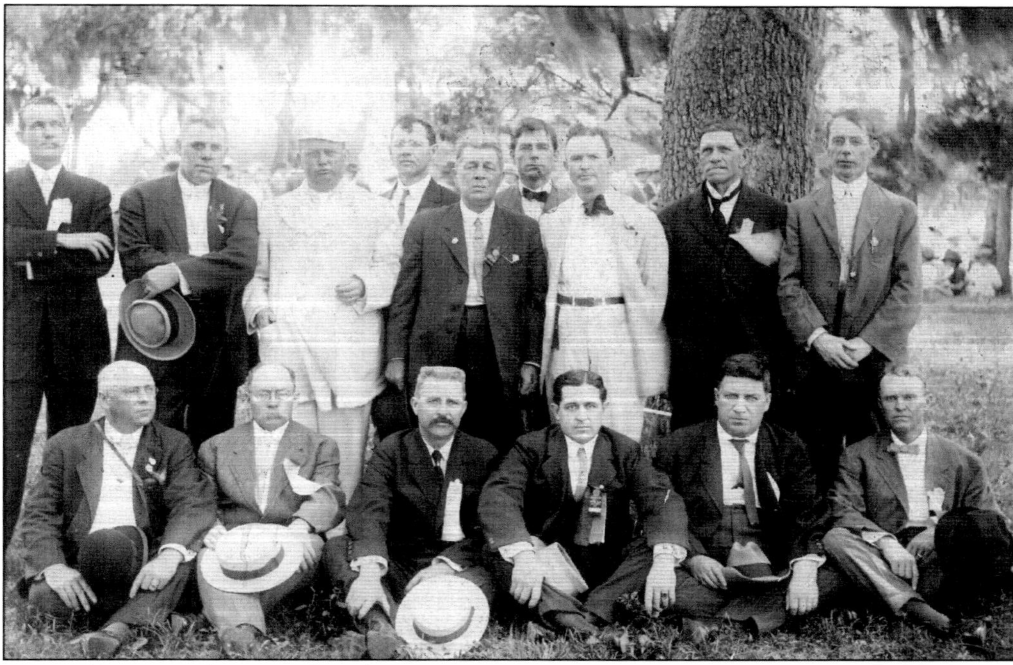

Pictured here at Sylvan Beach with some fellow Humble Oil directors, John Summerfield Bonner (standing in the back row) is wearing a white suit. Handwriting on the bottom reads, "Memories of the Golden Pack." Bonner had a wonderful wit and attitude. When Humble took a 20-year lease on the million-acre King Ranch in south Texas, he was quoted as saying, "A ranch of over a million acres was bound to contain at least a few oil fields." (Courtesy of Buck Bonner.)

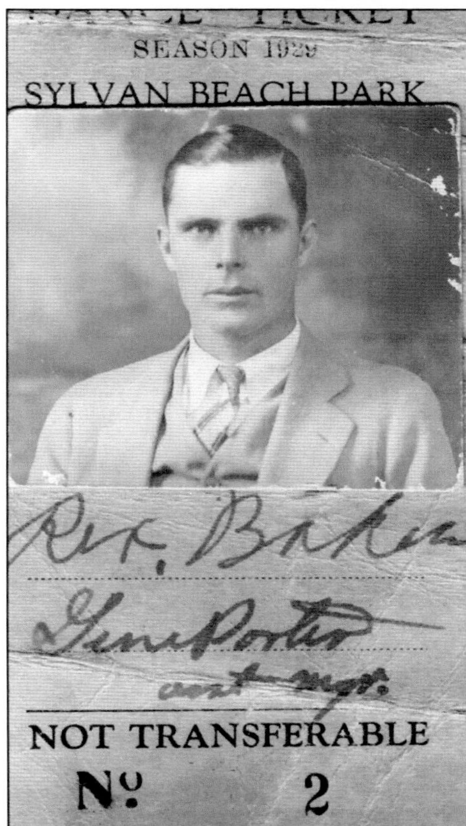

During the 1920s, Sylvan Beach Park sold passes for the dances held there. This photograph shows one such pass. It belonged to Rex Baker, a native of La Porte. People who lived in La Porte received a discount, and people from out of town paid full price. The manager wanted to make sure all visitors had a good time.

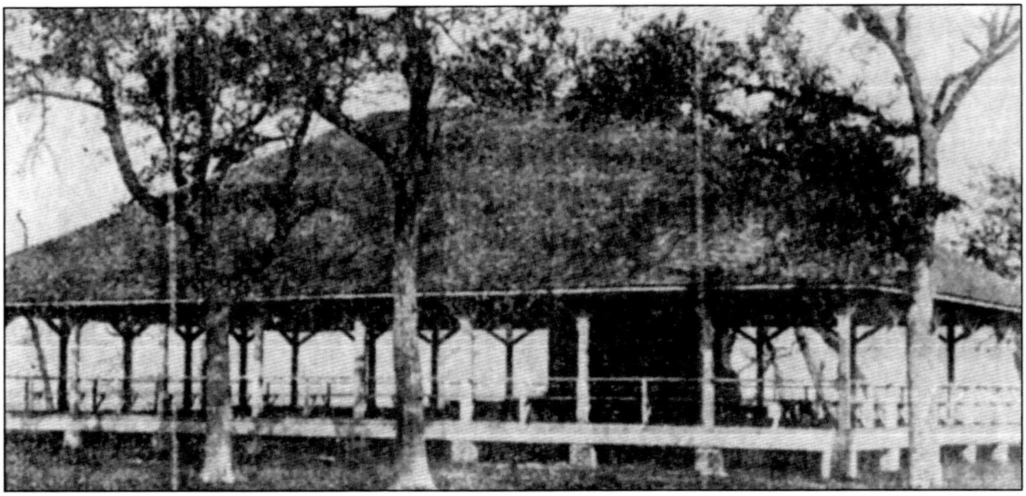

Around 1900, the first pavilion was built at Sylvan Beach Park. It was used for multiple activities such as dancing, meetings, and the Baptist Convention that was held in the park for several years. There have been many different pavilions over time and they have all been destroyed or damaged by storms or hurricanes. The last pavilion at the park is pictured below. Harris County bought the park and built the new pavilion, which opened in the mid 1950s. It has served the public well over the years. This pavilion was damaged in every hurricane since 1950s and has always been repaired. However, Hurricane Ike in 2009 took a great toll on the pavilion, and it has not been reopened to the public.

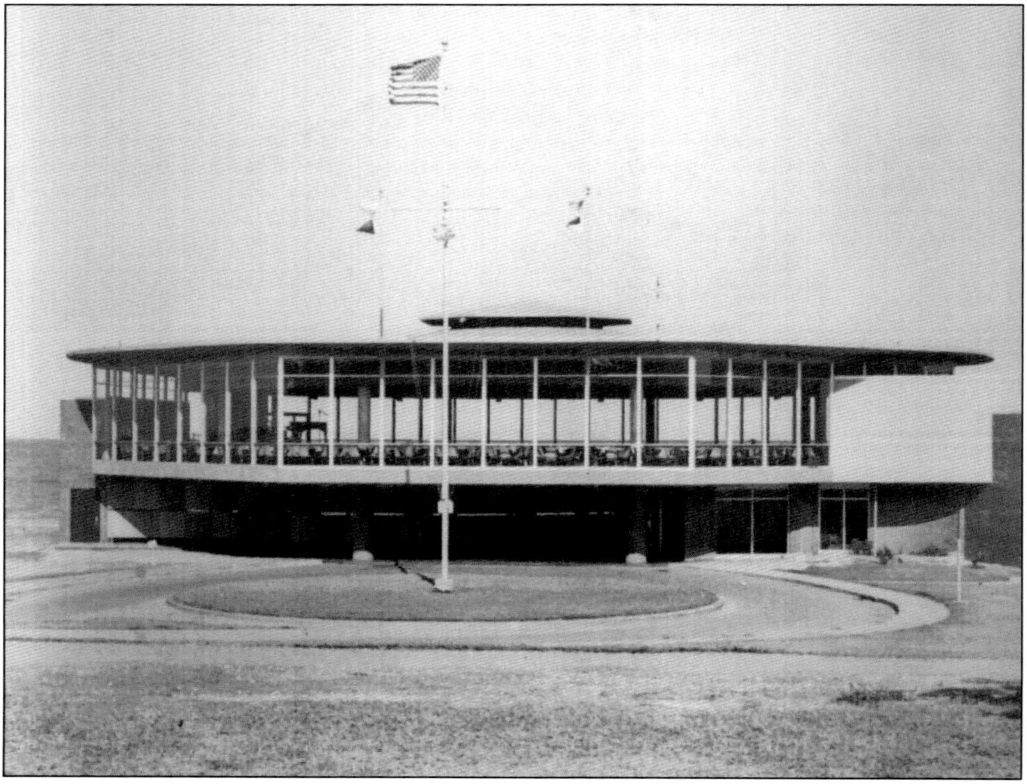

During the Big Band era of the 1930s and 1940s, Sylvan Beach Park had its share of celebrity visitors. This photograph was typical of the advertisements placed in newspapers. Harry James, Rudy Vallée, Tommy Dorsey, and Phil Harris were some of the entertainers that came to Sylvan Beach Park. It is said that Howard Hughes would often anchor his yacht and listen to the music.

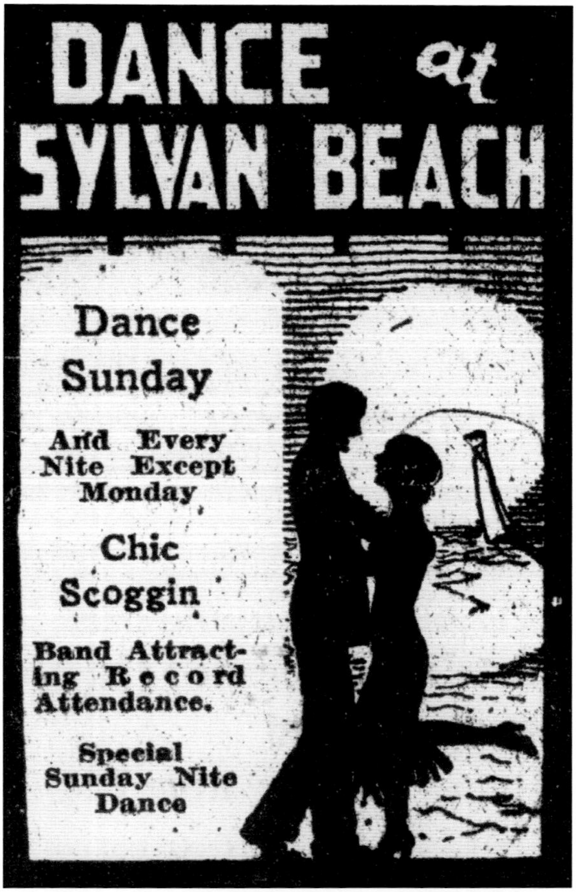

Dancing was the perfect way to spend an evening. Many of the big bands came to play at the Sylvan Beach Pavilion to be heard and seen. In this photograph, hundreds enjoy the music of the day and take a turn around the dance floor.

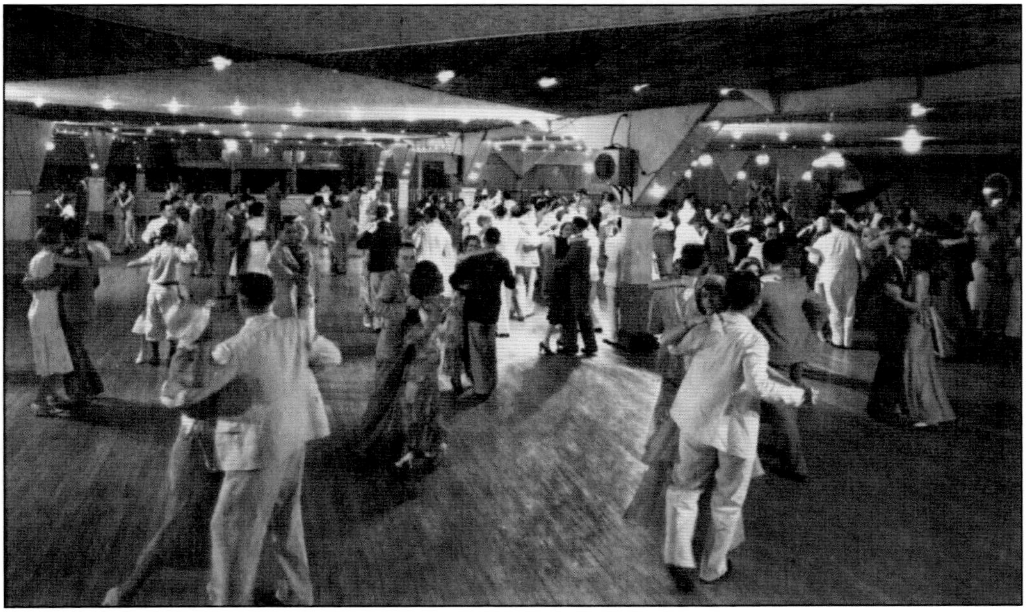

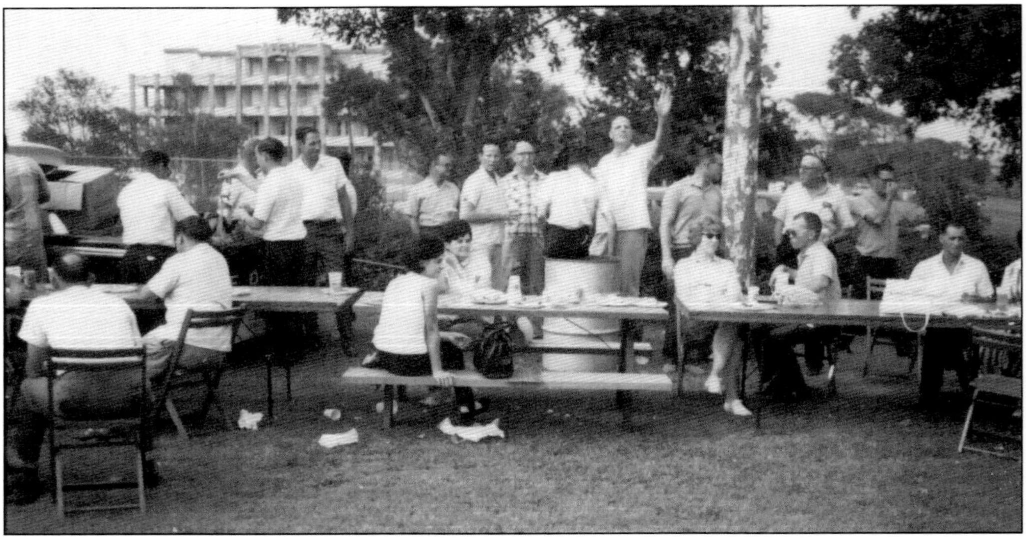

In this photograph from the 1950s, people are enjoying a company picnic at Sylvan Beach Park. In the background, St. Mary's Seminary can be seen before it moved to Houston in 1954. Sylvan Beach never regained this same level of popularity after World War II.

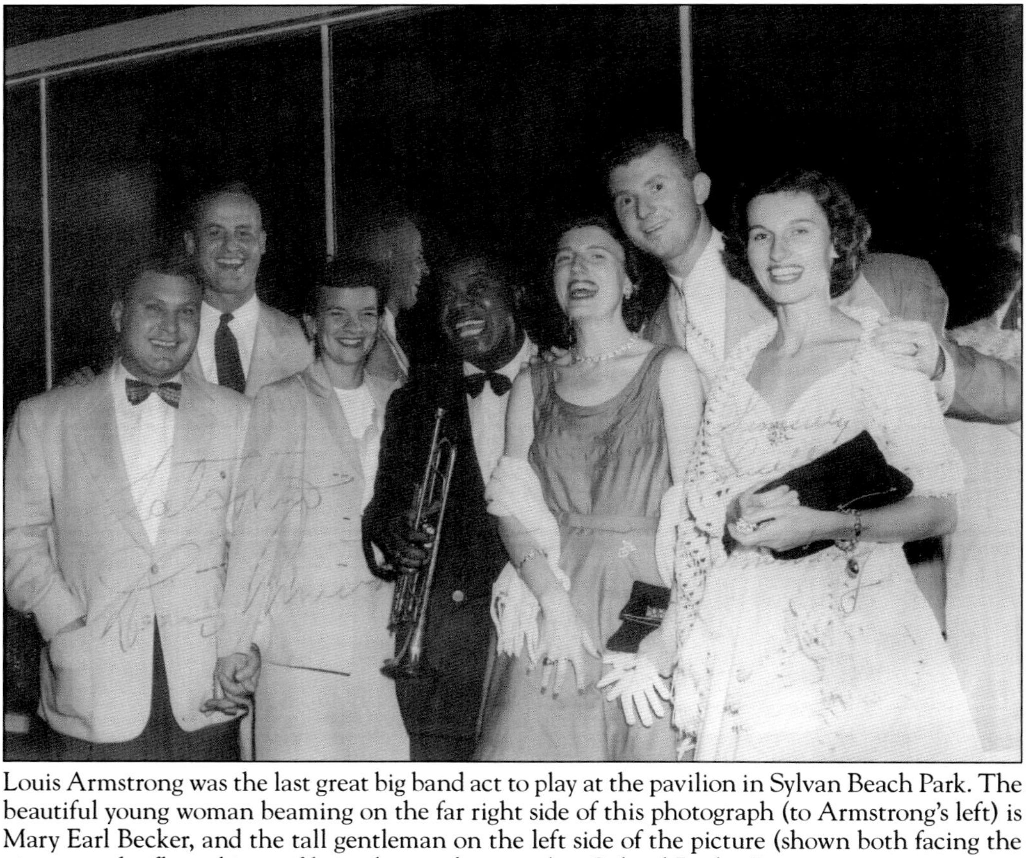

Louis Armstrong was the last great big band act to play at the pavilion in Sylvan Beach Park. The beautiful young woman beaming on the far right side of this photograph (to Armstrong's left) is Mary Earl Becker, and the tall gentleman on the left side of the picture (shown both facing the picture and reflected in profile in the window pane) is Gabriel Becker."

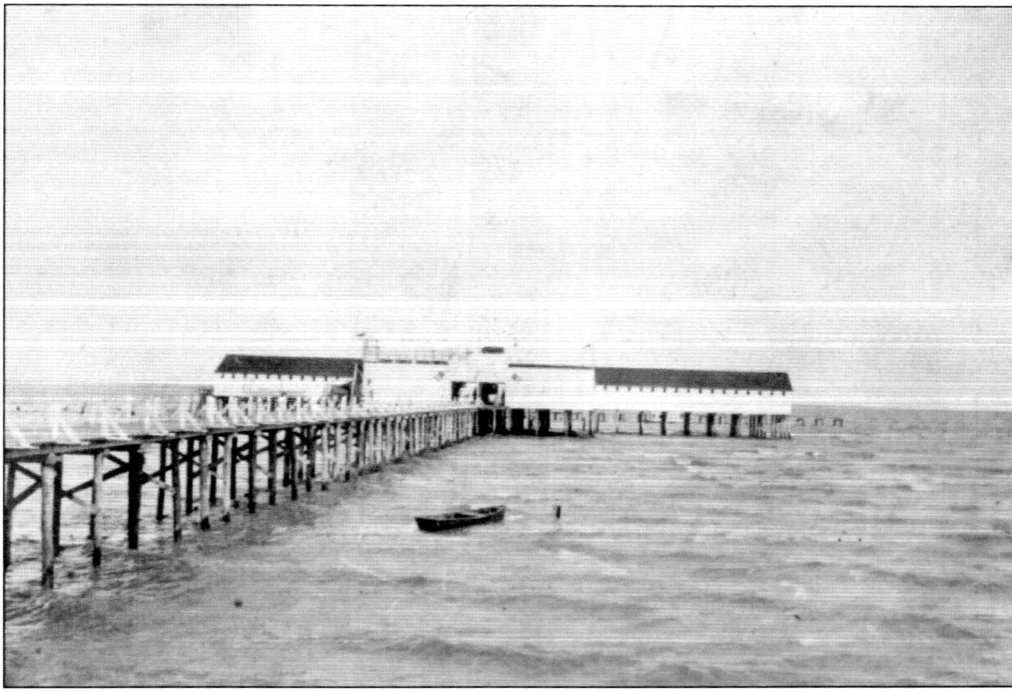

Bathing suits could be rented for the day for 5¢ each at the bathhouse on this pier. Over 100 lockers and baskets were provided for personal belongings under the watchful eye of Mary Sullivan, manager of the bathhouse.

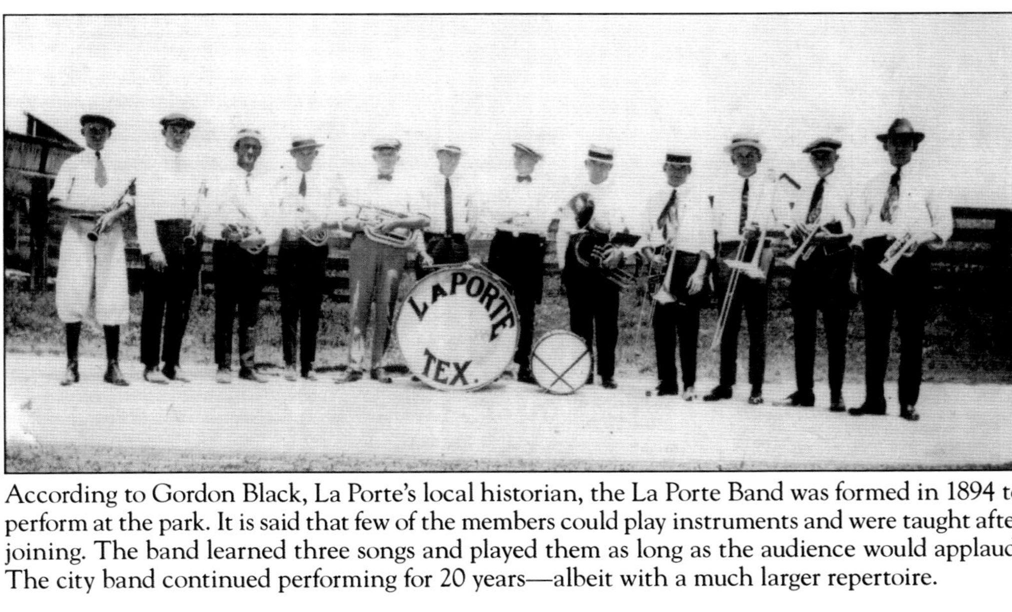

According to Gordon Black, La Porte's local historian, the La Porte Band was formed in 1894 to perform at the park. It is said that few of the members could play instruments and were taught after joining. The band learned three songs and played them as long as the audience would applaud. The city band continued performing for 20 years—albeit with a much larger repertoire.

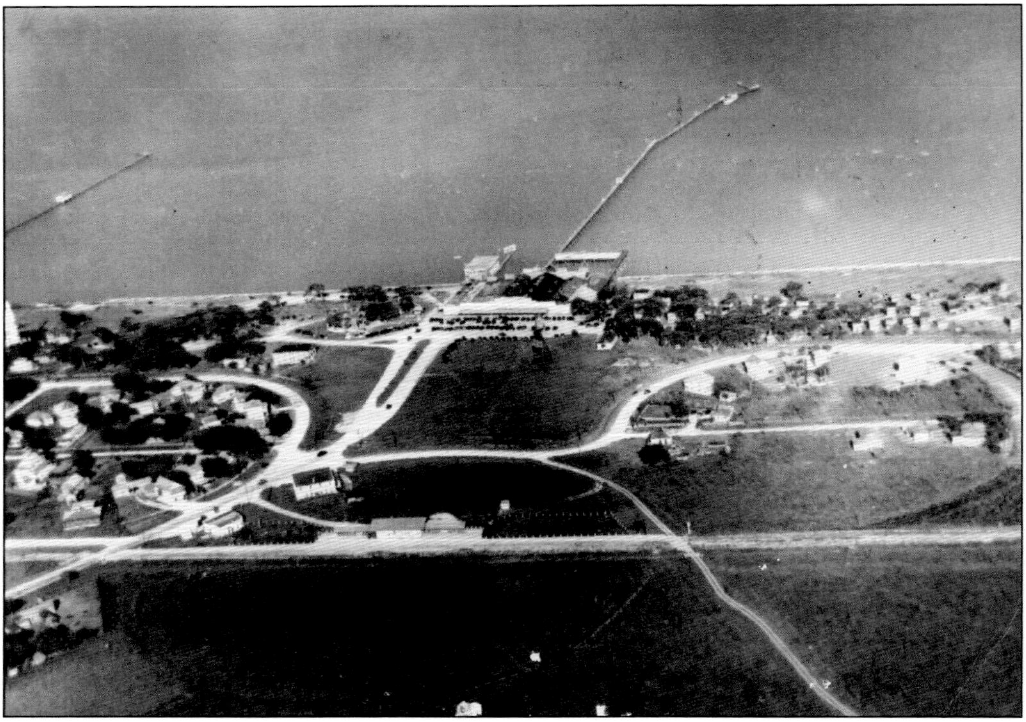

This aerial view of Sylvan Beach Park puts things in perspective. The depot is in the foreground. The gate to the park is on the left before the divided road that leads to the pavilion and pier. Cottages can be seen on the right, and the pier to the left is that of St. Mary's Seminary. The main road to get to the park at that time was San Jacinto Street.

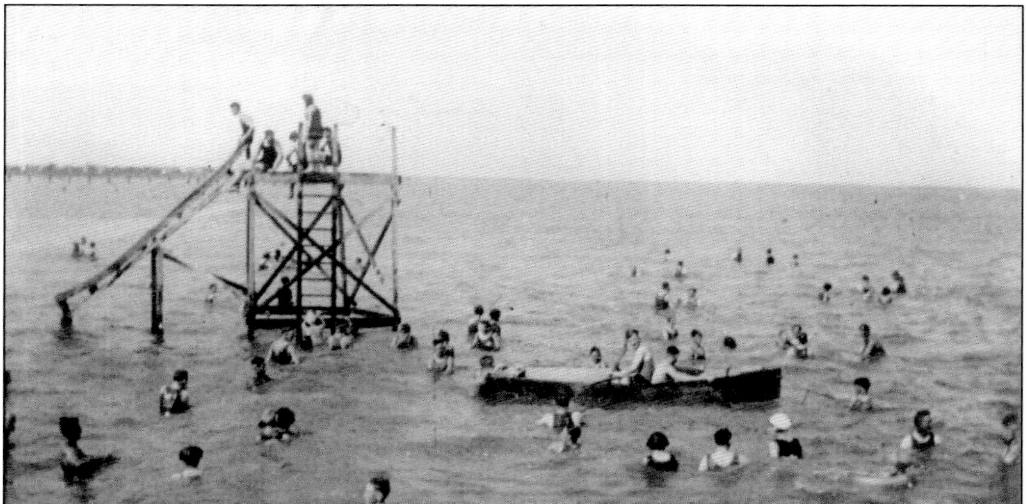

The water at Sylvan Beach was perfect for swimming. The waves were never too large, and the water was not too deep. Everyone—young and old—enjoyed playing in the water. This jovial summer scene shows a group of bathers mounting and descending a waterslide that had been erected for their pleasure.

Seven

Transportation

The fate and evolution of La Porte and Morgan's Point have been inextricably bound to Galveston and San Jacinto Bay, Buffalo Bayou, and, eventually, the Houston Ship Channel. The first regatta of the San Jacinto Yacht Club was held on April 21, 1860. With James Morgan at the tiller, the sloop named *Factories* won the race. He was 67 years old at the time and had been blind for 20 years. Such was the fiber of the men who plied the waters between Houston and the bay and on to Galveston. Capt. Frederick Allien was another man who plied these waters, eventually buying Colonel Morgan's plantation and introducing the members of the Nebraska Syndicate to the La Porte area.

Traveling from Houston to the La Porte area by horse or a hackney could easily take well in excess of six hours each way, perhaps more depending on the weather. Buffalo Bayou was the preferred route, particularly for heavy cargo. By 1895, the Galveston, La Porte & Houston Railroad had service from Houston to La Porte, and on to Galveston. By 1900, the Bayshore line ran regular routes through La Porte, Shoreacres, Morgan's Point, Seabrook, and on to Galveston.

The next 20 years saw the automobile and the oil it needed to run begin to change La Porte and its environs. By the 1920s and 1930s, 10,000–20,000 guests visited Sylvan Beach and the town's other attractions each weekend.

Today, the only remnant of the train traffic that flowed through La Porte for so long is the old Southern Pacific caboose down at the Heritage Society, and cars are now the preferred method for getting around. Yachtsmen, fishermen, and other local mariners carry on the proud traditions of Frederick Allien and James Morgan. But the vessels that dock at Barbour's Cut and further up the Ship Channel come from around the globe. The city of La Porte, true to her name, now truly is "the door" to Texas and the whole Southwest.

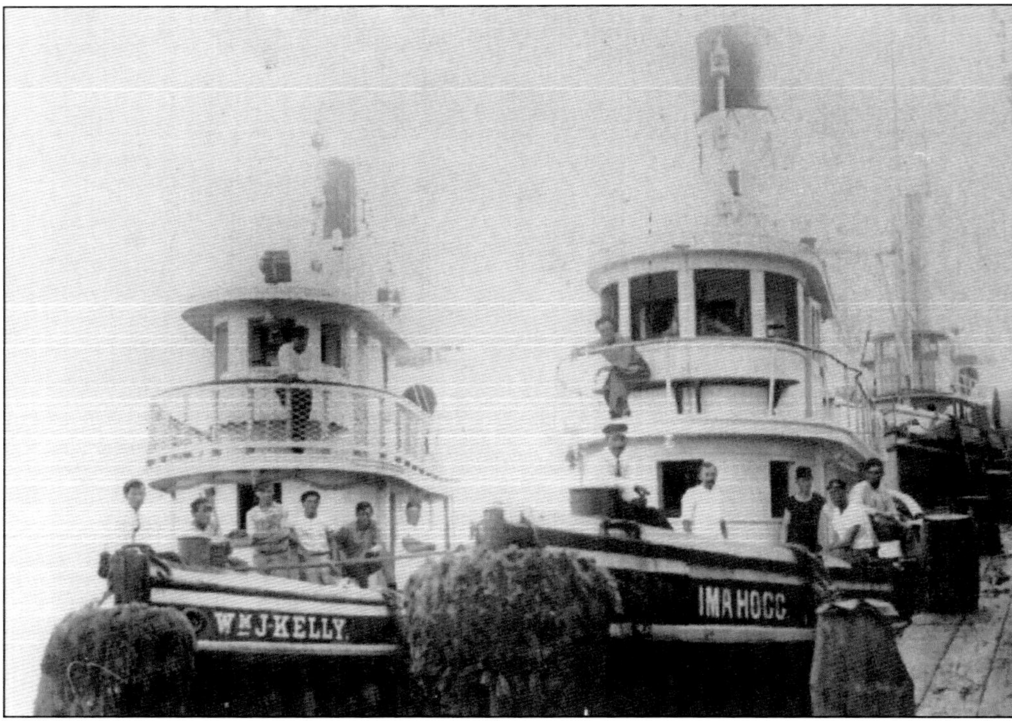

The M/V *Wm. J. Kelly* and M/V *Ima Hogg* tugboats are docked at Morgan's Point. This photograph probably dates from the 1930s, at which time seagoing vessels were frequently traveling through the canal Commodore Morgan had dredged in 1876.

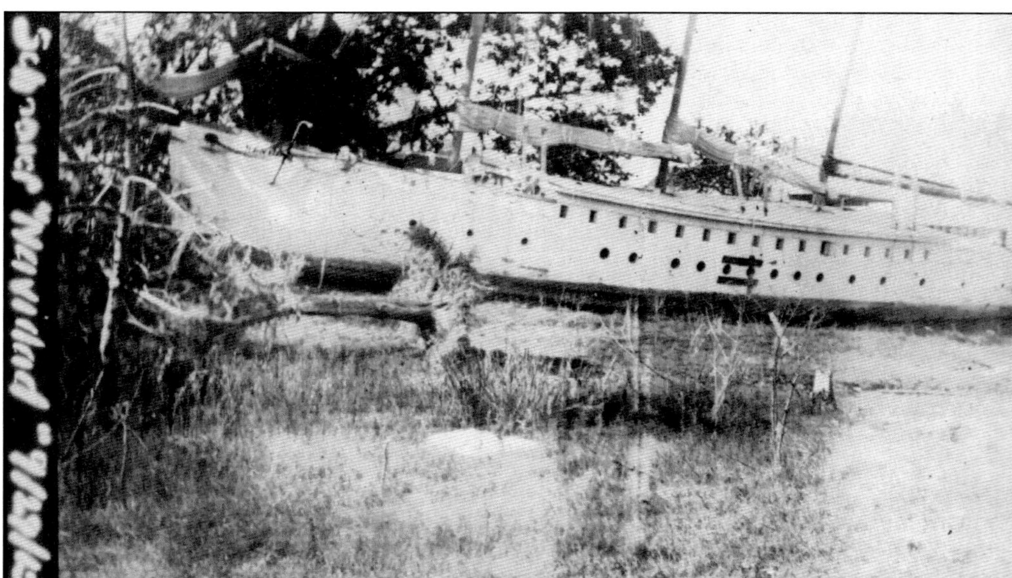

Low tide was a constant danger, and frequent dredging was the solution for schooners plying the shallow Galveston Bay and San Jacinto Bay waters. Here, the schooner *Navidad* is caught high and dry at low tide in La Porte.

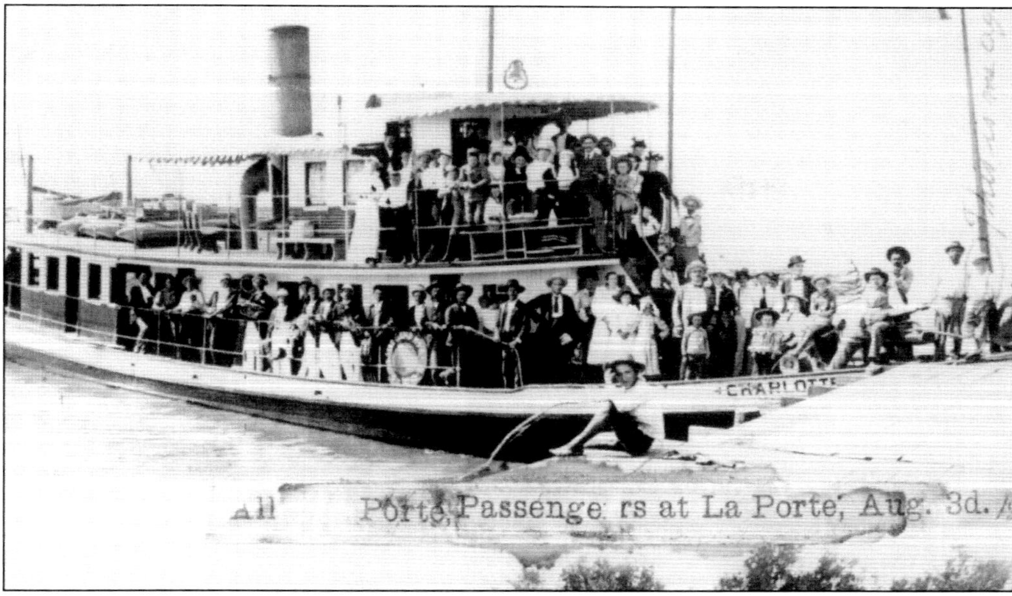

The *Charlotte* was one of the early vessels used to deliver passengers at the Sylvan Beach pier. This photograph was taken in 1895. In 1892, La Porte's census showed 52 permanent residents, so recreational visitors to Sylvan Beach easily outnumbered the towns' permanent population. By the early 1900s, the population had eclipsed 1,000.

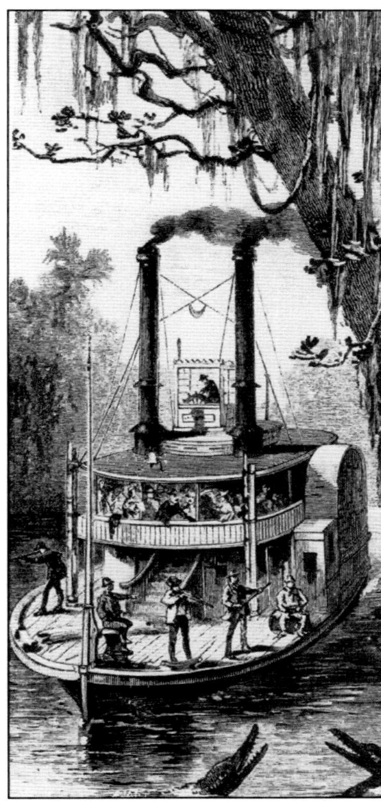

This image of an early steamboat sailing among dense foliage and alligators first appeared as an illustration in Sweet and Knox's 1883 book called *On a Mexican Mustang Through Texas* from the Gulf to the Rio Grande. Often mistakenly taken for an image of the steamboat *Laura*, it is still a remarkable view of an early explorative water way and the hazards found therein. (Courtesy of James D. Becker.)

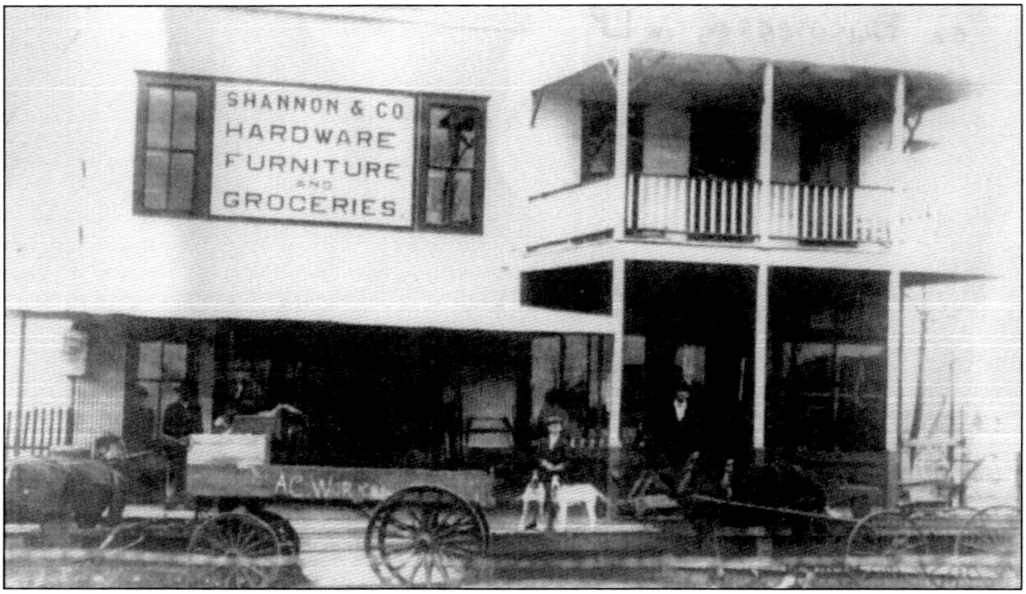

Above, Shannon & Co. Hardware, Furniture & Groceries, run by A.M. Shannon, was one of La Porte's first businesses. An advertisement in the *Galveston Daily News* on June 26, 1903, promotes La Porte as a center of commerce, recreation, and religion and catalogs this store as one of the 10 most prominent in the city. The only person directly quoted in the story is J.S. Johnson, a real estate agent, undertaker, and embalmer, who extols La Porte as the "greatest health resort on the Gulf coast." Note that the hackney in the foreground belongs to A.C. Workman. Temporary notoriety came to Workman when he was the prosecution's star witness in the J.L. Mitchell murder trial, which grew out of a collision between two early La Portians while in their hackneys. The accident occurred across from the East La Porte train stop and resulted in the shooting death of Mr. Bonner. In 1908, Workman had been a hackney driver in La Porte for 13 years. The photograph below shows hackneys waiting for riders at the East Depot.

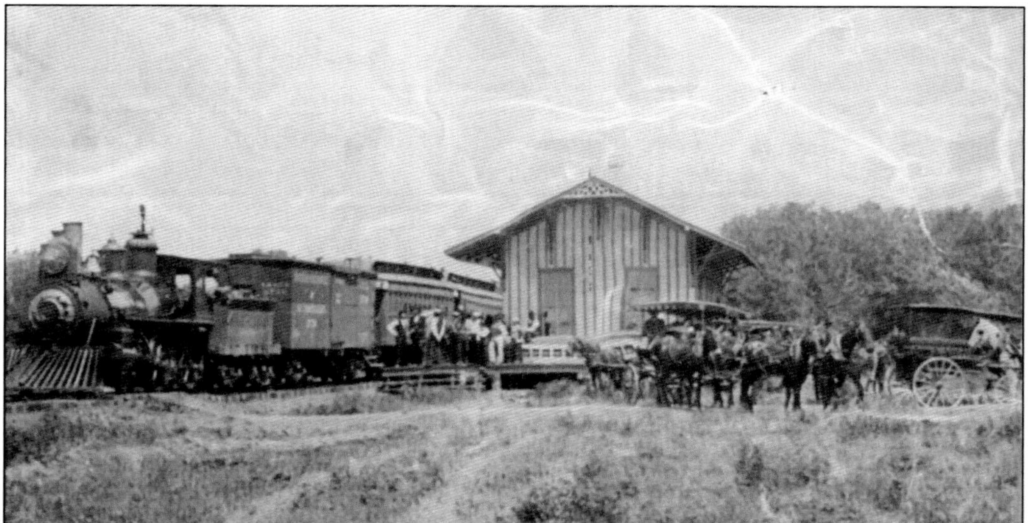

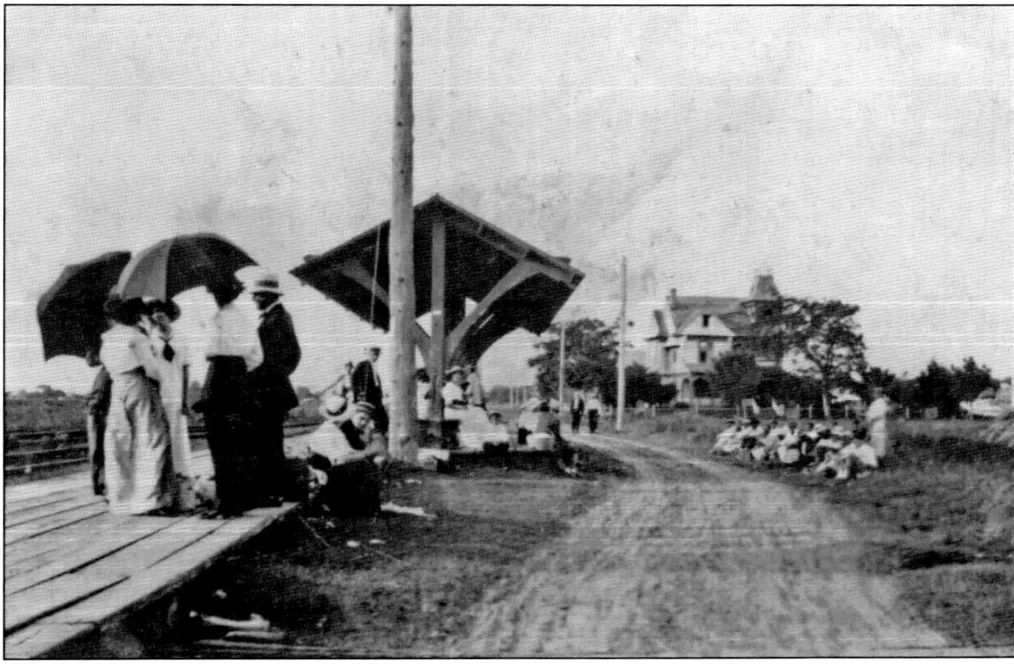

In 1895, the east side of La Porte started receiving train service and a depot was constructed, but with the popularity of Sylvan Beach Park, the decision was finally made that passengers would be better served if the East Depot was moved to Sylvan Beach. This photograph shows the shelter that existed before the move. Notice the Sylvan Hotel in the background.

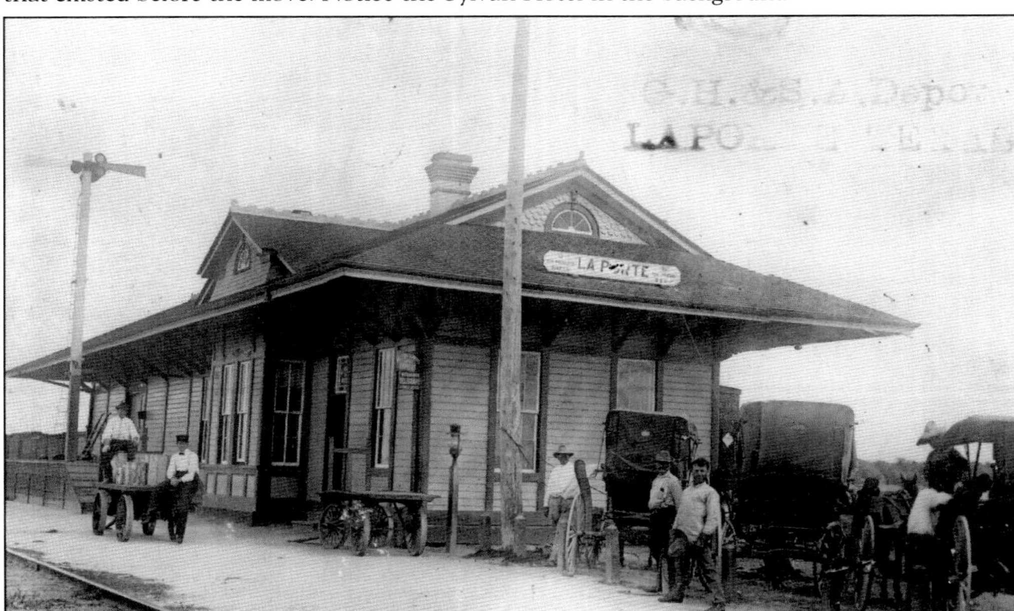

Train service finally came to the west side of La Porte and the same scenario came about. This photograph shows the hackneys and buggies lined up ready to take passengers to their appointed destinations, be it La Porte or Sylvan Beach.

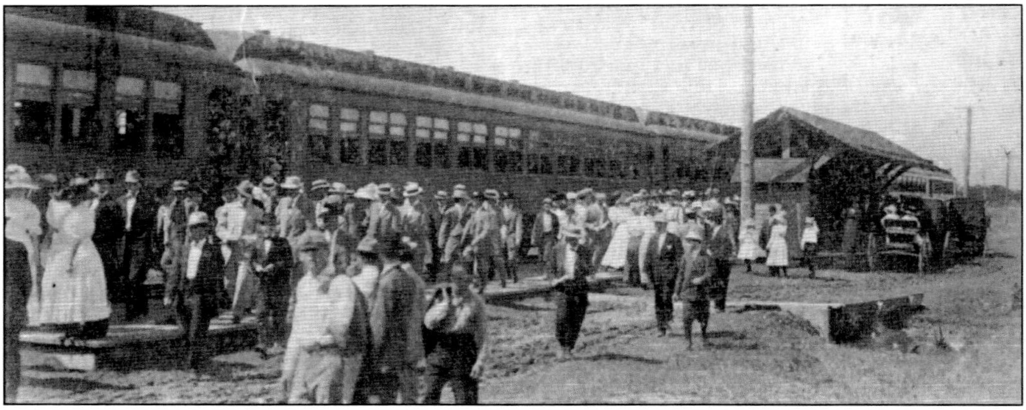

Passengers disembark for Sylvan Beach. At various times, railroad timetables and rate sheets showed stops for East La Porte, West La Porte, Sylvan, and Sylvan Beach. In 1929, the rate sheets were changed simply to La Porte, a helpful change for freight agents and deliverymen.

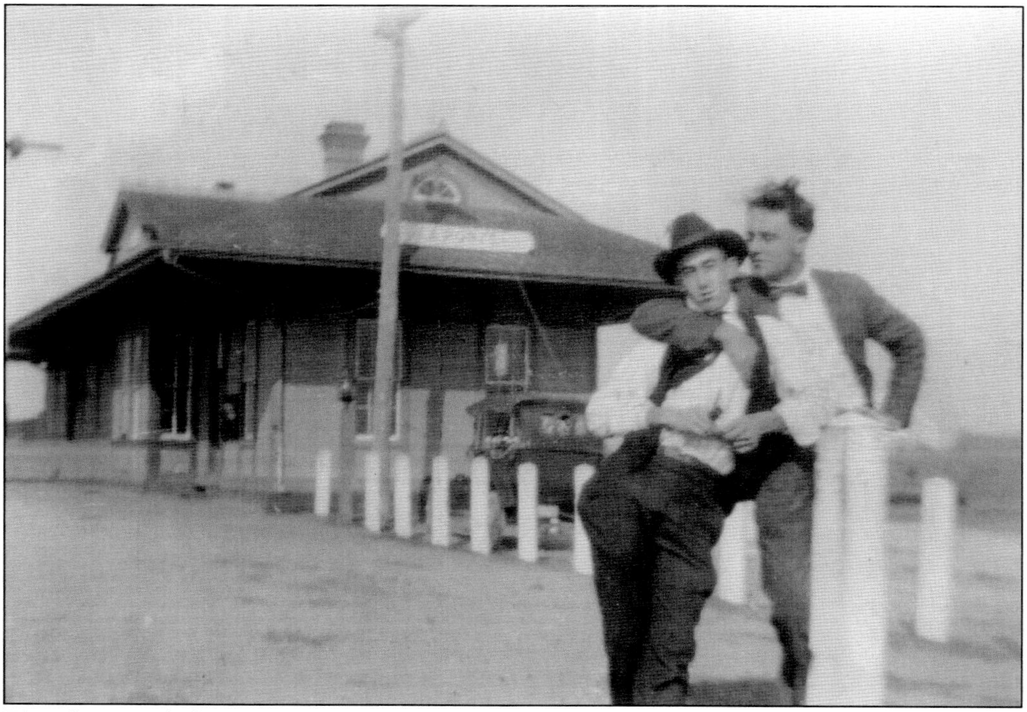

This photograph shows a couple of young men horsing around while waiting at the La Porte Depot early in the 20th century. The car in the background suggests the photograph dates to 1910–1920, and there does appear to be phone or telegraph line into the depot.

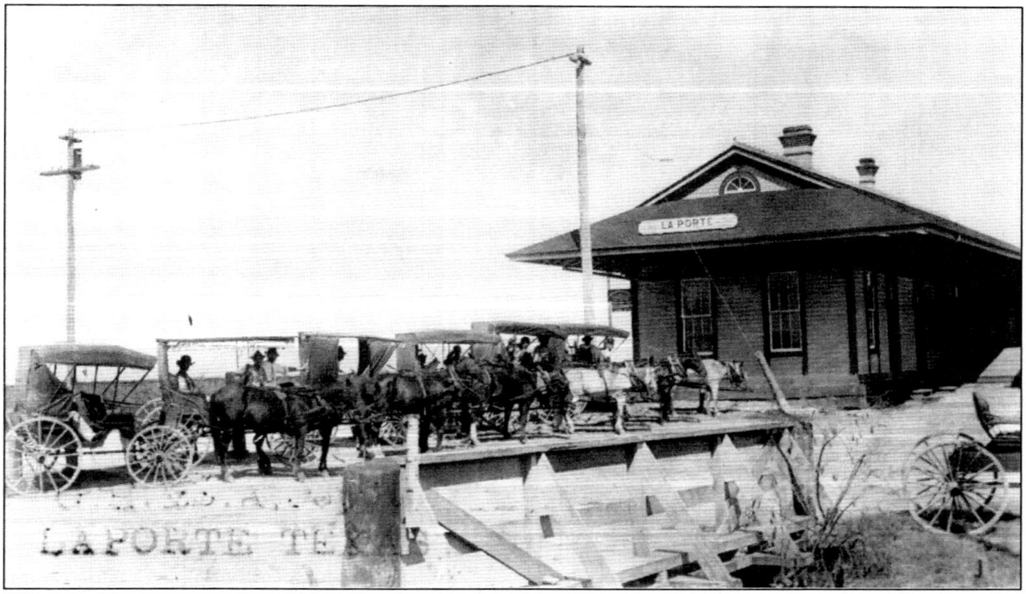

Horses and buggies were essential to travel any distance after La Porte became a city. At the West La Porte train station, before the train went to Sylvan Beach, buggies would line up for transportation. These same hackney drivers had at one time traveled to Deer Park to pick up passengers for a rough ride over the prairie.

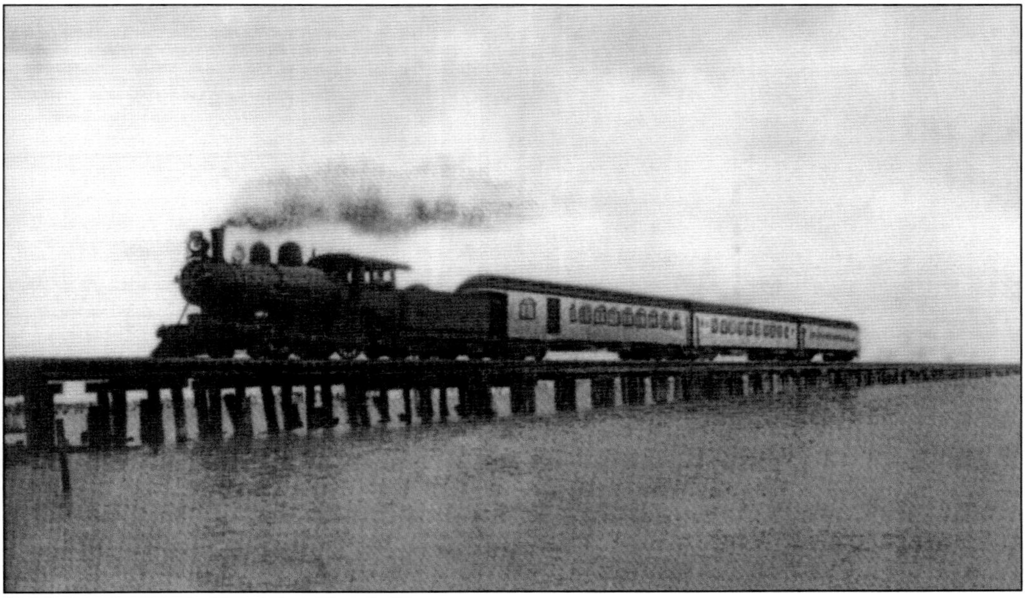

The Galveston, La Porte & Houston Railroad ran its first special train to La Porte on April 4, 1895. The train had two sleeper cars and brought excursionists from St. Louis to see the Bay Area and La Porte. By 1896, La Porte had regular through-trains to Galveston. By 1900, trains ran to La Porte, Morgan's Point, Shoreacres, Kemah, and Seabrook along the Bayshore line.

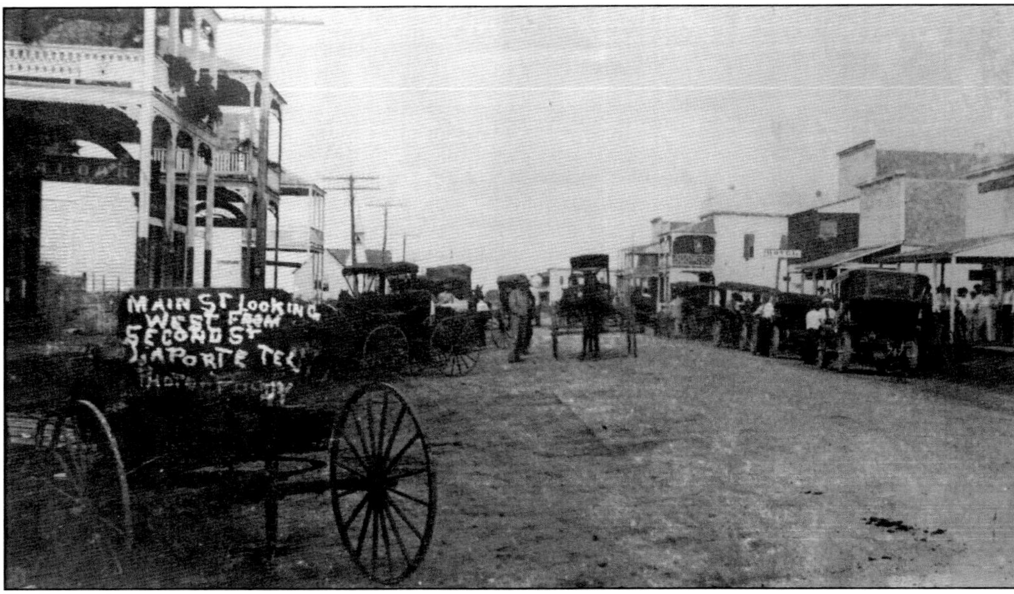

The old collides with the new in this shot of Main Street looking west sometime around 1910–1920. Horse-drawn hackneys jostle with cars and pedestrians for the road and for parking space. By 1916, there was a full-blown oil boom across the bay in Goose Creek, and much of the oil field business and many workers spilled across to La Porte to live and play.

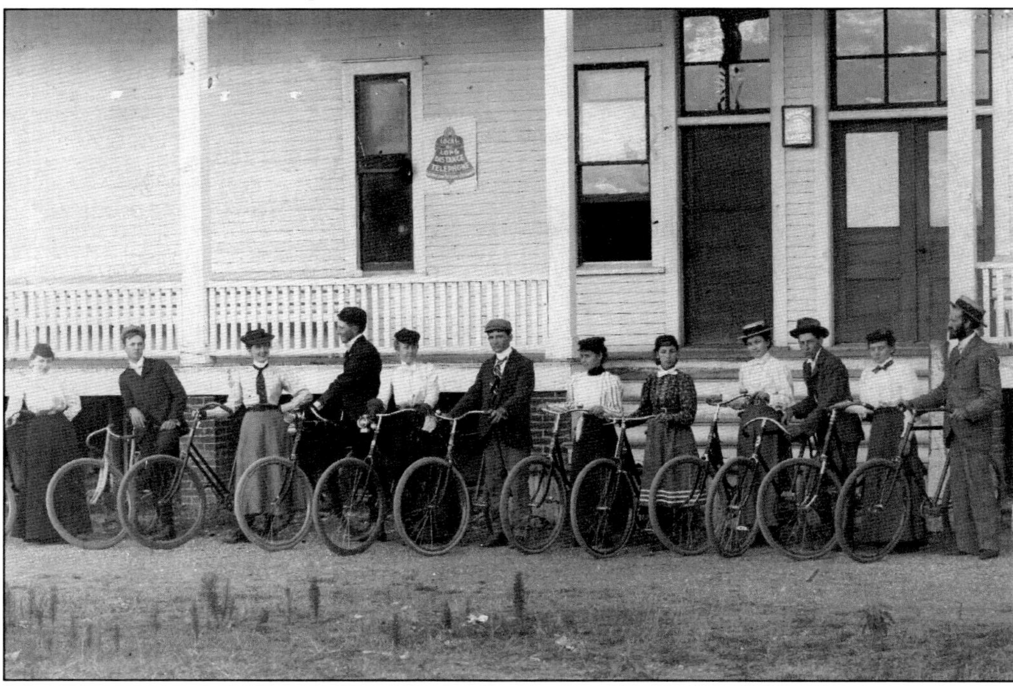

The La Porte bicycle club poses for a group picture on Main Street. By the late 1890s, bicycles were all the rage and were seen as a form of exercise, transportation, and social gathering. Suffragist Susan B. Anthony was quoted in print proclaiming the bicycle a "liberating invention" for women. Bicycle clubs like the one pictured here sprang up all over Texas.

Bibliography

Bate, W.N. *General Sidney Sherman, Texas Soldier, Statesman and Builder.* Waco, TX: Texian Press, 1974.

Black, Gordon. "Allien Interested Early Builders in La Porte." *Bayshore Sun.* Series: Heritage Society Presents La Porte. December 21, 1973: 12A.

———. "The Way It Was." *Bayshore Sun.* Series. December 30, 1990.

———. "The Way It Was." *Bayshore Sun.* Series: La Porte in 1906. 1991.

———. "The Way It Was." *Bayshore Sun.* Series. 1983: 9A.

Canada, J.W. *Life At Eighty.* La Porte, TX: self-published, 1952.

The Eyes of Texas Travel Guide. Houston, TX: KPRC-TV News Department, 1977.

Foxworth, Erna B. *The Romance of Old Sylvan Beach, a Hundred Years of Amusement and Nostalgia.* Austin, TX: Waterway Press, 1986.

La Porte Bay Area Heritage Society. *Summer Folks 'n Year-Round Neighbors.* La Porte, TX: Texas Marquee Publishing, 1992.

Nolan, Ray [president of the La Porte Bay Area Heritage Society]. Interview by Ann Malone. December 5, 2010.

Orr, Mary. *Bayshore Sun.* "Historian Maps LPISD Growth." July 4, 1976.

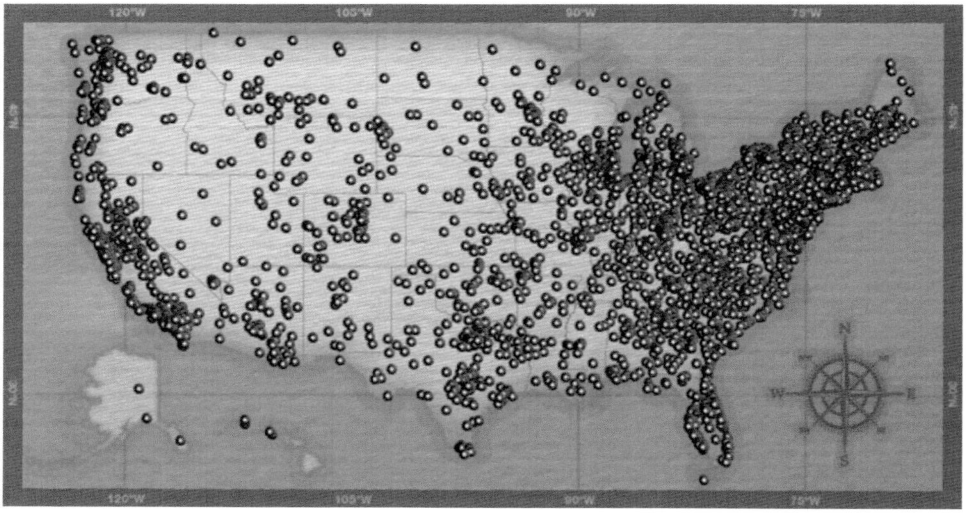

Consistent with our mission to preserve history on a local level, this book was printed in South Carolina on American-made paper and manufactured entirely in the United States. Products carrying the accredited Forest Stewardship Council (FSC) label are printed on 100 percent FSC-certified paper.

MADE IN THE USA

IMAGES
of America

AROUND LA PORTE

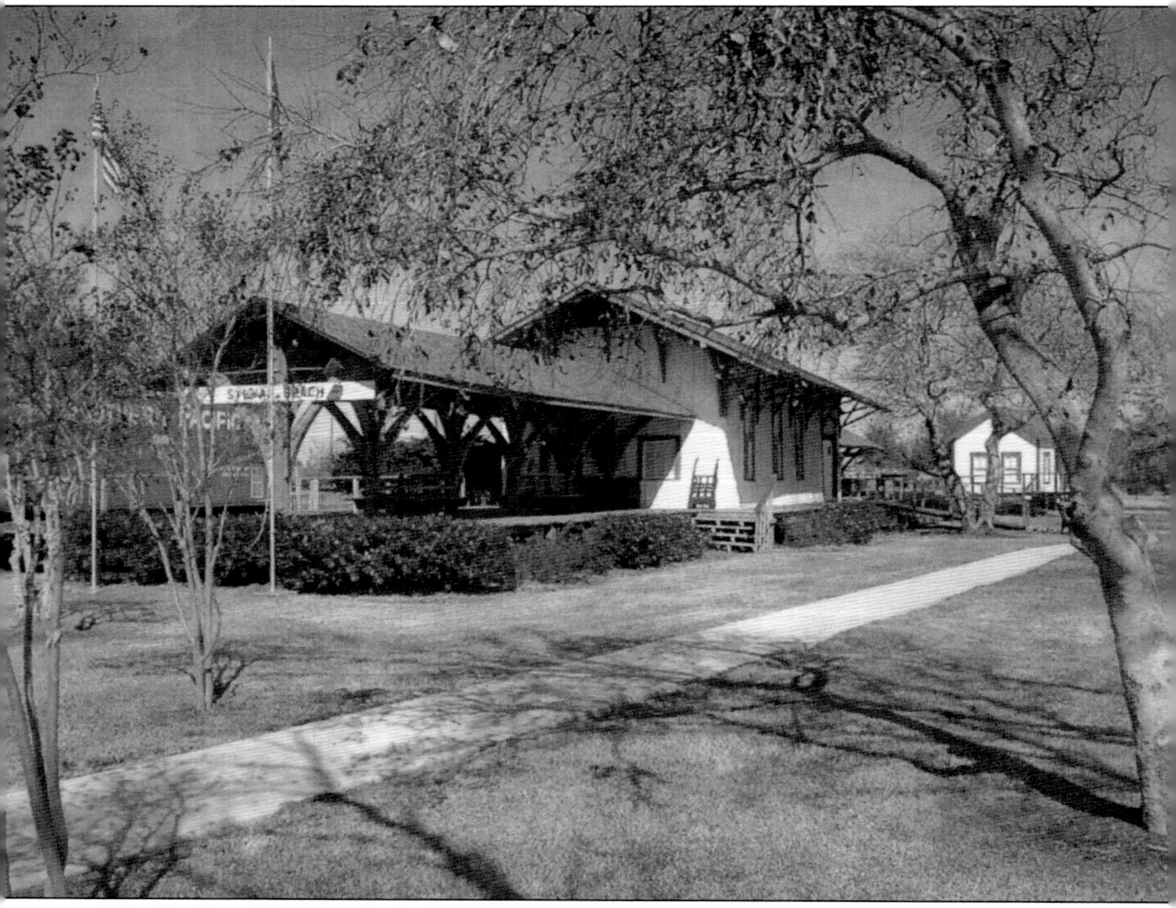

The La Porte Depot is the home of the La Porte Bay Area Heritage Society, whose continuing effort to collect and preserve the pictorial history of La Porte and the Bay Area is invaluable. This book could not have been completed without their archives. The vigorous efforts of local preservationists and the La Porte Bay Area Heritage Society returned the depot to the Sylvan Beach location, where it now serves as a museum. (Courtesy of Georgia Malone.)

ON THE COVER: La Porte loves a parade. The town still has them for the Fourth of July, Juneteenth, Sylvan Beach Day, and Armistice Day. La Porte celebrates local accomplishments with parades also, like when the La Porte High School boys' basketball team became the state's 5A champions in 1987 or when La Porte High School footballers became the district champions in 1947. (Courtesy of the La Porte Bay Area Heritage Society.)